The Priesthood of Believers

Ian Clayton

Son of Thunder Publications

Copyright © 2022 Ian Clayton & Son of Thunder Publications, Ltd.

All rights reserved. Short extracts, single chapters, activations and prayers may be copied for non-profit educational or devotional purposes only, without prior permission. Otherwise no part of this publication may be reproduced, stored in a retrieval system, or transmitted in any form or by any means, electronic, mechanical, photocopying, scanning or otherwise, without the prior written consent of the publisher.

Published by Son of Thunder Publications, www.sonofthunderpublications.org

Each chapter in this book is an edited and updated transcript taken from messages given by Ian Clayton at different times over several years. There are some minor differences from the audio messages.

Cover art hand painted © 2022 Derina Lucas, www.derinalucasdesigns.com
Cover design © 2022 Gabrial Heath
Interior Book Layout by Rachel L. Hall, WritelyDivided Editing & More
Ian and the Angel in the Wave surfing photo © Son of Thunder Ministries, 2016. Used by permission, www.sonofthunder.org.
Other diagrams & NFT graphics were produced from Ian Clayton's sketches by permission and form part of this book under copyright to Ian Clayton & Son of Thunder Publications Ltd 2022 and may not be reproduced for sale. Original sketches remain the copyright property of Ian Clayton & Son of Thunder Ministries.
Video excerpts, graphics & material from "The Foundation Nest" have been used with honour & gratitude in the creation of this book by permission. Copyright ©2016, www.thefoundationnest.com

Scripture quotations marked (AMP) are taken from the Amplified Bible, Copyright © 1954, 1958, 1962, 1964, 1965, 1987 by The Lockman Foundation. Used by permission.

Scripture marked EXB is taken from The Expanded Bible. Copyright ©2011 by Thomas Nelson. Used by permission. All rights reserved.

Scriptures marked KJV are taken from the KING JAMES VERSION (KJV): KING JAMES VERSION, public domain.

Scriptures marked KJ2000 are taken from the King James 2000 version. Copyright © 2000, 2003, 2001. Dr. Robert A. Couric. Used by permission.

Scripture quotations marked (NIV) are taken from the Holy Bible, New International Version®, NIV®. Copyright © 1973, 1978, 1984, 2011 by Biblica, Inc.™ Used by permission of Zondervan. All rights reserved worldwide. www.zondervan.com The "NIV" and "New International Version" are trademarks registered in the United States Patent and Trademark Office by Biblica, Inc.™

Scriptures marked NKJV are taken from the from the NEW KING JAMES VERSION®. Copyright© 1982 by Thomas Nelson, Inc. Used by permission. All rights reserved.

Scripture quotations marked (NLT) are taken from the Holy Bible, New Living Translation, copyright ©1996, 2004, 2015 by Tyndale House Foundation. Used by permission of Tyndale House Publishers, Inc., Carol Stream, Illinois 60188. All rights reserved.

Scripture marked (TLV) is taken from the Holy Scriptures, Tree of Life Version. Copyright © 2014,2016 by the Tree of Life Bible Society. Used by permission of the Tree of Life Bible Society.

Scripture quotations marked (TPT) are from The Passion Translation®. Copyright © 2017, 2018 by Passion & Fire Ministries, Inc. Used by permission. All rights reserved. ThePassionTranslation.com.

Scripture marked (VOICE) is taken from The Voice™. Copyright © 2012 by Ecclesia Bible Society. Used by permission. All rights reserved.

The Priesthood of Believers / Ian Clayton. —1st edition.

978-1-911251-60-6 *The Priesthood of Believers– Limited Edition* hardback
978-1-911251-59-0 *The Priesthood of Believers* paperback
978-1-911251-58-3 *The Priesthood of Believer– Limited Edition* NFT e-book

Printed in the United Kingdom, USA, and New Zealand
For Worldwide Distribution

CONTENTS

Acknowledgements 5

Praise for Ian Clayton & The Priesthood of Believers 7

Foreword 9

1. Living From a Different Kingdom 13

2. Throne of Grace 26

3. The Mobile Court 46

4. Man in the Fire 70

5. Solomon & The Queen of Sheba 87

6. The Priesthood of Jonah 101

7. The Priesthood of Hannah 121
    7.1: Model of the Temple at Jerusalem, 70 AD. 141

8. Thirteen Priesthoods 143
    8.1: The Interwoven Bench of Three Priesthoods 156

9. The Canopy of Angels 179
    9.1: Ian and the Angel in the Wave 181
    9.1: The Angelic Canopy 201

10. Heaven's Court System 211
    10.1: Explaining the Bench of Ten 212
    10.2: The Court System of Heaven 214
    10.3: Complex Overview of the Courts 229

11. He Made the Heavens 233
    11.1: The Menorah and the Realms of Heaven 234

About Ian 238

Acknowledgements

Working with Ian Clayton to create *The Priesthood of Believers* has been an honour and a privilege. Thank You, Papa, for great grace through Holy Spirit, in Yeshua Ha Mashiach, for Your continued help over the last couple of years, culminating in this volume, with the increased depths of understanding that Ian has gone into and the diagrams that illustrate what he sees in the spirit Kingdom world. We are especially delighted to be launching our first NFT e-book, which allows the work to become a permanent asset in the digital world and includes video clips that capture Ian's thoughts and perspective for the reader.

The chapters in this book are, in our estimation, some of the best work that we have done with Ian yet. We particularly enjoy the chapter illustrating our relationship with the angelic and the diagram showing the way Ian has experienced the angelic canopy. The first NFT set to be released is a digital animation of that view of the angelic canopy. The "Throne of Grace" is a chapter that has filled our atmosphere with the incredible, arresting presence of our Heavenly Father, and I commend that to you, reader, if you are dipping into this book, make sure you make a stop there.

I want to honour the help and support of so many team members, whose help has increased the pages of this volume in the time constraints we had. Thank you for praying blessing into them for their hours of tireless transcription, editing and proofreading. Rose Marie Gagnon was an incredible help! Ashley Hamilton also was such a help and support, and there were many other transcriber/editing team members who helped the project along, including Mark and Solomon Swift. Sheila Bunch was a huge help and support, and my eternal thanks go out to all the team members who contributed along the way.

Rachel Hall has been such a huge help through the proofreading, production and formatting of the book, and Donna Cruickshank has our great thanks for months of tireless editing and working on grammar with us.

Our special thanks go to Derina Lucas for hand painting the incredible cover art. Honour also to Gabrial Heath for the graphic design expertise on the cover, and our thanks to Iain Gutteridge, who helped us with the diagrams inside the book.

We give particular honour to Matthew Nagy who single handedly managed the design of the NFTs and created the web page containing the software that housed the NFT offer. Our gratitude as well to Anton Kasyan who so generously worked with us to create the incredible 3D animated NFT.

We also cannot give adequate thanks to the numerous precious sisters and several dedicated brothers who walked with us along the journey of creating this book, including proofreaders, intercessors and friends of wise counsel, without whom this book would still be a vision. They have chosen to remain anonymous, but they continue to be counted with affection as part of the Revelation Partners family.

We also want to express our love and gratitude for the kindness and encouragement of many who have opened doors along the way, including our beloved families of Global Community in Yeshua and Our Father's Business Alliance.

Finally, we want to express our affection and gratitude to Ian Clayton, his wife, family and team, especially Karl Whitehead, for their wisdom, support and oversight of this labour of love. Anyone who wishes to take a step into discipleship in this walk can find details about Ian Clayton's Nest programme at SonofThunder.org.

Revelation Partners
United Kingdom
June 2022

Praise for Ian Clayton
& *The Priesthood of Believers*

As a student of life and numerous subjects of interest, I find that books and their authors are inextricably linked together. Essentially, the author and his/her message are one and the same to me; therefore, when I choose to read, I open my mind and heart not only to the subject matter but especially to the perspective and influence of the author. If you are like me in recognizing that reading requires a measure of openness, even vulnerability, on our part, I assure you that we are in good hands with Ian Clayton and his excellent book, *The Priesthood of Believers*! The author and his subject matter are well-matched and thus powerfully impactful. *The Priesthood of Believers* is a must-read for all who endeavor to go deeper with our Heavenly Father in relationship and thereby to reflect and represent Him effectively on the earth.

I have had the exceptional honor and joy of walking closely with Ian Clayton for more than a decade. During this time, I have benefited immensely not only from his phenomenal teachings but also from observing and learning from Ian as a husband, father, friend, and business partner—overall, he is a genuine, integrity-filled, passionate, fun-loving, and super-cool son of Yahweh. In every area of life, Ian is the real deal; therefore, I wholeheartedly salute my friend and his remarkable contribution to humanity, and I greet with honor and much love all of you who join us on this amazing journey!

Marios Ellinas
Connecticut, USA
mariosellinas.com

The Priesthood of Believers encapsulates Ian Clayton's own personal encounters of a deep and intimate journey with God. Forged from a lengthy time of separation unto God, walking the ancient paths our forefathers once walked, honouring God and His creation.

It is a must read and it's difficult not to get more excited and hungry for God when listening to Ian's unfolding revelations from engaging Wisdom and Justice! Ian not only sees in the spirit but as he shares what he sees in the fear of the Lord, he helps others engage, too!

Jane Schroeder
Scotland, UK
janeschroeder.com

Foreword

We have known Ian Clayton for 13-plus years – and been good friends for at least half of that time. They say it usually takes a few months for a man to let his mask slip, revealing his true colours. However, Ian has consistently revealed himself to be a man of integrity and good character – whose sole purpose is to bring glory to God through his life and actions.

Although Ian is streets ahead in spiritual rank to anyone we have met, he is encouraging, exhorting, motivating and humble in his close relationships as well as with those he disciples. He has a father's heart and a desire to see those who have ears to hear and eyes to see come into their maturity as a son. Ian has spent decades travelling the globe, so he can share his valuable spiritual keys and insights with those whose heart is to grow into the full stature and measure of their identity in Christ.

You may be challenged by some of the things you read in this book. However, if you can change your mind, you can change your world. Ian presents truth that leads to life. The reader would do well to pay attention to a pioneer who has gone before, scouted out the territory and come back to lead those who would usually prefer to settle into greater depths in their relationship with YHVH. He demonstrates that there is much more to our spiritual walk than we've been led to believe through our religious programming. In *The Priesthood of Believers*, Ian offers many keys to the reader. If applied, these keys could unlock a level of freedom in your own life, but more than that, a generational legacy for those who follow after you.

Grant & Samantha Mahoney
The Foundation Nest

The Priesthood of Believers

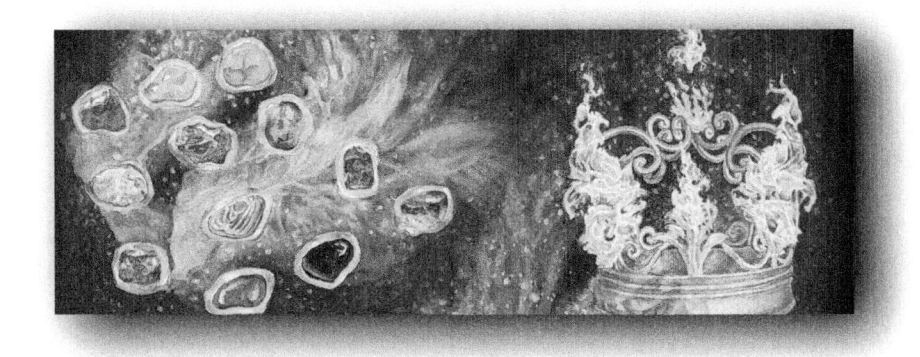

Chapter 1

LIVING FROM A DIFFERENT KINGDOM

The Lord is taking us through an interesting season as we learn to engage with what He is releasing now. Reviewing what has been done in the past and standing on the layers of the old, we begin to engage with what He is doing in our day. It is a great tragedy when we as a people try and take what is new back into the old system that was not designed to hold what YHVH is doing today.[1] We can honour what has been done, but we must not succumb to past habits and revert back to what we have always done. What YHVH did in the 1960s is not what He is doing today. We are now experiencing life within the Kingdom from a completely different perspective than we used to. Yesterday's knowledge will not suffice for us today. As we move

---

[1] YHVH is the Tetragrammaton used in the Bible in Hebrew to refer to the person of God. Its first mention is in Genesis 2:4. I refer to Jesus as YHSVH by inserting "S" to indicate the Shin in His Hebrew name.

into new understandings and function in the realms of the Kingdom in Heaven, our role is to let go of the old and embrace what is being released for today. Of course, that's a lot easier said than done. However, as you move through the chapters of this book, I hope to challenge and inspire you to do just that. As Paul said, *"forgetting those things which are behind, and reaching forth unto those things which are before, I press toward the mark for the prize of the high calling of God in Christ Jesus"* (Philippians 3:13–14 KJ2000). As we move forward and engage the presence of YHVH, the challenge will always be finding a way to function and walk with Him into maturity.

The Word says, *"But the hour is coming, and now is, when the true worshipers will worship the Father in spirit and truth; for the Father is seeking such to worship Him. God is Spirit, and those who worship Him must worship in spirit and truth"* (John 4:23–24 NKJV). YHVH is a Spirit. We must learn to live in the spirit within His realm, from a different Kingdom than the one our body has been accustomed to. We often try to superimpose what we know on earth onto what goes on in Heaven. Heaven is completely different to what is here on earth. Scripture is very succinct in its dialogue over this. It specifies *"on earth as it is in Heaven"* (Matthew 6:10), not in Heaven as it is on earth. We must learn how to engage with Him as a spirit being in the spirit Kingdom of our Father and how to function in both realms of the Kingdom, both inside and outside of us, that together operate as the spiritual realm.

You and I did not start out in this physical form of our bodies. In my opinion, one of our biggest issues is our need to come to the realisation that we are not just human beings. Once we get born again, we cease to be Adam's seed. We become connected to a different realm through this encounter as immature spiritual beings. The physical form of our bodies is not our origin: it is the last product of the choice we made to be able to come into this world and engage in the physical realm. We did this so we could have a physical inheritance.

What we see in the physical realm is creation. However, everything in creation is not only physical but also spiritual and dimensional. The corruption within the record of our DNA causes us to get so engaged in this physical realm that we overlook the other realms. Yet we can live out of the other realms because the physical world does not confine us at this point, even though it contains us. If this world confines us, this is all we will ever have. You and I are not confined to this world but are engaged as spirit beings with the Father, growing in awareness of our true identity and responsibility within His world.

The origin and source of your life was as a supernatural being in the Father before the foundation of the world. When YHVH framed creation, He released you to be an illumination in Heaven. This is found in the blueprint of Genesis 1 and with Isaiah's encounter in Isaiah 6. Isaiah's visionary encounter with YHVH and the burning coal helped unlock the truth of his assignment and the scroll given to him. As we mature, we pass through this process of remembering who we were and what our assignment was. Unfortunately, not everything we do is part of our original assignment. The seraphim came and prepared Isaiah for the task by placing a coal of fire from Heaven on his lips. When He asked, "Who will go?", YHVH caused a remembrance in Isaiah of what happened at the very beginning. Isaiah's response was to cry out and say, *"Here am I, send me"* (Isaiah 6:8).

You and I have gone through the same thing, even though many of us believers do not remember yet. As spirit beings and entities in YHVH before the foundation of the world, we registered our intent and said the same thing: "Here am I. Lord, send me. I will go for You." At that point, from under the Shepherd's rod, we came out of Heaven as spirit beings into the heavens in the created realm, bringing with us our scroll of destiny. Out of this realm of mystery, we were assigned to the earth as spirit beings. In our mother's womb, we joined with the union of the two DNA strands from our parents. Our bodies took on their physical forms in the agreement made by the records of our parents' DNA's union in the womb. The corruption within the record of our parents' DNA creates amnesia problems as we mature physically on the earth and frame the memory of the physical world over the record of the spiritual world. The union of our spirit beings with the physical seed of our parents materialised our souls into existence as eternal beings. The soul's purpose is to be the mediator for the spirit being, to be able to engage with the natural world as a spirit being through the body.

My desire has always been to be able to live out of the supply of YHVH's realm and not be subject to this physical realm and its limitations. Living within and from YHVH's realm completely changes our perspective and the way we view things. As we live our natural life in this world, we look into creation or the realm around us, almost as a 2D picture. When we ascend above the environment and our circumstances into YHVH's realm, the natural realm takes on a multi-dimensional framework with a completely different viewpoint, enabling us to function differently. As spirit beings, we have the capacity through YHVH to ascend into His realm and experience its full measure. When we are positioned in YHVH's realm, we get a completely different perspective of this world.

Often we struggle to hear the Father's voice while we are caught in this world, let alone see His face. The teachings on how to hear YHVH's voice (as opposed to seeing His face) have been one of the greatest detriments to our framework. YHSVH never said, "I do what I hear the Father is saying" – He only ever taught us to do what we see the Father doing (John 5:19). Our core desire is being with Him, engaging with Him and enjoying relationship, shoulder-to-shoulder and face-to-face. The only way we can have that relationship is to become reoriented as functioning sons in YHVH's world, being the supernatural spirit beings we are destined to become once again.

Engaging purposefully to retrain ourselves back to our first estate as functioning sons helps unframe the restrictions and limitations of the physical world. We are programmed to be in the world and change it through Christ back into the spirit Kingdom of YHVH. We already have the capacity to be completely changed and come back into the origins of what we were before. The key is that I am not just a human being; I am a spirit being that has a soul and lives in a physical body. My soul is the servant of my spirit, my body is a slave to my soul, and my soul is the mediator for my spirit being to engage with the physical realm. This perspective helps us to live from the Father's Kingdom realm.

YHVH is referred to by many different names, but the one I love is YHVH, spelt in Hebrew: Yod, Hey, Vav, Hey, or YHVH. Hebrew is read from right to left, but we are showing it left to right for ease of understanding. The framework of His Name gives us the ability to manifest what we are sitting in and reflect it into the world around us. This is called being in His name. We are then able to administrate what we are experiencing in the realm of YHVH and display His world in different measures in this realm. As sons (mature beings), we have the opportunity to bring understanding and knowledge of YHVH to the world around us. All this only comes through relationship with Him as an expression of maturity. The key is a minute by minute, hour by hour, day by day entwining with YHVH. It is written, *"He who is joined to the Lord is one spirit with Him"* (1 Corinthians 6:17 NKJV). The best way I can think of to describe this is as a many-stranded cord so tightly wound together that no individual strand can be identified. The key to remember is that you cannot become joined to someone properly until you know them, and the only way you can get to know them is to visit them, be with them and experience life with them.

THE PRIESTHOOD OF BELIEVERS

There is a huge difference between knowing about someone and knowing them personally. Let me explain it like this. If you read about someone in an autobiography or a book, you will get to know about them, what they did, who they were, etc. However, you do not actually know the person, even though you know about them. Knowing someone requires personal connection and doing life together, not just in an organisation but rather as part of a commitment to developing a personal relationship. You connect personally by going up to them, making physical contact, looking into their eyes, shaking their hand, walking beside them, and doing life in their world. It has always been the desire of the Father to walk, talk with and experience our life together with us in our world and environment, but even more that we do life with Him in His realm. The Holy Spirit came to bring us into the full measure of relational connection with YHVH so we could come into that life with Him. It is a minute by minute, intricate interaction with His presence woven into the fabric of our lives every day. He wants us to do the same thing with Him in His world. Relationship is interactive and is done together. It is not just a passing of information or task-oriented activity. Doing things this way helps believers transition to the priesthood because we witness what goes on within the relationship. Moses proved this in his relationship with YHVH.

When I first became born again, I read a book called *Practicing the Presence of God* by Brother Lawrence, a 17th-century French monk. It took me about two years of practice to become consciously aware of hosting the presence of the Holy Spirit all the time. It included being aware that He is with me and in everything I am doing. I realised that because YHSVH tore the veil, I could go through the veil and into His realm and experience life as He wanted me to experience it there with Him, not only Him here with me. When we first begin to engage with His Kingdom, it can be a very foreign place, an entity and realm that we are unfamiliar with. However, as we

LIVING FROM A DIFFERENT KINGDOM

become familiar with it by being there, we get empowered to begin to walk with Him and experience life with Him there.

I so value the access granted to me by YHVH through what YHSVH did when He tore that veil, giving us unrestricted access into our Father's realm, being able to be there as an observer at first, and then as a participant as we mature and become responsible. One of my greatest delights is to be able to watch what He does outside of time and space and then, with that knowledge, administrate the same thing into time and space, watching it unfold here and happen on the earth. That is the only thing YHSVH did on the earth: He watched what the Father did. Then He brought what He saw into time and space, unfolding and administrating it into the world around Him.

The unmeasured river that flows out of our innermost being (John 7:38) comes out of this type of relationship with YHVH. What we experience within the supply of YHVH within His world releases a supply that flows out of us and is for us to administrate on the earth. We do not need to beg YHSVH to come down. We can go up freely through the torn veil, which opens the way for us.

It is amazing how the devil has presented himself as so powerful and all-encompassing. YHVH said to me in one of our encounters, "Show the devil your future". After much discussion, I began to reach in and open the way of eternal life that is the doorway in our hearts. I remembered that it is written that YHVH put eternity in our hearts (Ecclesiastes 3:11). So, reaching into this realm, I went through my timeline looking for Lucifer to show him my future. As I reached into my future, I could not find the devil but instead found his complete absence. I was pondering this and heard YHVH begin to laugh at my consternation and belief system that satan had influence everywhere, which He had just exposed as false. YHVH spoke again and said, "The devil and all he does is completely immaterial and irrelevant to you and who you are in Me. Stop giving him your attention, your breath and your belief". That changed my life and how I engaged with everything around me. Up to that time, I had actively engaged with the devil in spiritual warfare and intercession. I never realised he needed my breath and my words to frame himself in to give him a place within the framework of my dialogue and thus in my life. I now no longer blame and frame the devil in anything as he is completely irrelevant. He is immaterial to my life. He has no influence or say in my future whatsoever.

You and I are co-creators with YHVH in this world. We speak life and frame not only our future but that of our children and the generations to come. In believing rapture theology and all the stupidity around it, we lost hope for the future and thought the earth was ending soon. So, we stopped sowing prophetically into the lives of the younger generation and did not give them a hope and a reason to live for the future. We should have given them a reason to live beyond tomorrow and shown them an endless, ever-expanding Kingdom to which there is no end, which is their future. Because of what we believed, we did not prophetically sow into their future but instead made a framework for the devil to have a residence in the world around us through spiritual warfare. We were blaming, framing and engaging with the devil at every turn. However, there has been a shift in focus towards the right place, which is that we have an amazing future paved by the ways of YHVH, and we are being fashioned to become the priests of the future within our generation.

"We know that whosoever is born of God sinneth not; but he that is begotten of God keepeth himself, and that wicked one toucheth him not" (1 John 5:18 KJV). I have taken and submitted my life to this scripture, entwining and becoming one with it. I am begotten of my Father, born again out of the will of the Spirit, renewed into life, and I am coming into remembrance of what I was before the foundation of the world. This scripture must lay the foundation for our lives. We need to

have a mind and heart to connect with the truth. We will not always be sinning, and the devil will not be able to touch us.

We dwell in a created light world as a creative light being that can only express creative light once we become born again. When we are born again, there is a struggle or enmity between created light and its influence and the creative light that now makes up the building blocks for the future. This life can be expressed through us as a supernatural spirit being because of the function of the body. Our supernatural spirit beings came out of Heaven and fused themselves into the physical form of the DNA strands in our mothers' wombs. As a spirit being, you were also fused into a complete record of everything your parents experienced and all their knowledge into your now physical being in the womb. The developing physical brain is utilised as a storage vessel for this information as a reservoir for the future. Revelation is not so much new knowledge but rather re-remembered knowledge. Unfortunately, many of us get amnesia about all this as we frame this physical world as our reality, and we forget.

It is said that most of us only use about five percent of our brain. I believe the rest of our brain is connected to the remembrance of all that we were before we were born on the earth. The truth is that you and I are creative light beings living in a created light world trying to express another realm through our physical bodies. We currently live in this physical realm framed by created light. We are supposed to be living in the glory of another realm, remembering who we were and what we are capable of as sons of YHVH. We then release that life here as the Kingdom of creative light, transforming everything we are engaged with and have influence over.

It is very much to our advantage to understand the source of what we are becoming, who we are and what is at our disposal when we are participants in YHVH's realm. We have been afraid of saying things like, "I am a Godlike being" or "I am made in the image of YHVH". If He is my Father, then my inheritance is all of His realm. Our Father is YHVH, and as such, I want to be like Him. He is the God of the universe and the creator of everything. If that is our Father, and we are going to take on His image and do what He has done, then perhaps we should change the way we think.

A great starting point is to become familiar with the different aspects of what Father looks like, which for me is dependent on where I see Him and in which way I view Him at the time. When I have engaged with Him on His throne, it has not always been a very pleasant experience because He is about His business. When Father is about His business, I have learnt to be an observer, and I have learnt to definitely not interrupt Him. There is a lot of protocol regarding how we engage with the Father on the throne. When He is off the throne, it is a totally different issue. I have seen Him take on an appearance like a man and be very approachable, loving and affectionate. When He is in this estate, His physical appearance is very interesting. His skin takes on what looks like a deep, iridescent blue colour and carries what looks like a woven fabric of laced diamonds with all the moving colours of the rainbow and other colours we do not have. A deep blue appearance emanates from within Him, rippling with white glory, lightning and fire. Every time He moves, there is lightning. I am always in awe of His appearance while He changes and morphs into lion, ox, eagle, and man.

We must believe in who we are. We are new beings, completely new creatures. We can categorically state we are no longer only human. We no longer just live in the created light realm but are totally empowered to function as sons within the creative light realm as priests and kings. We can function out of creative light now because of the unrestricted access we have to go into that light and become a host for it here within creation. Our bodies are gateways for the unfolding, influence and administration of that realm and its reality on earth today.

LIVING FROM A DIFFERENT KINGDOM

It is interesting that our physical body not only shuts us down but takes control by restricting us within physical limitations. In my opinion, our physical form often does not want us to know what we really are. You are going to be like your Father. If your Father is YHVH, you bear His Name and His nature, character, and image. This is our reality check. This is a growing, maturing process to come to the realisation that we are His children, seeded by His life. The full capacity for this is already within us.

The realm around us is not just a physical realm but carries many dynamic arenas, both spiritual and physical, quantum and energetic. Scripture says, *"We [who were with Him in person] have seen and testify [as eye-witnesses] that the Father has sent the Son to be the Savior of the world"* (1 John 4:14 AMP). Being a witness means being an eyewitness: one who has seen, not just heard. An eyewitness testifies to others of something they have seen or experienced. That is why YHSVH invited us to come up and draw near to experience our life in His presence and realm. Scripture says in 1 John 4:12, *"No man has seen God"*. This is not talking about the arenas of His realm in Heaven but rather here in this physical realm on earth. Only once in my life has He ever shown up in a physical way within this physical environment, and let me assure you, it was not pretty. We have been designed to see Him within His realm.

We can only administrate from Heaven what we have seen and heard. Hearing is only a tiny percentage of the way we are supposed to engage with the presence of YHVH. We need to see His face rather than only hear His voice. It is better to be in His presence, watching His face rather than just hearing His voice. Our function is to ascend into the Father's realm and be an observer of what He is doing – to actually see what He is doing. The point in doing this is to be able to bring what we have observed and be the administrators of it here on earth. It is so much more than just asking YHVH to bless something we are doing.

The Lord said, *"Go... and I will be with you"* (Matthew 28:19–20). He did not say, "Go and I will do it". He said, *"Go and I will be with you"*. We are the ones who cast out devils and heal the sick. We are a gate He flows through. Our spirit beings have the capacity to engage in Heaven and reveal Heaven here on earth. Engagement with the realm in Heaven and the things in this world goes beyond using spiritual gifts. The spiritual gifts are amazing but do not qualify our character or maturity. Moving in spiritual gifts does not mean that you are a mature spiritual person or that you have a good character. It only means that at the point of using the gift within the environment, you are graced to operate in it, regardless of your lifestyle. A gift is freely given. It does not require anything other than to believe.

One of the keys to unlocking that realm is to set our intent there. We must allow desire to engage with our hearts and imaginations. Then through faith (not by faith or with faith – there are three different functions of faith), our heart becomes the birthing chamber for our intentions, creating a germination bed for the desires of the heart to find root. The unfortunate part of this is that it operates for the good and the bad. The action of intent places, establishes and builds a germination environment in which our faith then builds a framework that has the capacity to materialise substance within that framework. We will then be able to bring substance out of the unseen realm and manifest it here in the physical.

We must engage in these things. They do not happen instantly just because we want them to happen. This engagement takes time. When YHVH graced us with His name, He gave us the capacity of His name to be the full measure of all that we can ever be. It is already woven into the fabric of who we are. His name is YHVH – Yod, Hey, Vav, Hey – which bears the insignia of the four faces of the lion, ox, eagle and man. We have been taught we are a three-part being with a spirit, soul and body. I realised that was incorrect because we actually have a fourth part, which is the evidence of YHVH living inside of us. YHVH makes and qualifies the fourth part Himself by taking up residence in us. We function as a three-part being until the fourth takes preeminence over the three-part being, as we become the full measure of what we are in Heaven, on earth – that is, as mature sons bearing the record of YHVH bodily, administrating as priests and ruling as kings.

There is a time coming when we are going to be completely different from what we currently are. Even our physical form and appearance will be completely different. When we begin to move into the full measure of creative light and take preeminence over created light, we will be able to come in and out of created light the same way that YHSVH did in the temple (John 8:59). We will be moving out of created light, into creative light and then back into created light, materialising from one realm into another. The sons of YHVH cannot be separated from what the Father is doing. I believe in the full measure of sons being fully revealed in the earth in their Godlike estate and appearance. This must come to pass if we are going to create a new Heaven and a new earth. YHVH has given us the capacity to do that, and it will be our job. The earth is now in its fourth estate. It has fallen three times from its first estate to where it is now. Its fifth estate will be the materialising of a new Heaven and new earth that we will be at the forefront of creating.

See you there.

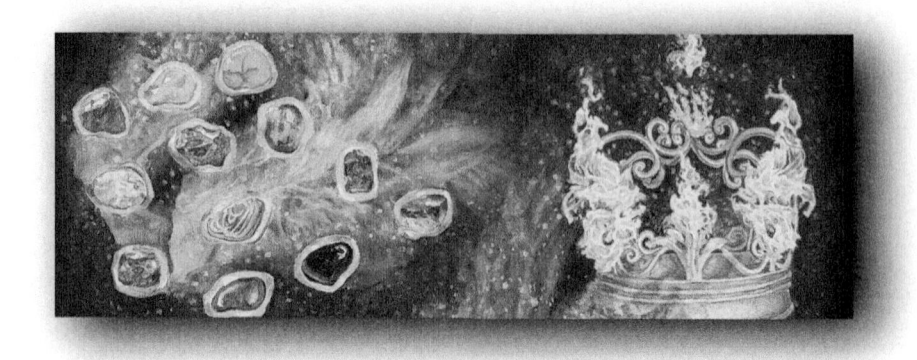

Chapter 2

THRONE OF GRACE

I would like to clarify the differences between the Throne of Grace, the Mobile Court, and the governmental court system of Heaven. First, we must understand and appreciate the scriptural provision YHVH has given, making every avenue available for us and showing us that there is a way of escape with every trial. By engaging with YHVH, there is an opportunity to find a way through the condition within us that creates the environment for repetitive sin patterns. *"...With every trial God has provided for you a way of escape that will bring you out of it victoriously"* (1 Corinthians 10:13 TPT).

I love that YHVH has made a way for us. In the Old Testament, before YHSVH became our high priest and mediator, it was very difficult to become a priest because the office of the priesthood was passed down through blood lineage. I am very excited about what YHVH has done to facilitate what we now have through Christ: a way for you and me, any time of the day or night, to be able to come to the

THRONE OF GRACE

Throne of Grace. *"Therefore, brethren, [have] boldness to enter the Holiest by the blood of Jesus, by a new and living way which He consecrated for us, through the veil, that is, His flesh..."* (Hebrews 10:19 NKJV).

The Word is the love invitation of YHVH for our life; it is able to bring us into connectedness and union with Him. We know that they that are joined to the Lord are one spirit with Him (1 Corinthians 6:17). YHVH has always been pursuing that union. I do not believe this has ever changed.

> *"For the word of God is living and powerful, and sharper than any two-edged sword, piercing even to the division of soul and spirit, and of joints and marrow, and is a discerner of the thoughts and intents of the heart."* (Hebrews 4:12 NKJV)

In my opinion, anyone who teaches that the Throne of Grace and the Mobile Court are the same thing is not teaching good doctrine and has never seen either. Too often, because of the need to be seen as spiritual, people teach from a basis of mental assent to information they have learned, but they have not personally encountered the realms they are teaching about. Seeing how things work for ourselves is very helpful as it brings us to a point where we no longer have to stand in faith. We come out of a knowing that empowers us to go deeper. This does not negate faith and hope as necessary and essential for us as believers. Seeing, though, is another tool that helps us get where we need to be.

> *"And there is no creature hidden from His sight; but all things are naked and open to the eyes of Him to whom we must give account. Seeing then that we have a great High Priest who has passed through the heavens, Jesus the Son of God, let us hold fast our confession. For we do not have a High Priest who cannot sympathise with our weaknesses, but was in all points tempted as we are, yet without sin. Let us therefore come boldly to the Throne of Grace, that we may obtain mercy and find grace to help in the time of need."* (Hebrews 4:13–16 NKJV)

THE PRIESTHOOD OF BELIEVERS

The first thing I want you to see about the Throne of Grace is that it does not operate in the atmosphere of the earth. The Kingdom of YHVH is within you. The Kingdom of the earth is around the outside of you, and the Kingdom of Heaven is enduing the power of YHVH coming down out of Heaven around you. The Throne of Grace is in the realm of the government of YHVH's Kingdom, in His world, in Heaven. We access it through faith, in faith and by faith by the blood of YHSVH that gives us unrestricted access into this realm.[2] We must go to it because it does not come to us. We can engage with the Mobile Court, which will come to us through high praise. However, we still have to be in the spirit kingdom in the world of YHVH within the Kingdom of the earth to administrate around the Mobile Court. The Throne of Grace is not and does not come within the atmosphere of the earth.

When we come to the Throne of Grace, we come to the centre point of our connection to Heaven. I am not talking about the Great White Throne of His government. When you look at Heaven, you cannot say it is a small place. Heaven is a multi-dimensional, multi-universal place that is everywhere. It can also be found in one place because it is where our Father sits. YHVH sits at the very centre of it. The Throne of Grace is one of the many layers of the function of what the Father does and administrates. This is one of the things that occur within the realm of His government, but it is not part of the court structure of YHVH. The Throne of Grace is not a court.

The Sea of Glass is before the Throne of Grace. The Throne of Grace is where you and I have to go to engage the supply that is there for our daily lives within the environmental circumstances we live in. You cannot sit on earth outside of Heaven and engage the Throne of Grace. You must go there.

---

[2] Through faith is an access point of our entry, in faith is the overshadowing of Christ's faith, which is the law of faith found in Christ. Paul says, "This life I now live I live by the faith of the Son of God." *By faith* is a mobilising of your own actions, desires and intents.

THRONE OF GRACE

The Word of YHVH says that we must come boldly to the Throne of Grace (Hebrews 4:16). You have to go where the Throne of Grace is: it will not come to you.

There is a difference between the Throne of Grace and the Realm of Grace. The Realm of Grace is the overshadowing of the goodness of YHVH in the land of the living. Grace is the power and the will to do His will. Grace is meted out to us as believers to empower us to walk into a godly lifestyle. This is not the Throne of Grace. The Realm of Grace is something YHVH pours out over us because of His love for us. His grace comes to us because He loves us, but when we are dealing with our own stuff, we go to a throne and there, grace is given because we are surrendering to a higher realm. Grace is given to us here, and we experience it as an outworking of YHVH's union with us in Christ. It is our relational union with YHVH that leads us to go to deal with our stuff.

The Throne of Grace is a seat of government, and we are to *"...come boldly to the throne of grace, that we may obtain mercy and find grace to help in the time of need"* (Hebrews 4:16 NKJV). We go to the Throne of Grace to obtain the ability to look into the four faces that YHVH presents to us, which are grace, mercy, help and time. Going to this place called the throne, which is a seat of government and a place of assistance given to us by YHVH, requires no effort of ourselves, but it does require us to go and receive. Without any requirement whatsoever, we go boldly to obtain, and it is given to us by our Father when we go there.

Going to the Throne requires faith because you need faith to engage with what you cannot necessarily see at first. I was fascinated when I first discovered the Throne of Grace in 1991. I knew about it before I knew about the court governmental systems, Heaven and all that exists there. I found that the Throne of Grace was where I could bring my petitions to make them known. There is no agenda in the Throne of Grace. It is a place for you to be completely expressive and abandoned in making your needs known. This is not so in a court system. The court system has an agenda, is very ordered and has protocol regarding when and what can be done. The Word tells us to come boldly to the Throne of Grace. *Boldly* means unashamed, with everything open and uncovered, with no worries and no stress.

The thing I love about the Throne of Grace is that none of us is rejected there.

The Lost Son

When the Lord was teaching me about the Throne of Grace, He was talking to me about the lost son:

> "Then Jesus said, 'Once there was a father with two sons. The younger son came to his father and said, "Father, don't you think it's time to give me the share of your estate that belongs to me?" So the father went ahead and distributed among the two sons their inheritance. Shortly afterward, the younger son packed up all his belongings and travelled off to see the world. He journeyed to a far-off land where he soon wasted all he was given in a binge of extravagant and reckless living.
>
> 'With everything spent and nothing left, he grew hungry, for there was a severe famine in that land. So he begged a farmer in that country to hire him. The farmer hired him and sent him out to feed the pigs. The son was so famished, he was willing to even eat the slop given to the pigs, because no one would feed him a thing.
>
> 'Humiliated, the son finally realised what he was doing and he thought, "There are many workers at my father's house who have all the food they want with plenty to spare. They lack nothing. Why am I here dying of hunger, feeding these pigs and eating their slop? I want to go back home to my father's house, and I'll say to him, 'Father, I was wrong. I have sinned against you. I'll never be worthy to be called your son. Please, Father, just treat me like one of your employees.'"
>
> 'So the young son set off for home. From a long distance away, his father saw him coming, dressed as a beggar, and great compassion swelled up in his heart for his son who was returning home. So the father raced out to meet him. He

swept him up in his arms, hugged him dearly, and kissed him over and over with tender love.

Then the son said,

"Father, I was wrong. I have sinned against you. I could never deserve to be called your son. Just let me be—"

The father interrupted and said, "Son, you're home now!"

Turning to his servants, the father said, "Quick, bring me the best robe, my very own robe, and I will place it on his shoulders. Bring the ring, the seal of sonship, and I will put it on his finger. And bring out the best shoes you can find for my son. Let's prepare a great feast and celebrate. For this beloved son of mine was once dead, but now he's alive again. Once he was lost, but now he is found!" And everyone celebrated with overflowing joy.

Now, the older son was out working in the field when his brother returned, and as he approached the house he heard the music of celebration and dancing. So he called over one of the servants and asked, "What's going on?"

The servant replied, "It's your younger brother. He's returned home and your father is throwing a party to celebrate his homecoming."

The older son became angry and refused to go in and celebrate. So his father came out and pleaded with him, "Come and enjoy the feast with us!"

The son said, "Father, listen! How many years have I been working like a slave for you, performing every duty you've asked as a faithful son? And I've never once disobeyed you. But you've never thrown a party for me because of my faithfulness. Never once have you even given me a goat that I could feast on and celebrate with my friends like he's doing now. But look at this son of yours! He comes back after wasting your wealth on prostitutes and reckless living, and here you are throwing a great feast to celebrate—for him!"

The father said, "My son, you are always with me by my side. Everything I have is yours to enjoy. It's only right to celebrate like this and be overjoyed, because this brother of yours was once dead and gone, but now he is alive and back with us again. He was lost but now he is found!"'" (Luke 15:11–32 TPT)

The son went into the wilderness in his thinking and left the father's house. He went into a far country and spent his money in sin. He was a drunkard and ended up tending pigs and eating food from a pig's trough. Eventually, he came back to the father. The father ran out to meet him, put a new garment on him, placed a ring on his finger and celebrated his return.

For me, the Throne of Grace is like the father's response to the return of the son. In the story, the father does not go to the younger son, saying, "You naughty, filthy sinner. I am going to chastise you. You will have nothing to eat for three weeks. You are going to fast!" The father did not do that. Instead, he opened up his heart in love towards the son to embrace him and bring him back into the house. The Throne of Grace is where YHVH sits as Father. In His function as Father, He embraces and brings the son back into the house of YHVH and back into the way, renewing his activity and the processes of his life. The Throne of Grace is an important place for you and me to go. I believe that the development of my relationship with YHVH really got underway when I understood the Throne of Grace. I understood the capacity I have to engage with Him there, and that brought me to the point where He can engage with me so that I can make my requests known unto Him.

I come to the Throne of Grace to make all my requests and petitions known, particularly those focused on my own life and those I have lodged in my heart. We must walk through our own lives and experience YHVH in the middle of them before we try to take someone else to the Throne. Otherwise, if we try to petition for others, our own stuff is in the way. We cannot take another where we have never been ourselves.

If we really understood the Throne of Grace, half of the intercession we do would never be necessary. Too often in intercession, someone tries to take others to a realm they have never been themselves. Doing so actually creates more chaos. Instead, we need to go to the Throne of Grace with most petitions. It is a shame that in the Church Age, intercessory prayer evolved into a process of praying for others without the necessity of them encountering the Lord and the realms of Heaven for themselves. I often find that in this type of intercessory environment, people are so busy blaming and battling the devil and the demonic that they miss the point that there is no war in YHVH's world. He is the God of war in our world: *"The LORD will fight for you, and you shall hold your peace"* (Exodus 14:14 NKJV). Rather than remaining on the earth trying to fight with the devil, we should come to the Throne of Grace. Remember – the devil is not our enemy; he is our adversary. Our true enemy is death.

As I stated earlier, grace is the power and the will to do His will. A throne is a governmental seat of authority where the power and will to do His will is continually unfolding and engaging in the supply of that power. The will to do His will is found there. When I go to the Throne of Grace, it is to engage with the supply of the power and will to do His will, to walk out that process within my life. I go to this governmental seat of authority where the power and will to do His will is continually unfolding and working around me. The supply and the boundaries of this power and will sit within His world, but their functionality is here in our world, within creation, where they supply to us what we have engaged with. The key to remember is that it is not about your will or wants but about His will and what has been revealed within your engagement at the Throne of Grace.

The Word says to approach the Throne of Grace boldly (*boldly* means open-faced and unashamed). Therefore, there is nothing to be afraid of, and there is no shame in any form whatsoever when we go by faith and engage with the Throne of Grace. Nothing is hidden. YHSVH has already applied everything necessary for us to engage with the provision of YHVH. Understanding this is another key that will help unlock some things for you and me. At the throne, I make petitions for things. I say, "Father, this is what I would like to present to You today. Here are some solutions that I think would be appropriate, but I want to ask for Your guidance to help me process this". Suppose I am praying for someone I am actively engaged with within my heart who is in great lack at that moment, perhaps with sickness. In that case, I do not go to the Mobile Court to make my petitions for them known. I go to the Throne of Grace to obtain the power, the will to do His will from the position of government, to engage with the supply for this person's life. I engage with a supply from the Father who sits on the Throne of Grace.

Mercy, the Unmerited Favour of YHVH

> *"Let us therefore come boldly to the throne of grace, that we may obtain mercy and find grace to help in the time of need."* (Hebrews 4:16 NKJV)

Mercy is the unmerited favour of YHVH, and grace is the power and the will to do His will, which is to engage in the full supply of the unmerited favour of YHVH. Favour is amazing – it is a weapon of war and a loving tool that YHVH has available for us when we come to that throne. I believe that accessing mercy is the most important and vital ingredient in this whole process, and it is readily accessible. So, to obtain mercy, which is the unmerited favour of YHVH, we go to a governmental seat to engage with the supply of the power and the will to do His will to obtain the unmerited favour of YHVH in every circumstance of our life.

I want you to see how different the Throne of Grace is from the Mobile Court. It is not the place where judgment happens. I do not make my requests known in the Mobile Court – that is a place of presentation and judgement of what has gone on through my encounter at the Throne of Grace. The court brings the outcome of what I have presented myself for. There is a supply of oil for our needs at this throne, and that supply never runs dry. It is continually flowing towards you and me as the sons of YHVH. The only issue is that we must go into His world where the Throne of Grace exists because it cannot come into this world around us. We must go to this throne to obtain His unmerited favour. When I think about unmerited favour, it is where everything is abounding, precious and amazing, where the joy of YHVH is lavishly inclusive, and where we find fulfilment.

At the Throne of Grace, we find the unmerited favour of YHVH, the joy of YHVH, the rest of YHVH, and the peace of YHVH. This reveals the four faces of love. Here we find tranquillity – the ceasing of our own works and striving on our own to accomplish what we want, of trying to get things done in our own way through performance.

> "Now if this promise of 'rest' was fulfilled when Joshua brought the people into the land, God wouldn't have spoken later of another 'rest' yet to come. So we conclude that there is still a full and complete 'rest' waiting for believers to experience. As we enter into God's faith-rest life we cease from our own works, just as God celebrates his finished works and rests in them. So then we must give our all and be eager to experience this faith-rest life, so that no one falls short by following the same pattern of doubt and unbelief." (Hebrews 4:8–11 TPT)

Some people find themselves continuing to try to perform before YHVH or others. I advise them to try presenting themselves as spiritual to YHVH and then see what kind of conversation they have! I think you would end up with a few different results in the way you feel about things. I personally go into that arena to unlock what is there. The guidance through Hebrews 4 addresses this *rest* that we have: the place of rest, the way of rest, the seat that we have, who Christ is and the Order of Melchizedek. The functionality and government of the Throne of Grace is part of a greater throne; it is a dimensional expression of the greater throne. We have direct access to that throne to engage with the supply there.

We go to the Throne of Grace, a governmental seat, to obtain mercy and find grace to help in time of need. *Grace* means the ability to accomplish something that seems impossible. So we go to this seat of government to find the power and will to do His will, receive unmerited favour, and be empowered to walk out this process of grace.

Forgetting Our Lists

Twenty-five years ago, I used to go to the Throne of Grace with lists of needs. No one taught any of this process at the time. I would go with my list and begin to engage with YHVH by opening my life to Him and presenting my needs. I would feel His love and then forget about my list. The love of YHVH constrains us, directs us, and brings us into union with Him. I would engage in this love and begin to forget why I had gone to the Throne of Grace. I would forget about my list because I was so engaged in what YHVH was doing.

That experience taught me how immaterial our stuff is. Instead of being focused on what He wants, we tend to be centred on what we want. I would come out of those encounters and realise I had not made a single request known before Him because I had been so engaged with His love. The funny thing is that because I forgot my list, I got more done. I did not even have my list anymore. It was almost like YHVH would take the list, fold it and put it away, and I could not find it anymore.

I began to see that my issues were not the true need. We go to the Throne of Grace to engage with the goodness of YHVH and obtain unmerited favour and the ability and power to do His will. At the end, like an afterthought, we think, 'Oh – here is my need'. Over time, I have come to engage with this realm and unlock the process, and now I repeatedly go in. I have found that the needs I have and the things I want have become less and less, to the point where all I want is what He wants. Now I go to find out what He wants and what I need to do to function with what He wants within creation. I then find the grace to function in the way He wants. My concerns do not really come into it because my needs have already been met. I believe that the biggest need in all of humanity is to find acceptance and favour with YHVH. The Throne of Grace is where we find it.

> *"For every high priest taken from among men is appointed for men in things pertaining to God, that he may offer both gifts and sacrifices for sins. He can have compassion on those who are ignorant and going astray, since he himself is also subject to weakness. Because of this he is required as for the people, so also for himself, to offer sacrifices for sins. And no man takes this honor to himself, but he who is called by God, just as Aaron was."* (Hebrews 5:1–4 NKJV)

I believe that there is a way YHVH has for you and me to engage in the process in which our life fulfilment comes from walking out His desires. Although we bring our petitions to the Throne of Grace, it is not a place like a cash box or exchange platform where we put something in, thinking we will get something out. The Church Age teaching about tithes and offerings is very interesting. You give thousands per year and perhaps hundreds of thousands of dollars to your church over the years. We were in one church for twenty-four years. If you calculate it at ten thousand a year, that is two hundred and forty thousand dollars we gave to that church. There were times that I did expect to get something back from YHVH, but I want you to see that the Throne of Grace is not a machine where you put something in to get something else out. The only reason to go there is to find the grace and goodness of YHVH, that YHVH's reflection would be seen in the land of the living in the areas of your life.

Becoming a Blueprint

The Throne of Grace positions you to become a blueprint of *"as it is in heaven"* (Matthew 6:10 NKJV). After engaging in the process of approaching the Throne of Grace for ten years, I would still go with my lists, but my desire was really to engage with Him more and more. During times of worship, I would engage with Him and find that I actually wanted to discover what He wanted to do. He put desires in my heart, and I began to engage with those desires. The Throne of Grace became a place to engage as a priest of YHVH's desires. I could then find out what was on His mind and heart towards humanity. Over ten years, I went through the process, shifting from my needs to finding out what His needs were within creation. I could then petition for His needs and stand with Him in agreement as His reflection on earth. I found that I had become a blueprint on earth for something going on in Heaven. It unlocked a realm that is the unmerited favour of YHVH. From that unmerited favour, I could engage with the Spirit of Wisdom.

"Jesus grew in wisdom and favor with God and people" (Luke 2:52 EXB). The Throne of Grace unlocks the capacity for you and me to find favour with YHVH and with people. When the throne operates, it is a governmental seat; it is one of the ways promised by YHVH:

> *"Thus says the LORD of hosts:*
>
> *'If you will walk in My ways,*
> *And if you will keep My command,*
> *Then you shall also judge My house,*
> *And likewise have charge of My courts;*
> *I will give you places to walk*
> *Among these who stand here.'"* (Zechariah 3:6–7 NKJV)

Engaging in this process is one of the ways of YHVH. It is also a way of maturing us to take responsibility. So please, **do not be afraid of going in**, asking for your needs and engaging. It does not necessarily mean that you will always get things the way you want them or just because you have asked for them. This is not a machine. This is a way to develop relationship so that YHVH can honour who you are, and you learn how to honour who He is.

The Word talks about us becoming clean (1 John 1:7,9). His world is about Him, not about us, so when we present our needs, we present as unclean beings. However, we are able to go in because the blood of YHSVH was applied to the heavenly temple so that we, as the only beings, could come to Him through that blood and find unconditional acceptance. YHSVH did what He needed to do to make a way for you and me to come through the veil into the full supply of the Kingdom in the simplicity of just going in. The moment we present ourselves through the veil into His world, He cleanses us because we cannot be in His world as unclean beings. We come boldly – our job is to go. You cannot just stand here in creation and expect YHVH to come to you. We go there to engage with the supply that YHVH has so that we can participate in His world that is around us.

Do not be afraid of making your needs known. The Throne of Grace is about your needs, not everyone else's needs. This is not necessarily where I make everyone else's needs known. It is awesome to do that, but the principle is first in Jerusalem, then in Samaria and then to the uttermost parts of the earth (Acts 1:7). If I cannot make my needs known, how can I engage where I have never been myself to make the needs of others around me known? You engage with your life and your lifestyle first. Then, once your lifestyle is flowing in the revelation YHVH is releasing there, and you are functioning within that process, you start bringing the needs of others in with you. Others can then become part of your petition within creation. This is not a demanding thing where you go in saying, "I want this", making your wants known like someone having a tantrum. YHVH is not interested in demanding people's tantrums. One of the key ways of accessing this area is to learn humility. Your internal attitudes are important in how you present yourself in these arenas.

I went through this process over a ten-year period of learning how to go to the Throne of Grace, but it took me about three or four years before I could begin to see anything. I want to emphasise – three to four *years*. When I engaged in this process, everything was done by faith: I worked it through with scripture, got pictures of what a throne looked like and how it would potentially look and then, by faith, engaged with the throne. I would go there to engage with the governmental seat of the unmerited favour of YHVH, to engage with the full supply of what was necessary within creation for me to move in. I would engage with and by faith, bring the supply down and release it into my circumstances. It is no good just receiving something. You have to release it and administrate it within your environment. I was going in, engaging with that supply, bringing it into this world and then administrating it here. Through that process, I found out what it was to sit at the table in the presence of my enemies, sit at the table of rest and eat from the supply of YHVH, and sit when all chaos broke around me. This is the rest that the Throne of Grace brings us into. This is how YHVH will unlock the full measure of what we are to become in the future.

You and I have the capacity to walk in this process, but that does not mean that we will fully understand it the first time we go in. We have to actually walk it out. This is a walked-out process. So, if you have messed up and assumed or been taught that the Throne of Grace is the same as the Mobile Court, it is not. Go in and say, "Father, forgive me for this. I did not understand". Then walk your way through it.

From His Presence Within To His Kingdom Outside

We must recognise that the throne is not here in this atmosphere. It is far above everything to do with this world and all the conditions and connections of our world. It is in our Father's world, which is in the realm of Heaven. We go inwards to the realm of His presence within us because our connection with it transitions us into the realm on the outside of us, which is the Kingdom of Heaven. So, the arc between the Kingdom of YHVH within you and the Kingdom of Heaven on the outside of you opens a window. Through it, we can go by faith into the realm of Heaven to engage with the seat by faith.

I would walk through the process something like this: "Father, open my heart so I can engage with You. I allow this realm of Your presence within me to engage with the realm of Your presence on the outside of me, to form an arc and a window that I would come through". By faith, I would go through that window to present myself to the seat of government as a realm where the dominion of YHVH is fully revealed to me, to engage with the supply that comes from that arena. I would then make my request known, and I would start to engage.

"Father, I want to thank You for my wife and children. Today I ask for Your grace to sit over them. Father, I present them before You and ask for Your glory to sit over them so that their minds and hearts would be clear during the day. I ask for Your loving kindness to touch them, that You would open up conversation for us around the family table at mealtimes to be able to talk about Kingdom things."

This is the kind of thing I pray when I engage with that throne and the supply of unmerited favour of YHVH so that what is around me can engage and be administrated in the earth.

When I had gone through that process and made my petitions known, I would receive that unmerited favour, that flow, that glory, that realm, that love – everything I needed. I would bring it back down here into the earth and over my family, wife, circumstances, and business. I would begin to release and administrate the glory, goodness, favour, blessing and grace of YHVH so those around me would begin to walk in those processes. I did that for ten years, going in by faith and walking through the process, in and out and in and out. I learned how to pray there. Sometimes, while here on the earth, I would pray in the Spirit. I do many things when I am involved in the spirit realm by praying in the Spirit and letting my mind and heart get caught up in the process of what is going on. I would find myself beginning to pray in English, but actually, it was in the Spirit because I was not thinking about what I was saying. I would be processing this information, listening to myself pray and listening to myself making petitions before YHVH for things.

The first time I went to the Throne of Grace to ask for connectedness with the Seven Spirits of YHVH, I asked that they would begin to mentor and tutor me and begin to engage with me. I would ask, "Lord, how do I find these things? What do I do?" I would be asking questions, but I would also be hearing answers. I found that the Throne of Grace was a two-way conversational portal that helped me develop my relational connection with YHVH and with all those surrounding His throne. This is a developing process that does not happen overnight. It happened over many years as I learned the way.

Entering the Place of Rest

> *"There remains a rest for the people of God. For he who has entered his rest has himself also ceased from his own works as God did from his. Let us therefore be diligent to enter that rest, lest anyone fall according to the same example of disobedience."* (Hebrews 4:9–11 NKJV)

I have found that when people continually strive towards something, sometimes they are full of unbelief. The Throne of Grace has positioned me to be at rest in my environment and within my circumstances. Even in dire circumstances where difficult things have happened, I have found a place of rest because of the Throne of Grace.

When my mother passed away many years ago, I was overseas ministering. I had already said everything I needed to say to her. I told my brothers that if my mother passed away while I was travelling, I would not be coming home to the funeral. Since she was being cremated, I would take her ashes and celebrate her life with my family on my return. We would sort the ashes out and put them in her special place that we went to every year. When my mother died, I thought I would go through the normal grieving cycle even though I could not come home. However, I had already said what I needed to say to her and was at peace with her passing. Due to my engagement with the Throne of Grace and out of that place of rest, I found that I continued in the place of rest. Please do not get me wrong, I had lost my mother, and I was sad at her passing, but grief did not grip me. I was absolutely fine for two conferences. I walked through everything, came home and was completely at peace with not actually seeing my mother and not attending the funeral because I had made my petitions known. I had worked my way through the process, and I had found a supply of rest that came out of the grace of YHVH from the goodness of the Throne of Grace because the presence that sits on that throne had been turned towards me.

I had built a relationship with YHVH in this way, which proved helpful when I was going through stressful circumstances. I was able to find a way, to the point that I was learning how to administrate in the Throne of Grace, which is one of the abiding places of YHVH and part of His house. I was also learning how to engage from that house for others, to administrate this supply from Heaven to earth – not by simply praying for others in the physical realm, but by being at the throne and administrating from there.

The Throne of Grace is a place of relational development where you receive all you need. Sometimes you do not even get to pray about your needs because you receive the supply of YHVH before your needs are even mentioned. I have found it has been a place of administration for me, for YHVH to do what He is going to do there. I love the way you change your priorities to His. This is a worthwhile process to invest in.

Not Our Will But His

In developing my relationship with YHVH through the Throne of Grace, my priorities shifted away from me. First, I had to walk through my stuff. Then, because of the process I walked through with Him, my priorities changed. They shifted to His priorities for my life and the administration of my function within creation. To me, that is a loving Father teaching me how to engage with the arena that He wants to see manifest here.

It is amazing that eventually, He changes our needs to become His needs. Your focus shifts from what you want to accomplish in your life to what He wants within His love. In scripture, we read that when YHSVH was in the garden, He said to the Father, *"Father, if it is Your will, take this cup away from Me; nevertheless not My will, but Yours, be done"* (Luke 22:42). I think that there was an exchange there where YHSVH was presenting Himself around the throne.

When taking others before the Lord, I take my heart for them into the Throne of Grace, and I present my heart for them so that YHVH can do what He has to do. I do not go there demanding, as it is not a place for demands. I present others there so that YHVH can do what He needs to do within their lives. It is about literally surrendering to His will, not your will. Nevertheless, not my will, but Yours be done, Father.

Remember, everything is done on the other side of the veil, not this side. It means going in. I set my intent not to engage the Mobile Court but to go into the Throne of Grace. So, my intent becomes a framework to anchor me into the truth of the way that supplies my life. Before you can mediate for others, you have to learn about mediating for yourself.

I ask YHVH to unlock His will for others' lives. I hold them and whatever He wants to do for their life in my heart. In the Church Age, we would say, 'I will stand in the gap through intercession for someone'. I have seen minimal fruit from the outworking of this process, which has been done for the last fifty years. However, there is a way for us to come into the full measure of what YHVH will unlock. You cannot take anyone where you have never been yourself. If you try to, you will feed them dry straw, and nothing will happen anyway because it has to be processed within you. You have to be the shadow of the reflection of what YHVH is doing for you and through you.

Decrees and declarations are not made before the Throne of Grace. They are made in a different place. We go to the Throne of Grace to receive grace and obtain mercy and favour in the time of need. This is about your life and what you do, not about decrees and declarations. You make decrees and declarations in some of the other courtroom processes, e.g., in the Court of the Kings, the Court of the Fathers and the Court of the Angels, where you become an administrator of what you already know YHVH is doing. You can only do this once you have been trained and mentored by others, including the Cloud of Witnesses, as this is where you become a priest of what you already know. So, decrees and declarations really are what I would call learning how to be an oracle or a legislator under the priesthood function within the Order of Melchizedek. Decrees and declarations become nothing unless you understand your function within that priesthood.

It does not take long for us to recognise how fruitless some of what we have done in the past has been when we start to see the reality of what goes on in our lives unfold. Because of the junk that I had in my heart, I spent many years being a participant in dealing with my own life before I tried to mediate for others. It is intrinsically important that we walk through the full process and not try to take shortcuts, particularly regarding our personal lives and learning the process of the Throne of Grace. It is also vitally important that we learn to understand the protocols of the love of the Father that is mediated around the Throne of Grace. In turn, we become mediators for the love of YHVH to be manifested through us, around us and towards others.

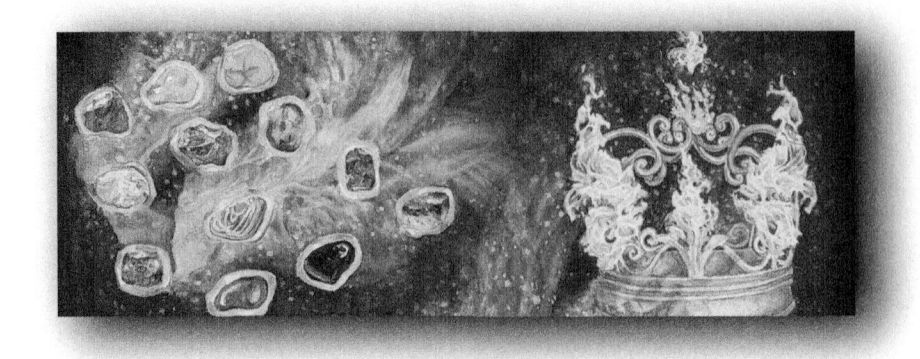

Chapter 3

THE MOBILE COURT

The Mobile Court has been instrumental for me in engaging with YHVH and dealing with the issues deeply rooted in my life. I want to lay this foundation from the very beginning. Here in the kingdom of the earth, we can present ourselves in the Mobile Court or Mobile Throne of YHVH. The Mobile Court is where the accuser has access to accuse us before the Father day and night. It is not a place to get what you want. You go to have your life judged so that YHVH can get what He wants and facilitate His desire for you. Then He can release you to do what you need to be doing. Many of these things are now such a part of my life that practising them has become second nature.

A recent series of court sessions I encountered dealt with things that happened in the business arena. I had to deal with my internal emotional upheaval while trying to find answers for difficult things which I had no answers for. Going through vain imaginations to find a solution was not a good scenario. I had to go into court and allow YHVH to judge me in this arena of my life so He could facilitate intrinsic change inside me. It took me about three months of going into court every day, perhaps eight or nine times a day, whenever I felt tension coming around me. I would then go straight into the Mobile Court. I would stand in front of the Father and say,

> "Search me, O God, and know my heart.
> Examine me, and know my anxious thoughts,
> and see if there be any offensive way within me,
> and lead me in the way everlasting." (Psalm 139:23–24 TLV)

After three months of submitting to the process, there were no more issues. I have found this is vital. You can go through processes such as the simple process about the blood and about YHSVH as your High Priest. All these are very alive within the Mobile Court and how it functions within creation. I never do this in a religious way. By that, I mean I do not become religious about the process. Everything is about relationship. Honour is the key for the approach and how you engage.

The Purpose of the Mobile Court

I access the Mobile Court with a purpose. I go because I want to check my life and because I want YHVH to judge me. I go to deal with my own personal life. The Mobile Court is where you go to be judged. YHSVH is our mediator in this courtroom process. All that He has done by His passage through death to the grave, into His resurrected body, and His subsequent cleansing of the heavenly temple makes it possible for us to be judged and have the consequences of that judgement laid on Him. It is a place of exchange, through judgement, that enables a transfer into what He has done and a removal of those present influences. You do not go there to get what you want. You go there so He can judge you to get what He wants. Through this process of divine exchange, we are able to receive newness of life and often unlock a new perspective. Sometimes I find that due to my unconscious and subconscious thought processes, I have to go there repeatedly, especially when changing my lifestyle or dealing with challenging issues. Our role is to be an observer of Christ's mediation of the answers given to us. As a priest of YHVH in Heaven, we learn how to mediate these answers into our lives and circumstances. It is awesome to receive freedom and answers in Heaven. Yet, as it was for Daniel, sometimes that freedom and those answers can take time to land, and our mediation for them is necessary.

I have found that people have completely misapplied what the Mobile Court is for. It has been very frustrating to watch. I hear statements like, "Let's take your brother into court" or "Let's take your grandma into court". Remember, the key to being a priest is mediating YHVH to man, not trying to bring man to YHVH. You can only take anyone else into court if you have their full consent and you stand with them, not against them. The same judgement that falls on them falls on you in just the same measure, but you need them to be with you. You cannot do it as a proxy without them having knowledge. Much of this goes back into Christian witchcraft. Because of this, I believe, at times, people are being drawn into things they should never have been drawn into.

Remember, the Throne of Grace is not the Mobile Court. Some circumstances we might bring before the Mobile Court have other people involved in them. When holding these things in my heart, I am always very careful to have YHVH judge me alone. I ask Him to judge the conflict in me, not the others who stand within that conflict. As an example of this, many years ago, through a misguided and deceitful process, accusations were publicly made about me and what I was doing here in New Zealand. When I presented myself in the Mobile Court, it was specifically for me to have my life judged, so I could see if the accusations had a root in me. As the scripture says, *"Like a flitting sparrow, like a flying swallow, So a curse without cause shall not alight"* (Proverbs 26:2 NKJV), I found YHVH activated His judgement when I went through the process of allowing my life to be judged. YHVH gave me a great piece of

THE MOBILE COURT

advice in this environment: "Go up your mountain, stay there, engage and do not give them a man to fight with".

I want you to see that I did not take these people into the Mobile Court as accusers. Lucifer is the only accuser. If an accusation has no truth and cannot alight on you, it will go back to where it came from. However, if the accusations are true, then repentance is required. Within this earthly environment, I have found that there is fruit that carries the consequences of our actions. For example, if I am caught speeding down the road by a policeman, I can repent of speeding, but I will still have the consequence of having to pay a fine. This is how I create a perspective on my own actions regarding others: consequences still have to be dealt with.

We are able to go into the Mobile Court as a corporate group and have YHVH judge us. As a corporate group, we ask YHVH to judge issues in all our lives. I have experienced corporate court engagements where people have walked through the court process and allowed their own bodies to accuse them on behalf of what they have done to them. I have seen people healed in these times without the laying on of hands, simply because of the way the judgement of YHVH came. It released healing within their bodies. There are many fascinating things in the court process. Part of this process in the administration of divine exchange through Christ in the court involves the fruits of gladness, joy, holiness, righteousness, truth and justice.

As we have said, the Mobile Court is not where you go to get what you want. You go there so YHVH can judge you to get what He wants. It is the submission to the authority of what He wants within the court system of His government that operates here within creation. In reality, if I was to go physically into a court here on earth (which is, to some degree, a reflection of the Mobile Court in Heaven), and I was to start demanding what I wanted from the judge, I would be held in contempt of court and potentially put into prison. I want you to see this is what it is like when believers who are not in the place of submission come into the Mobile Court in a place of demanding that things go their way.

One of the keys is to always listen to the accusations so they can be answered, with YHSVH as our mediator. At times I have had people accuse me personally of things that they have become fixated about. When I heard their accusation, I went in submission to the government of the Mobile Court. I presented myself so that the accusation could be heard. In waiting on the accusation, nothing was presented in the Mobile Court, and I left content. This happened because there was "no thing" in me for the accusation to sit on. It is as YHSVH said, *"[T]he ruler of this world is coming, and he has nothing in Me"* (John 14:30 NKJV). As you deal with your stuff, allowing the Father to prejudge you helps negate any resting place for accusations. This, in effect, is the scripture quoted above (Psalm 139:23–34). As priests of YHVH, our role is to wear a garment of holiness as an underlying garment, because without holiness, no man shall see YHVH.

Entrance into the Mobile Court

> *"Make a joyful shout to the LORD, all you lands! Serve the LORD with gladness; Come before His presence with singing. Know that the LORD, He is God; It is He who has made us, and not we ourselves; We are His people and the sheep of His pasture. Enter into His gates with thanksgiving, And into His courts with praise. Be thankful to Him, and bless His name. For the LORD is good; His mercy is everlasting, And His truth endures to all generations."* (Psalm 100 NKJV)

The earth is part of Heaven. In Genesis 1 when YHVH created the firmament, it included the structure of physical creation, and He called it all *Heaven* (Genesis 1:6–8). The spirit world is a different abode from the physical world. The spirit world was created first to be the container for the physical world to have an existence in. In the spirit world, there is a place of glory – our Father's world – and a place of corruption. The place of corruption was precipitated by Lucifer's trading and fall, which

THE MOBILE COURT

created an existence in the spirit realm for his realm of corruption. Due to his choices and fall, Lucifer now has no access into YHVH's world. Therefore, the Mobile Throne of our heavenly Father comes into our creation so that the accusations of the prince of the power of the air can be addressed through Christ's victory.

Because worship brings union with YHVH, engaging with YHVH is a key component before ever engaging the Mobile Court. Without union in connection to the Father, we risk engaging with our own stuff and precipitating what I would describe as a shadow court. A shadow court is a demonic reflection of the Mobile Court. A shadow court can be formed when we attempt to engage with the Mobile Court by demanding what we want or making accusations against someone else. One way to activate union with the Father is through singing. Remember, worship helps us transition into the presence of our Father, so we can engage there. Worship is about Him, not about us. Even the singing must be about Him and not about us, and we must consciously remain in the place of worship. I have found the way this union and connection with the Father unfolds comes more naturally as you mature and gain understanding.

Psalm 100:4 says to enter His gates with thanksgiving and to come into His courts with praise. Thanksgiving is a process available to help us enter His gates. A gate is a place of government that helps facilitate the authority of YHVH to be released in our circumstances. That is why you find it written that the king, prophets and officials sat in the gate – a gate is a place of government.

> "Then the king arose and sat in the gate. And they told all the people, saying, 'There is the king, sitting in the gate.' So all the people came before the king." (2 Samuel 19:8)

> "Then all the officials of the king of Babylon came in and sat down at the Middle Gate... and all the rest of the officials of the king of Babylon." (Jeremiah 39:3 NASB)

In the book of Ruth, we see that *"Boaz went up to the gate and sat down there"* (4:1 NASB), and in Esther, we see *"Mordecai was sitting at the king's gate"* (2:19 NASB).

With our hearts open, we have an entry point of engagement to establish spiritual government in Heaven so that this government can be reflected on earth as it is in Heaven. From this place of government, through our union on earth with our Father, we can now begin to activate the Mobile Court within the earthly realm.

After we enter with thanksgiving, Psalm 100:4 says to enter His courts with praise. The word *praise* means a high, sustained, long, loud shout. When I first started doing this, I found I needed to be activated by this shout. The shout brought me into the realm of the Mobile Court, where I was able to engage with YHVH so He could judge me. After about three months of using that, my revelation was no longer stuck on the process of going through, and I was able to enter the Mobile Court through the already established process of high praise. I could now more easily transition into the Mobile Court because I had learned the point of access through the continued activation of high praise. The more I used this activation, the quicker it would facilitate the precipitation of the Mobile Court where His government presides and engages here with creation.

The Role of the Accuser

YHVH's Mobile Throne comes into this arena here, in this atmosphere, to engage with creation itself and with you and me in the kingdom of the earth. Through the Mobile Throne, we have access into His world. The kingdom of the earth contains the spirit world – kingdoms such as the realm of YHVH and the realm of Lucifer. They are both in this world, and your choices open or close these realms to you. If we are walking in the light, in incorruption, then corruption has no access. Where corruption has access, we address that in court, and it is broken by

THE MOBILE COURT

being judged. This is the reason for the Mobile Court. Through it, corruption does not have access and the light can shine. However, if corruption has preeminent existence within you, you cannot shine properly. We sometimes do not shine due to corruption sitting deep inside our hearts. I want you to understand this: there is a way through.

Lucifer cannot leave the atmosphere of the earth. YHVH confined him and called him *"the prince of the power of the air"* (Ephesians 2:2). Only where the air is breathable does the adversary have legal access in this realm. That is why the Mobile Throne comes down into this world. It engages here specifically within the atmosphere of the earth because the Word says that Lucifer stands accusing us day and night (Revelation 12:10). This happens in front of the Mobile Throne.

When we access the Mobile Court and stand before YHVH, the accuser stands next to us to engage with any area of our life that he still has access to. We go to the Mobile Court to submit to the government of that seat and to understand it. Understanding has nothing to do with head knowledge. Rather, *understanding* is a legal term of *standing under* the government of the seat that you look up to. Whatever you lift your eyes to has a position over you, and you automatically come under its government. The Word tells us to lift our eyes to the mountain of YHVH, where our help comes from. People look at Lucifer as in the second heaven: they look up as if he is over them, and they get in a mess.

Second heaven is a church term, a theological term that in my opinion has no clear Biblical reference point. It likely comes from a linear-thinking Greek mentality. We see it in 2 Corinthians 12:2, where Paul mentions a man *"caught up to the third heaven"*. For a linear thinker to get to *three*, there must be a *one* and a *two*. The *three* implied in "third heaven" has nothing to do with the number 3. Rather, it has to do with the Hebrew three and the letter Gimel. The Gimel is about the supply of YHVH, so Paul knew someone caught up into the full supply of YHVH.

The spirit world in the kingdom of the earth contains both the corrupt demonic and YHVH's world. This is why the Kingdom of Heaven is as close as the air you breathe. Whichever one you lean into has its influence over your life. Entanglements with the demonic are often triggered by the corruption within our own DNA records. Therefore, even when we go to the Mobile Court voluntarily, the accuser must stand in the place of accusing us. Personally, I will go there voluntarily to see where I am in my own life, what is being said and what I am being accused of. As the years have gone by, there have been times when I have gone voluntarily into the Mobile Court and found no accusation being levelled against me. It is important to note that people cannot accuse you in the Mobile Court. According to scripture, only Lucifer can.

If we go into court with accusations against a brother or sister, we place ourselves in the position of the accuser of the brethren. This heart attitude will position us into a demonic shadow court, not the Mobile Court of our heavenly Father.

We must purposefully go in to engage with YHVH so He can bring judgement to us and remove any rights the accuser holds against us. When we do this with prevalent or hidden issues in our lives, the demonic connected to the corruption in us must turn up as the accuser. If there is something which he has a legal hold on in our life, then we go through the agreement process.

I have never been pulled into a court involuntarily. This is a voluntary engagement with YHVH's Kingdom through a process precipitated by our action of high praise. High praise is the beginning process when you first learn how to access the Mobile Court. Once the pathway has been learned, it becomes a much quicker and easier journey to stand in the Mobile Court. When I first started, it could take me ten minutes of continual high praise to activate the Mobile Court. Corporately, when high praise is given in unity by a body of people, it can get activated far more quickly. When I was first teaching about the Mobile Court, I found that a shout of praise would open up access to the Mobile Court spontaneously. It opens up the way of liberation for me from the confines and detrimental record within my life of my behaviour – the things I have done, the things that have been done to me, and the things that my genealogical line has triggered inside of me. These all create a platform for corruption to take hold.

I have never been pulled into a shadow court. Some are, though, because they have detrimental behavioural patterns. When you are pulled into a shadow court, it is usually because of pride. Suddenly someone may think they are something they are not, and this can happen. Taking other people to court without their consent will draw you into a shadow court. I have never taken another person to the Mobile Court. This is not a place to settle your disputes brother-to-brother: you do that face-to-face. Entering a shadow court will release the demonic around your own life. If the glory of YHVH's presence and preeminent dominion, power and authority is not present, I question which court I am standing in front of. If His glory is not present, I step out of where I was and present myself to the Lord with high praise until I see YHSVH, the Father, myself, and the accuser, and that is all I behold. There will only ever be on the floor in the Mobile Court the Throne with YHVH sitting on it, YHSVH as our mediator, you as the accused and the accuser. Above this will be Men in White Linen, the angelic realm connected to the court case and any other believer learning about the court process as an observer.[3]

It must be noted here that these have no right to speak in court on the floor where you are standing before YHVH. Again, the Mobile Court is not a place to present your needs or

---

[3] Every time we refer to Men in White Linen, it has nothing to do with the masculine. Rather, it has to do with spiritual maturity, whether they are masculine or feminine.

petitions for others. It is fascinating to me that people seem to have forgotten that there is something called the Throne of Grace (Hebrews 4:16), and it is there that this part of our engagement with YHVH needs to be presented. Everything must be obedient to YHVH: if anything is not obedient to Him, it is not where you need to be. Lucifer cannot rant and rave in this place. He is completely subject to the government of YHVH's presence, and all he can do is present the process of accusation.

Much of what goes on depends on our hearts' internal thought structures because the Kingdom that Christ presented deals with the intrinsic control of the heart and the thoughts of the heart of man. Inordinate obstacles positioned as idols in your heart could become obstacles that need a process of repentance, not a court case. Repentance is not saying "sorry" but rather is turning to YHVH to face Him and deal with issues. In facing Him, the stuff that needs court process will come to the fore. Remember, repentance in the traditional sense of the Hebrew understanding is not turning away from something but turning to something. As you turn, your eyes become filled with the right thing. The very act of turning to YHVH shows you are turning from what you were doing. If we go into the Mobile Court with iniquity such as accusations, offense and anger against others in our hearts, YHVH will judge that iniquity. We will find ourselves in a mess, as He will judge it all. When we do this, He does not take our side. He just takes over. For anything to be able to have a foothold and engage with us in our lives, it needs a tether or an image of itself in our hearts. If there is nothing in us, anything anyone says or does cannot land (see Proverbs 26:2). That is why dealing with your life is important. The church age preoccupation with being demonically slimed and having no responsibility or power in your experience is garbage in my opinion.

Do not pretend to be something and get into a spiritual act because you think people will look up to you, believing you to be more spiritual than they are. That is pride. It can pull you into a shadow court fast. Just be yourself. Learn how to be in what you are doing, and do not try and get the approval of others. I find so many people today looking for the approval of man. Sometimes it is to promote their ministries. Sometimes it is because it makes them look good around other people, which makes them seem spiritual. Just because you have information does not mean you are experienced enough to drive the Lamborghini. The sports car may be sitting in your garage, and you might have the key to it, but this does not mean you have the right experience. As far as I am concerned, anyone being paid for helping others to go to court is operating out of a shadow court. We teach others, and then we leave them to it as a process of discipleship. This trading floor is not something that I would ever choose to be a part of.

The Pattern Revealed From First Creation

The book of Job was one of the first books of the Bible, and I see it as the only book left from first creation. It records, "Now there was a day when the sons of God came to present themselves before the Lord, and Satan also came among them" (Job 1:6 NKJV). Then later it says, *"Again there was a day when the sons of God came to present themselves before the LORD, and Satan came also among them to present himself before the LORD"* (Job 2:1 NKJV). Between Job chapter one and Job chapter two, you have Lucifer thinking he is a son and has the rights of a son.

Even in the book of Job, the sons of YHVH had to present themselves before Him. There was a protocol of engagement. The pattern was established in first creation, and it flowed over into second creation. In Job's day, he was the first to experience sin and corruption because he was crossing over between first creation and second creation.[4]

---

[4] See Ian's teaching on creation at: www.sonofthunder.org

Joshua, the High Priest

I find the book of Zechariah interesting in the way that it presents itself. Zechariah speaks about Joshua's administration as the high priest. We need to understand that the high priest prepared himself for an entire year to go in through the veil. Remember, the veil was not torn. Some rabbis teach the high priest was breathed into YHVH, which means that his body would dematerialise, and he would walk through the curtain. They believe he was able to walk energy through energy by what YHVH was doing. He was able to go through the material world in the same way YHSVH was able to appear and disappear. The high priest walked through the veil in the same way. It was not until YHSVH passed through death to show us resurrection life and give us the ability to apprehend it in this life that the veil was torn. The veil was torn to give us unlimited, unrestricted access to the presence of YHVH as His priests.

In the New Testament, we are all priests. We all have the ability to go in before YHVH. We are all called into that arena to engage with our future and with what YHVH is doing within us. This is why we are called priests of our God and of His Christ. However, in the Old Testament, only the high priest could do that. The high priest would go through an entire year fulfilling all the requirements of his function as a priest just to stand before YHVH once to present Him with all the sin of his nation. I do not recommend that you go representing all the sin of your nation. Remember, we are the priests of YHVH, not the priests of man. Today we go in as individuals. In Zechariah's day, it was about Israel's sin, not the sin of the world. Because of their relationship with YHVH, Israel had right of access.

> "He showed me Joshua the high priest standing before the Angel of the LORD, and Satan standing at his right hand to oppose him." (Zechariah 3:1 NKJV)

Here we see Joshua, the high priest, coming in with the record of all the sin of the nation. He comes to stand in what is

THE MOBILE COURT

necessary to transact the release for the entire nation. The high priest goes and stands beyond the veil. This was the function of the high priest in those days. This was his mandate. So, Joshua stands before YHVH. Notice that Lucifer comes immediately and stands next to him. Lucifer is there because Joshua is presenting the sin of his nation. Do not forget: he was the priest for the people of Israel, so he spent an entire year preparing to engage YHVH in this arena.

> "And the LORD said to Satan, 'The LORD rebuke you, Satan! The LORD who has chosen Jerusalem rebuke you! Is this not a brand plucked from the fire.' Now Joshua was clothed with filthy garments, and was standing before the Angel." (Zechariah 3:2–3 NKJV)

At that point, Joshua was the holiest man in all of Israel, according to the Aaronic and Levitical orders. Because of what he had gone through in obedience to the law, through the shedding of the sacrificial blood and the preparation of his body, mind and heart, he was the holiest man at that time, prepared this side of the veil to be able to go into the presence of YHVH. Yet when we see the high priest, Joshua, he is standing before YHVH, and the Bible says he had a filthy garment on. I love this about YHVH. YHVH said, 'Filthy garments? I have the answer: new garments!' This is where grace comes in for you and me in the arena on this side of the Torah.

If Joshua's preparation was not good enough in the Old Testament, if Joshua still had filthy garments on, I want you to see how much grace and love YHSVH had for us when he passed through death. He made us able to stand righteous the moment we enter in.

> "'Take away the filthy garments from him.' And to him He said, 'See, I have removed your iniquity from you, and I will clothe you with rich robes.' And I said, 'Let them put a clean turban on his head.' So they put a clean turban on his head, and they put the clothes on him..." (Zechariah 3:4–5 NKJV).

THE PRIESTHOOD OF BELIEVERS

YHVH has an answer to Joshua's filthy garments. He says, take the garments off, put a ring on his finger, stick a fair mitre on his head, clothe him with a new garment, and it is done. YHSVH does the same for us, except we do not have to prepare. We, as the sheep, go in as a sacrifice. That is why the Word says, *"I beseech you therefore, brethren, by the mercies of God, that you present your bodies a living sacrifice, holy, acceptable to God, which is your reasonable service"* (Romans 12:1 NKJV).

In this presentation where you and I go in, the moment we present ourselves through the veil, our High Priest, YHSVH, has taken all our sin, and we are cleansed. It happens the moment we enter in. It is not cleansed here in this realm, but the moment we go in through the veil, He pronounces it *done*. No matter what lifestyle I have had, no matter my condition, I can go in, and I can be made clean. This is the greatest statement of love YHVH could express. We have this capacity to go in, and instantaneously, YHSVH makes us clean so we can present ourselves as holy and acceptable before YHVH.

I find it interesting that in the same way Joshua appeared and Lucifer stood on his right side, when we go in to present ourselves before YHVH, Lucifer also comes in. In the same instant, YHVH prepares us, cleanses us and makes us fully capable of engaging with the confession of our mouth. Doing so in that arena brings the process here so that your body on the earth can come into the full measure of your presentation in Heaven. Then, it is "on earth as it is in heaven". The process we go through to engage with this is not hard. It is to go through the veil here in the kingdom of the earth and present yourself before the Mobile Court of YHVH so He can begin to judge you.

In the Old Testament, when YHVH said about Joshua, "... put a new garment on him", this is the last time we see Lucifer in the court with Joshua. YHVH does not pay attention to the accuser anymore. YHVH is disinterested in him. The accuser is immaterial to who YHVH is and what you have now become, which is holy and righteous. The adversary has nothing to do with your life unless you want him. However, with the broken parts of our life, we give him legal access to the dust of our record. This was what his food was in Genesis. YHVH said to Lucifer,

> *"You shall eat dust
> All the days of your life."* (Genesis 3:14 NKJV)

Dust is the record of the corruption of the fallen nature of man. Because we are made of dust, Lucifer will have access to this within our fallen nature. The internal corruption held in the record of our DNA is one of the keys that allow access to the record of who we are. Corruption will always look for a handle to use as a lever to leverage us to bend the way that will allow it an expression through us. It is here that presenting ourselves and our bodies as living sacrifices becomes very helpful in maintaining a lifestyle of holiness. Additionally, dealing with the autosomes of our DNA becomes intrinsically important. They often carry the record of the enmity held against us that is accessible to corruption (the demonic realm) engaging with us.

Therefore, we come into the Mobile Court to deal with the access points in us and our fallen nature. The moment you present yourself, YHSVH stands there as your High Priest. I have had the accuser start a railing accusation against me, and it is amazing that YHSVH does not pay any attention to him. He does not turn to the accuser and say, 'Oh, I need to hear what you are saying'. He just looks at you to see whether you will acknowledge the sin of the accusation. The moment you agree, YHSVH smiles and says, 'I have that'.

Our High Priest

YHSVH is our High Priest who has transacted the release for all of humanity. He has done that for us, once for all time and for all mankind. It is all done, all recorded. All we are required to do is engage with the supply that is already there. We go into the Mobile Court to receive the full supply and the provision given by Christ. When YHSVH said, *"It is finished"* (John 19:30 NKJV), it was all finished. However, we still need to apply this victory to our lives. For this reason, you must engage in the court.

The process does not just happen because of a belief in the Father's grace. People say, "It is all grace; therefore, there is no sin". This is not true. In Heaven, it is all grace and there is no sin. However, here on earth, until your body starts its metamorphosis out of the record of humanity, you are still dealing with sin. When you undergo metamorphosis and start to glow white, maybe by then corruption will not have a hold on you. Until then, you need to work on your issues.

There is literally no warfare in any of this. Warfare is immaterial. YHSVH has already won the war and made an open show over Satan, triumphing over him totally. *"Having disarmed principalities and powers, He made a public spectacle of them, triumphing over them in it"* (Colossians 2:15 NKJV).

Our Saviour looked down to this day with joy. He knew that even though railing accusations would be made against us, we would be able to say, "Yes, Lord, I agree. I have done that". Then, YHSVH would answer, "I have got that. Is there anything else?" Instantly, at that point, Lucifer becomes immaterial to the function of the courtroom of YHVH. He has no more access there (unless there is another accusation that he can accuse you of).

Sometimes I find accusations will come when I am dealing with stuff, and they will try to remind me of my iniquity. I will respond and say, "Yes, I agree," and carry on doing what I am doing. I do not get caught up in the religious system of trying to make everything right or making sure everything is done. As you walk through into maturity, you will find these details become more and more important.

The sacrifices that were received by the priests from the children of Israel were for sin and for transgression. Therefore, iniquity could not be judged. Yet while Joshua was standing there, YHVH dealt with the iniquity inside his heart, inside his record.

> *"Then He answered and spoke to those who stood before Him, saying, 'Take away the filthy garments from him.' And to him He said, 'See, I have removed your iniquity from you, and I will clothe you with rich robes.'"* (Zechariah 3:4 NKJV)

When you go into the Mobile Court, YHVH will deal with access points. This way, the accuser cannot have access to you while you are dealing with your stuff. When we are walking through something, YHVH will overshadow it. He will protect you from the smiting of the enemy here in this world while you are walking through it. If you are continually being smitten by the enemy in what you are walking through, you have not yet presented yourself in a deep way. I would advise going back in and going back repeatedly until the accuser becomes irrelevant to your function within the Father's world and within this realm here. This way, YHVH can do what He needs to do around you. I have learned this process, and it did not just happen overnight. I had to walk through the protocol of learning the ways of YHVH.

Heavenly Participants

Speaking for the Lord, an angel said to Joshua:

> *"If you will walk in My ways,*
> *And if you will keep My command,*
> *Then you shall also judge My house,*
> *And likewise have charge of My courts;*
> *I will give you places to walk*
> *Among these who stand here."* (Zechariah 3:7 NKJV)

YHVH said He would give Joshua a place to walk among these that stand by here. I want you to note this. There is a promise given to Joshua to be able to abide on the other side of the veil within the court system. The process is this: I go in, I get judged, I learn, and I get a clean garment put on me. My whole lifestyle begins to change. I receive a fair mitre on my head. In the translation of the original Hebrew words, a *fair mitre* means an interlocking crown with two sides. One side is a king, and the other side is a servant. When I go into the court, I go in as a servant. When I see what I need to do, I can become a king. You can operate in these things. I have learned how to function there by being in the court system and understanding the protocols.

Joshua was walking on the earth when YHVH said to him, *"I will give you free access [to My presence] among these who are standing here"* (Zechariah 3:7 AMP). When I read that, I said in my heart, "YHVH, I want to be among these that are here in this court". That is when the process began for me. I began learning and being instructed by the chancellors[5] within the court system. I spent time observing and participating in a very small way with the changing of people's garments and engaging with the process of the courtroom system. I learned how to govern and then sat behind the bench, watching how the judge judges and engaging with that process. This is where you learn the ordination of lordship and where you see others come and surrender. I have watched people come into court like little children yelling, screaming and what I would call pitching a hissy-fit or demanding right of access to get what they want. It simply follows this form: if they make a massive mess, YHVH boots them out. The courtroom is a place of submission to YHVH's government, not a place for you to try to enforce what you want. Often I find that because they put their personal desires in a preeminent position, a person's life is

---

[5] Chancellors keep the records and sit in the court moving papers like court assistants, making sure everything the Judge says happens. They look after security for the court system, making sure no one rants or rails in court but is escorted out if found to be in contempt of court.

worse after doing this than it would have been had they not come into the court. Remember: this process is all about surrender.

The Council of YHVH in the Antechamber to the Court Governmental Systems, Including the Mobile Court

This is one of the many places of the Councils of the Lord connected to Heaven's governmental court systems. Here the opinions of heavenly hosts and people of maturity are a part of what comes to pass following the rulings of the Judge (YHVH) in the Mobile Court. This is not a part of the Mobile Court and is therefore not part of the procedure of that court. This is like an antechamber of the Mobile Court or a meeting hall connected with the Court governmental system of Heaven. It would be like a chamber where an earthly judge pulls the lawyers in to discuss what has been going on in court. The actions of this antechamber are generally the end result of the proceedings in the Mobile Court. We go into the Mobile Court and get judged, and the judgments from the Mobile Court are outworked from this chamber. This is one of the places known as the Councils of YHVH, where, through the process of maturity, you get the capacity to sit and watch how judgement precipitates and works out through creation.

This place taught me my function in the Table of Seventy. I go to this antechamber to receive my assignments on the earth. Because the Father is omnipresent, He is simultaneously in the Mobile Court and in this Council Antechamber. No system on earth can match what goes on in Heaven. Behind the scenes of the Mobile Court, a whole host of things go through the process of mediation in the antechamber afterwards. This is not a place we need to go to after we are judged. We leave the Mobile Court free. The rest of the courts are mobilised without requiring you to go to them to get everything signed off. Once judgment has passed by YHVH, it gets signed off by Him.

In 1 Kings 22:22, a spirit comes in and gets an assignment from YHVH to go out and persuade Ahab, the king of Israel. I often wonder what would have happened if someone had stood and suggested something different. What sort of discussion would have occurred? I admire this about YHVH – He is open to negotiation. Some people claim that YHVH's will is *this* and only *this*. However, His will is also to mature you, which means you need to learn how to take responsibility and negotiate as Moses did. Moses changed YHVH's mind from a burning, fiery YHVH who was about to kill all of Israel to telling Him to repent. That sort of persuasion requires someone with strong inner fortitude! This type of relationship is so important. This is another one of the Councils of YHVH where we get to negotiate with Him for outcomes. This negotiation can only be done through a place of maturity, deeply personal relationship and union with the person of YHVH Himself, with the understanding of His mind, His heart and His will for humanity.

The Courts in the New Testament

In the gospel of Luke, we find YHSVH saying, *"... Simon, Simon! Indeed, Satan has asked for you, that he may sift you as wheat. But I have prayed for you, that your faith should not fail; and when you have returned to Me, strengthen your brethren"* (Luke 22:31–32 NKJV). After I understood the court system, I started to ask questions, such as where and how did YHSVH know that Lucifer had come in and asked to be able to sift Peter like wheat? If I understand what I have read in 1 Kings 22:22, Lucifer came into the court to petition YHVH to sift Peter.

What I find fascinating is that YHSVH was able to intervene with the circumstances which happened in the court system because of who He was and because He had gone up into the mountain to pray. It says He was able to facilitate a change within the court system. Where it says, *"I have prayed for you, that your faith should not fail..."* (Luke 22:32 NKJV), we see an

THE MOBILE COURT

unlocking of something within that realm. YHSVH set boundaries around what Lucifer could try and do within a person's life. Once you learn about being mature, you learn about boundaries and how they work. You then learn the process for the administration of boundaries.

This is not a simple thing. This is an in-depth unwrapping of only a few things YHVH does for us within the court system. You will find these things all through the Bible, and as you study them, they will open your understanding. Remember, YHSVH is the high priest of your confession.

> *"Therefore He is also able to save to the uttermost those who come to God through Him, since He always lives to make intercession for them."* (Hebrews 7:25 NKJV).

He is always making intercession for us. He engages with us even when we are unaware of the accuser standing and railing accusations against us. YHSVH is already standing on your behalf. The moment you go into court and present yourself, the whole realm lets out a massive sigh, and you hear, 'Finally! They are here! Someone is here so we can actually deal with this instead of just setting boundaries and limitations'. I often hear this when I am engaged in this process during the night watch.

Once you have accepted the accusation before the presence of YHVH and you have owned it, it is terminated. The accuser can no longer use it. It is terminated. Done. Finished. There is no more record of it. In Heaven, your record is expunged, and the accusation is completely removed from you. It is removed permanently. The accuser no longer has access to accuse you of it ever again.

If we do not make use of this process, we may feel condemned by the ways we have behaved and not find freedom. The Bible says to confess your sin. So, you confess and ask Him to forgive you. Three days later, you are busy praying about the same thing again. You ask YHVH to forgive you all over again. You feel condemnation because you have not been in court where YHVH can expunge it. The protocol is to go in and deal with it there.

Do not try and deal with it on this side of the veil. The church age taught us to stand on this side of the veil. Because YHSVH has torn the veil, the invitation is there to go up into His world and begin participating with it on that side of the veil.

When the Bible says that YHSVH is the high priest of our confession, the word *confession* in Greek is *homologeo* (*Strong's* 3670), which means "to say the same thing". It is not just about agreeing with the accusation; it is also about agreeing with your release from the condition of what Lucifer is accusing you of. Then, we thank the Lord that we have been released. We are now saying the same thing. We are free from this accusation because of what YHSVH has done, and we receive it here. I am *homologeo*; I say the same thing as He is saying. I do not look at the accuser to hear what he is saying. I look at YHSVH to see what He is doing and hear what He is saying so I can do and say the same thing.

He is saying I am free.

I am free. It is expunged. It is done. It is dealt with in my life.

Maturity is the Objective

The objective of all this is maturity. So when I say I spent two years learning from the chancellors in the courtroom how to govern the court and participate with the court, and then I went through an ordination process to be there without their supervision, I mean it was *two years*. That is all I did for two years. I was dedicated to dealing with my stuff and learning what it was to be within the court's governmental system of Heaven. I was learning how to function within that court. If I am going to judge angels, I certainly need to learn how to be judged by the court. I need to know how to administrate judgments within that court and how to sit on the bench and judge

THE MOBILE COURT

within the court system. So again, this is a maturing process. It does not happen overnight.

As believers, we seem to want shortcuts. I am sorry, but if something has a shortcut, it can be taken away just as quickly. Someone can come along and take it away because it has no true foundation in your life. It is not something that has been carefully laid inside you. We must walk through the process so that it becomes effective within our lives. If we do not, the process and its effectiveness can be negated. Because of my experience and the process of longevity and learning that I have gone through, I know that no one can come to me and steal it away.

Years ago when I started teaching on the courtrooms, some people writing books on the courtrooms today said I was in blatant deception because the blood of YHSVH was enough. While yes, it is enough, there is a way for us to apply it to ourselves because the blood comes to cleanse us: that is what YHSVH does. The moment you agree, "Yes, I have done this", His blood cleanses you from the record of that which is held against us. Therefore, do not stand in court and try to fight for your position. Do not stand and try to defend yourself. It is easy to understand why you want to defend yourself, but do not do this. YHSVH is our defence. He is our high priest and the mediator of our confession. All we do is agree, and YHSVH answers because He has it covered. It is as simple as that.

We need to process all this. We need to allow YHVH to teach us about our function as a priest and a judge within the courts of YHVH. Again, it does not happen in one night just because you now have information. You need to go and learn. In the Mobile Court, you present yourself to be judged so that YHVH can do what is necessary to bring you to maturity.

Chapter 4

MAN IN THE FIRE

I have been engaging with revelation about Daniel for years. I would like to talk about this because we often take what we have heard in the past without fully understanding the depths of what YHVH went through to engage Daniel. The Father prepared Daniel, and the preparation was not easy. If you have read the book of Daniel, you know his journey had challenges. In this chapter, I would like to look at some of the things that happened with Daniel, Shadrach, Meshach and Abednego. This is all about the dwelling place of YHVH.

I can remember when the Lord was speaking to me out of the book of Daniel. YHVH began to open the book to me. He gave me new understanding of the depths He went through to prepare a man to take His image into a circumstance and bear that image to rescue sons that had not compromised. YHVH prepares us and brings us to a point where we are willing to die to become a gate of the realm of eternity.

One of the things I love is that when YHVH's presence comes around us, He puts the realm of eternity into our hearts (Ecclesiastes 3:11). To administer that eternity, we must become like Him so we can be a complete gate that can move. I would like to read from the scriptures and walk through this with you. As we go through this journey, you will realise some weird things happened. If you have previously read about Daniel as a Sunday school story, like Noah's Ark, what we are about to look at now will change the way you think. What you have been told is not necessarily everything that went on.

We'll start with Daniel chapter 2, in which Daniel describes an encounter.

> "...that they might seek mercies from the God of heaven concerning this secret, so that Daniel and his companions might not perish with the rest of the wise men of Babylon. Then the secret was revealed to Daniel in a night vision. So Daniel blessed the God of heaven.
>
> "Daniel answered and said:
>
> "Blessed be the name of God forever and ever, For wisdom and might are His."" (Daniel 2:18–20 NKJV)

Because we see Daniel had an encounter, a good question is this: What is the function of an encounter? The answer is to open a door to take us into the world of YHVH and translate us into the realm of the beginning and end, where we can find secrets.[6] We have encounters to bring the revelation we see back into this day and reveal it in season in the earthly dimension. I praise the Lord for the dream schools we have today, but these do not share the same function that Daniel did. Today's dream schools teach the knowledge of circumstances, information and imagery gleaned over years concerning the meaning of patterns and images in dreams. The unfolding of this has come from situations in other people's lives. We may learn the pattern of

---

[6] The secrets are connected to the upper waters and the mysteries are connected to the lower waters (Genesis 1:7).

interpreting dreams from this approach, but Daniel's wisdom and dream interpretation were not like that. Sometimes, I wonder if all we do when we interpret a dream is divine what we think it means from a limited selection of current information.

Daniel went to YHVH to engage with the mercies and the unmerited favour of YHVH. Daniel blessed His name because the name of YHVH is the gate that leads us into the world of the mysteries and secrets of YHVH, where we can find secrets from the beginning and end and know a matter before it has begun.

Daniel brought back such a secret, and not only was he able to give the interpretation of the dream, but he also told the king what his dream was without the king first telling Daniel what the dream was. Then Daniel gave the king the interpretation. That is true dream interpretation. It is not trying to figure out what all the little symbols mean. You need to go back to the beginning where the dream started. YHVH places dreams inside our hearts. We need to understand the functionality of the spirit man in that dimensional world. YHVH reaches into the testimony of what has been to bring it into this reality, so we can live into or out of the supply of the future.

Daniel continues:

> "... Blessed be the name of God forever and ever, For wisdom and might are His. And He changes the times and the seasons; He removes kings and raises up kings; He gives wisdom to the wise And knowledge to those who have understanding. He reveals deep and secret things; He knows what is in the darkness, and light dwells with Him."
> (Daniel 2:20–22 NKJV)

I have often wondered if wisdom and might are the two pillars of the door to this realm of interpretation. The mystery of dream interpretation as a priest mediating all that is here is simply amazing. From the record of the first day of creation, the Holy Spirit knows what is in the darkness and in the light. We are born into this physical world that we call light, but to our spirit being, it is darkness because it has no reference for this realm. Therefore, to bring the mystery into the light from within the darkness, we must go back to the source to understand what He spoke in light. I believe this is what transpired with Daniel. Daniel was bringing the light of the mystery of YHVH into the corruption of the world and revealing a new record of the future.

As we move forward through a couple of passages in the scriptural narrative, we find that King Nebuchadnezzar made a great big golden image of himself (Daniel 3:1). Then, the king got all the officials of the provinces to come to the dedication of the image he had set up.

"So the satraps, the administrators, the governors, the counselors, the treasurers, the judges, the magistrates, and all the officials of the provinces gathered together" (Daniel 3:3 NKJV). Daniel had oversight of many of these positions, which is a clue regarding their importance. The positions dictate the extent of this man's authority in the government and show what is underneath him. When you become a king, you will have all these positions reporting to you. With them may come the responsibility to administrate Heaven through engaging the realm of YHVH's government to execute justice on His behalf. Did you think you would just be a king sitting on a throne, singing "Hallelujah" for all eternity? I do not think so. There will be too much work to do.

A friend of mine had travelled with her husband for many years doing ministry together. He died suddenly. They were soulmates, so she grieved deeply in the first couple of weeks after his death. She began asking the Lord, "Why did You take my husband? Why, after all these years, did You take him from me?" One morning, she was inside her house praying the cry of her heart: "Why? Why did you take him from me?" She felt a shift inside the room and looked up, and the wall of the room rolled back. In front of her was her husband dressed in white linen with a load of scrolls tucked under his arm. He looked at her and said, "Woman, get up, get on, and get over it". This was very blunt, as was his way with her when he was here on the earth. When he looked at her, because of the love in his eyes, she said it was the most amazing look she had ever had from her husband. With that, he walked out of the room. She said the feeling and attitude that came from him was, "I am too busy for you to be like this." Within half an hour, she felt her grief had lifted.

Please do not get religious and say she was necromancing. Necromancy involves having someone talk to the dead for you. They then manifest or channel the deceased person's personality with information connected to what's familiar in that person's life. My friend was talking to the Father, and a man in white linen showed up. A man in white linen can be described as the spirit of a just person made righteous before the Lord. It is interesting that her husband still had the capacity to engage with this world.[7]

Daniel had gone through so much and was then made the chief of nearly everything in Nebuchadnezzar's realm (Daniel 2:48). All the men who practised magic arts and rituals, worshipped pagan deities and operated in the occult realm hated Daniel. I believe this was so because they could not do what Daniel, a son of YHVH, could do. This is one reason why they wanted to try and destroy anything to do with the "one true God" out of Egypt. Through relationship and holiness, Daniel was given the ability to engage this world of YHVH as a priest. Often, a lineage with a religious, active seed will reveal itself by attempting to destroy the seed of godliness and the seed of the Kingdom world in another's life. Daniel was in the middle of precisely this. It can be recognised in the attempt to strip away and dislodge a person from having significant influence. I call this religious seed lineage the reptilian seed

---

[7] I have a teaching on the Men in White Linen in the Limited Edition of *Realms of the Kingdom Volume 2*. You can also hear my teaching available at www.sonofthunder.org.

line. It will always function this way. When speaking to the religious order of his day, YHSVH said, *"Serpents, brood of vipers! How can you escape the condemnation of hell?"* (Matthew 23:33 NKJV), and *"You are of your father the devil"* (John 8:44 NKJV). Through those words, He was displaying a different kind of shepherding.

The Fiery Furnace

In Daniel 3, we read that King Nebuchadnezzar gathered together all these men and the herald shouted:

> *"... To you it is commanded, O peoples, nations, and languages, that at the time you hear the sound of the horn, flute, harp, lyre, and psaltery, in symphony with all kinds of music, you shall fall down and worship the gold image that King Nebuchadnezzar has set up; and whoever does not fall down and worship shall be cast immediately into the midst of a burning fiery furnace."* (Daniel 3:4-6 NKJV)

In those days, furnaces were massive. They had enormous doors that would open wide so they could throw all sorts of things in as fuel to heat it up. This passage says you would go into the fire alive for not worshipping the king. Burning is one of the worst deaths you can experience. When you go into the midst of a fire like the one in the furnace in the book of Daniel, there is no oxygen, and you suffocate instantaneously. You cannot breathe because when you take a breath, the fire goes into you and burns you from the inside as well as the outside. It is the most horrendous death you can imagine. It is a worse death than drowning or being gassed.

> *"At that time, when all the people heard the sound of the horn, flute, harp, and lyre, in symphony with all kinds of music, all the people, nations, and languages fell down and worshiped the gold image which King Nebuchadnezzar had set up. Therefore at that time certain Chaldeans came forward and accused the Jews. They spoke and said to King Nebuchadnezzar, 'O king, live forever!'"* [...] *"You, O king, have made a decree that everyone who hears the sound of the horn, flute, harp, lyre, and psaltery, in symphony with*

> *all kinds of music, shall fall down and worship the gold image; and whoever does not fall down and worship shall be cast into the midst of a burning fiery furnace."* (Daniel 3:7–8, 10–11 NKJV)

One of the key issues here is that worship opens up a gate to another kingdom. In this situation, the worship was idolatry. King Nebuchadnezzar was trying to take this image of himself and use it to form a gate to show off his power. Nebuchadnezzar required that every knee bow to him, thus creating an image of himself as a deity.

Worship of someone captured in corruption is intrinsically connected to idolatry. They develop a driving need to become the centre of focus and attention and feel the need to be worshipped or accepted by others. For us, worship is an abandoned expression of love for another, but for those caught in corruption, it becomes a driving need to be the centre of all activity and to be worshipped. You either worship one another, or you worship YHVH. There are no two ways. There is always only one way.

> *"There are certain Jews whom you have set over the affairs of the province of Babylon: Shadrach, Meshach, and Abed-Nego; these men, O king, have not paid due regard to you. They do not serve your gods or worship the gold image which you have set up."* (Daniel 3:12 NKJV)

A golden image is an image of pleasure and sin. It is made of gold to show its spiritual perspective. In the end, it all becomes about self. We set up golden images in our own hearts about things we think are the best things for us outside of the presence of the Lord. That is why it is important to die daily in YHSVH. Outside of this, nothing is possible. Because the flesh wants to become a gate for corruption to manifest itself through, the flesh cries out to be worshipped. In reality, our cry must be in response to His love, which enables His glory to manifest through us.

MAN IN THE FIRE

> *"Then Nebuchadnezzar, in rage and fury, gave the command to bring Shadrach, Meshach, and Abed-Nego. So they brought these men before the king."* (Daniel 3:13 NKJV)

When we say "No" to a religious spirit expressing itself through the medium of a human being in self-idolatry, it will reveal itself. You will get two things: rage and fury.

> *"Nebuchadnezzar spoke, saying to them, 'Is it true, Shadrach, Meshach and Abed-Nego, that you do not serve my gods or worship the golden image which I have set up? Now if you are ready at the time you hear the sound of the horn, flute, harp, lyre, and psaltery, in symphony with all kinds of music, and you fall down and worship the image which I have made, good! But if you do not worship, you shall be cast immediately into the midst of a burning fiery furnace. And who is the god who will deliver you from my hands?'*
>
> *"Shadrach, Meshach and Abed-Nego answered and said to the king, 'O Nebuchadnezzar, we have no need to answer you in this matter. If that is the case, our God whom we serve is able to deliver us from the burning fiery furnace, and He will deliver us from your hand, O king. But if not, let it be known to you, O king, that we do not serve your gods, nor will we worship the gold image which you have set up.'"* (Daniel 3:14–18 NKJV)

The king of the most powerful nation on the face of the earth in that day made a decree, and three of his servants refused to obey it. Unless the king gave you permission to speak, you would be executed on the spot for disobedience.

The king spoke to these three, and something began to happen. Shadrach, Meshach, and Abednego said to the king, *"We have no need to answer you in this matter"*. They were talking back to the king! They answered him, saying, *"Our God whom we serve is able to deliver us from the burning fiery furnace and He will deliver us from your hand"*. With hundreds of his chancellors and courtiers standing around him, can you imagine how the king must have felt to have a slave of his house saying, "Well, listen O King, our God is able to deliver us out of your hands" (paraphrased in my words)? Talk about a left eye twitch! The king of the known world was making a decree to these young men, and they were replying, "Aaah, NO. I don't think so!" *"...Let it be known to you, O king, that we do not serve your gods, nor will we worship the gold image which you have set up."*

> *"Then Nebuchadnezzar was full of fury, and the expression on his face changed toward Shadrach, Meshach, and Abed-Nego. He spoke and commanded that they heat the furnace seven times more than it was usually heated."* (Daniel 3:19 NKJV)

King Nebuchadnezzar must have seen these men as three little upstarts as they said, *"But if not, O king!"* Do you know how much of a mockery that statement was? Their confidence was the result of their focus from a seat of administration within another realm. The king thought he had that seat, but the slave now challenging him was functioning from within it. *"Then Nebuchadnezzar was full of fury, and the expression on his face changed...."* Often, the image we hold in our hearts will become the thing we reflect out when we are challenged. This happens because we take on the express image of the thing we serve and allow it to capture our hearts.

Nebuchadnezzar commanded that they should heat the furnace seven times hotter than it was already. This was seven, one upon seven, i.e., Father, Son, Holy Spirit as one and the Seven Spirits of YHVH that dwell before His throne, which is the blueprint of a realm of government. Numerics are important. Nebuchadnezzar was trying to establish the domain of his own kingdom to rule over these men. So, he heated the furnace seven times hotter than usual to empower the provision that comes off the seven mountains of rulership. [That is what YHSVH was shown by the devil – the kingdoms of this world, not the kingdoms of the earth (see Matthew 4:8–10).]

The king commanded some of the mighty men in his army to bind Shadrach, Meshach, and Abednego and to cast them into the burning, fiery furnace. Shadrach, Meshach and Abednego were chancellors in the king's court, yet Nebuchadnezzar was so afraid of these Jewish youths who were slaves in his household that he got mighty men from his army to bind them. Remember, *mighty men* were cross-seeded and not genetically totally human.

> *"Then Nebuchadnezzar was full of fury, and the expression on his face changed toward Shadrach, Meshach, and Abed-Nego. He spoke and commanded that they heat the furnace seven times more than it was usually heated. And he commanded certain mighty men of valor who were in his army to bind Shadrach, Meshach, and Abed-Nego, and cast them into the burning fiery furnace. Then these men were bound in their coats, their trousers, their turbans, and their other garments, and were cast into the midst of the burning fiery furnace. Therefore, because the king's command was urgent, and the furnace exceedingly hot, the flame of the fire killed those men who took up Shadrach, Meshach, and Abed-Nego."* (Daniel 3:19–22 NKJV)

Strong men bound them and took them up to the entry of the furnace. The fire was so hot that the furnace slew the men who took them up. When a furnace is burning that hot and you open the door, you become a crisp. Can you imagine what it would have been like for Shadrach, Meshach and Abednego to stand there, watch the doors open, and see the strong guards getting burned up right next to them? But when we walk within the foundation of the administration of our priesthood, nothing will harm us.

"And these three men, Shadrach, Meshach, and Abed-Nego, fell down bound into the midst of the burning fiery furnace" (Daniel 3:23 NKJV). Can you imagine what that must have been like? Soldiers take you up to the door, and when they open the door, heat comes out with a tremendous roar, and you are still standing there as they are burned to a crisp! Whoa! My God rules! The Bible says my God is a consuming fire (Hebrews 12:29).

The New Testament talks about the strong man who keeps his plunder unless a stronger one than he comes along and takes his goods as his own (Mark 3:27). The *strong man* can be seen as a demon spirit that seeks to keep you bound and immobilise you through fear. These men were bound while wearing their hats, shoes, coats and garments. Isn't it amazing how the adversary tries to engage you on your level in your walk with the presence of YHVH, to tie you up in your circumstances so that you do not understand what you are carrying, what you are wearing or who you are until the adversary has got your attention so that you are looking at them instead of looking at the coming provision within the fire? The provision is in the fire. YHVH is a consuming fire.

> *"And these three men, Shadrach, Meshach, and Abednego, fell down bound into the midst of the burning fiery furnace."* (Daniel 3:23 KJV)

They were not cast into the fire; they "fell down into" it. I believe this is an expression out of a place of worship that they were engaged with, bowing the knee and falling onto their faces in the fire to worship YHVH.

> *"And the satraps, administrators, governors, and the king's counselors gathered together, and they saw these men on whose bodies the fire had no power; the hair of their head was not singed nor were their garments affected, and the smell of fire was not on them."* (Daniel 3:27 NKJV)

The fire did not touch their coverings. Their hats, which were coverings for their heads (the head is a symbol of government), were not burned. The hand and overshadowing of YHVH over their lives held fast, no matter what trial was coming at them. It says, *"These men on whose bodies the fire had no power; the hair of their head was not singed nor were their garments affected, and the smell of fire was not on them."* Have you ever wondered about this? It must have been a wonder to them, being in it. As a side note, you cannot physically breathe in a fire. For them to have been able to breathe, there must have been an overshadowing of something else going on within the fire. Their bodies (a symbol of the dwelling place of YHVH) were not affected, and their hair (a symbol of their humanness in a right place of submission) was not singed, nor their garments (a symbol of their station and function within a community as mediators of YHVH). Even the smell of fire was not on them (a symbol of the incorruptibility of their bodies in union with YHVH).

Right about now, you should be asking a question. If Shadrach, Meshach and Abednego were such good friends with Daniel, where was Daniel?

> *"Then King Nebuchadnezzar was astonished; and he rose in haste and spoke, saying to his counselors, 'Did we not cast three men bound into the midst of the fire?' They answered and said to the king, 'True, O king.' 'Look!' he answered, 'I see four men loose, walking in the midst of the fire; and they are not hurt, and the form of the fourth is like the Son of God.'"* (Daniel 3:24–25 NKJV)

Why couldn't the chancellors and councillors that were with the king see what the king was seeing? Maybe because the king had already seen a man of light in operation, and his name was Daniel. When you become a man of light, you take on the image of YHVH.

> *"Did we not cast three men bound into the midst of the fire? ... I see four men...."*

Three sets up government, the Beit Din. *Four* is the door. Numerics are all the way through the Bible. There were four men walking in the fiery furnace, which was a door that had opened that another man could walk through because he was already in the midst of the fire at the very beginning.

The king approached a four-cornered door: Meshach, Shadrach, Abednego and a son of God. The king does not say he saw God in the fire. He saw a son of God, which means one bearing His likeness and image.

How did the king know this being was like a son of God? Until you experience a son, you do not know what they look like. The king must have known what a son of God looked like to see him like that and then name him. A *son* means one who carries His mark, His name and His express image. It is always the fourth part to the three that makes it possible for a door to open.

In the same way, YHVH's face contains the Lion, Ox, Eagle and Man. The fourth is the Man: he is the door through which YHVH will move. The name opens the door. The new name that He is going to give you will open the door. That is why we are going to have three things written on us: *"He who overcomes, I will make him a pillar in the temple of My God, and he shall go out no more. I will write on him the name of My God and the name of the city of My God, the New Jerusalem, which comes down out of heaven from My God. And I will write on him My new name"* (Revelation 3:12 NKJV). Three things – but the pillar is the fourth.

> *"Then Nebuchadnezzar went near the mouth of the burning fiery furnace and spoke, saying, 'Shadrach, Meshach, and Abed-Nego, servants of the Most High God, come out, and come here.' Then Shadrach, Meshach, and Abed-Nego came from the midst of the fire."* (Daniel 3:26 NKJV)

After the mighty men opened the door and got burned to a crisp, the king looked in and saw four men, so the king came to the door.

> *"So wake up, you living gateways!*
> *Lift up your heads, you doorways of eternity!*
> *Welcome the King of Glory,*
> *for he is about to come through you."* (Psalm 24:7 TPT)

The king could look in from the door. When a door is opened, it brings protection to everyone who draws near to it. When your door is open, you bring protection to everyone who draws near to you. The Word says, *"Come to Me, all you who labor and are heavy laden, and I will give you rest"* (Matthew

11:28 NKJV). When you draw near to YHSVH, then He becomes your protection. If you are not near Him, the adversary will have a playground with you, and you will learn the hard way what it is to come to the door. *"I am the door. If anyone enters by Me, he will be saved, and will go in and out and find pasture"* (John 10:9 NKJV).

> *"Then Nebuchadnezzar went near the mouth of the burning fiery furnace and spoke, saying, "Shadrach, Meshach, and Abednego, servants of the Most High God, come out, and come here." Then Shadrach, Meshach, and Abednego came from the midst of the fire."* (Daniel 3:26 NKJV)

Why did the king not call the son of God to come out as well?

I believe the king knew who he was. He had seen that man in the lion's den, in his position as a son of light. The king knew that the only way for Daniel to be like the light was for him to be near his Lord. I believe that Daniel became the fourth person, in the form of light with the image of a son of YHVH, to be the door and become a priest to mediate the protection of YHVH's provision in the furnace around the other three. I believe that the king knew he could not call Daniel forth because what he was seeing was so significant that for Daniel to manifest himself back into physical reality would not have been good. In my opinion, Daniel was standing as a boundary stone for Shadrach, Meshach and Abednego – standing as the fourth part to the door, becoming a boundary stone to the fire of the furnace.

Being a Gate

> *"And the princes, governors, and captains, and the king's counsellors, being gathered together, saw these men, upon whose bodies the fire had no power, nor was an hair of their head singed, neither were their coats changed, nor the smell of fire had passed on them."* (Daniel 3:27 KJV)

Can you imagine how the princes, governors and captains would have felt? Perhaps they were in shock, fear or dismay.

Suddenly, these Hebrews were walking around after being in the fire that was supposed to burn them up! Yet only the bindings that the king had commanded them to be tied up with were burnt.

When we become a gate like this, whatever has bound us gets burned. The liberty and knowledge of YHVH are revealed. Due to the actions of the three, combined with the fourth man in the fire as the priest of his people in captivity, YHVH's name was made famous.

> *"Then Nebuchadnezzar spake, and said, Blessed be the God of Shadrach, Meshach, and Abednego, who hath sent his angel, and delivered his servants that trusted in him, and have changed the king's word, and yielded their bodies, that they might not serve nor worship any god, except their own God. Therefore I make a decree, That every people, nation, and language, which speak anything amiss against the God of Shadrach, Meshach, and Abednego, shall be cut in pieces, and their houses shall be made a dunghill: because there is no other God that can deliver after this sort. Then the king promoted Shadrach, Meshach, and Abednego, in the province of Babylon."* (Daniel 3:28–30 KJV)

> *"I have even heard of thee, that the spirit of the gods is in thee, and that light and understanding and excellent wisdom is found in thee."* (Daniel 5:14 KJV)

Daniel was already known as a man of light, a son of God. The word *angel* means a "messenger of light". I had been taught that it was YHSVH walking in the fire. In my opinion, that is wrong. Daniel was able to stand in the gate and experience the fullness of sonship in his day, in the Kingdom world, by becoming a gate and bearing the Lord's name. This is because Daniel knew relationally who the Father was and who he was himself as a priest before YHVH.

To become a gate bearing His image and His name, we have to draw near to YHVH and become like YHVH is Himself. Then, as we reach into the future and apprehend who we really are, we will be able to do the same kind of things. We will be able to intervene in the circumstances of the world around us.

Do you think Daniel intervened there? I think he changed everything in this kingdom by that one act of intervention. The day is dawning for this to become our reality, too.

YHVH has more than one person willing to draw near the gate. I see a whole lot of people who are willing. So the question is this: are you going to spend the time cultivating that name until you stand in the midst of it and you become a gate to be able to intervene in the circumstances of the lives of people and the environments of nations?

We are so busy praying, "I bind that thing! I take dominion!" Yet this is going about prayer the wrong way compared to what YHVH has been bringing us into. Those still of the church age pray like this because a hundred years ago, this type of prayer was practised, and the method of prayer has not changed since. Yet what worked then will not work today. The cloud has moved, but because of instigated religious systems, forms and traditions, we have not moved with the cloud. We are not priests of humankind; we are priests of YHVH. We have to come near to Him in His world to be conformed into His image so we can become a gate to intervene in the affairs of humanity. Only when we bear His image will we be able to behave like this – not out of mental assent to information but from a union with YHVH, which produces a reality within that can be seen externally.

> *"To all peoples, nations, and languages that dwell in all the earth:*
>
> *Peace be multiplied to you.*
>
> *I thought it good to declare the signs and wonders that the Most High God has worked for me.*
>
> *How great are His signs,*
> *And how mighty His wonders!*
> *His kingdom is an everlasting kingdom,*
> *And His dominion is from generation to generation.*
>
> *I, Nebuchadnezzar, was at rest in my house, and flourishing in my palace."* (Daniel 4:1–4 NKJV)

I think this may have been Nebuchadnezzar's born-again experience. What a difference we see in this man as it becomes very personal for him in the scriptures above. This is his view of the fruit that came from what occurred in the fire.

The Word says, *"... as we have borne the image of the earthy, we shall also bear the image of the heavenly"* (1 Corinthians 15:49 KJV).

You and I have to make a choice to draw near. It is our choice. You are the sum of all your choices, the good and the bad. I want you to see that YHVH can change the effects of those choices when you draw near to Him. YHVH can remove their effects so you can begin to make the right choices and be cleansed and purified.

Activation

Father, today I want to give thanks for Daniel's willingness to stand and pay the price to draw near the door and become a son in his day. Thank You for Daniel, who bore witness in his day. Father, we want to witness in our day that each of us is a son of God, born in this season to bear Your name, be revealed as a gate, and bring forth the life of the Kingdom as an expression through our lives. Father, thank You that You lead us, and from this day, we will be forever changed. Amen.

CHAPTER 5

SOLOMON & THE QUEEN OF SHEBA

My whole heart is for the revealing of humanity and our function as a species within creation. The sons have been hidden for so long, but YHVH is about to reveal us to creation in a greater way so that humanity as a species can begin to have a say within creation itself. In my opinion, the framework for YHVH doing this is found in 1 Kings 10, with the interchange between King Solomon and the Queen of Sheba.

The story of Solomon and the Queen of Sheba is about honour and what it looks like in scripture when a priestly king is revealed.

Solomon had established Israel, built a city and was in the midst of having his fame fully revealed to all the nations of the earth. YHVH was in the middle of Solomon's life and was beginning to reveal Solomon. There is a key to recognising the process of being revealed. If you notice others talking about the presence of YHVH around you, and you don't feel a need to talk about yourself and what YHVH is doing for you, YHVH may be in the process of revealing you. Marios Ellinas, who does an amazing teaching on the differences between being fully revealed and fully hidden, describes it as the hiddenness life cycle coming to an end.[8]

> *"And when the queen of Sheba heard of the fame of Solomon concerning the name of the LORD, she came to test him with hard questions."* (1 Kings 10:1 KJV2000)

YHVH was with Solomon, and His hand was being revealed in all that Solomon was doing. Amazing things had been going on in Israel and within Solomon's life. In 1 Kings 10, we see that out of Solomon's engagement with the Spirit of Wisdom, a revealing lifestyle cycle was precipitating Solomon's priesthood. When I talk about being *fully revealed*, I am not just talking about you as an individual, although you, as an individual, are important. Being fully revealed is about all the works of your hands being in full fruit all the time and everything you do prospering.

Solomon was not busy promoting himself. Solomon was busy labouring within the nation to make the House of YHVH famous, not himself. In my opinion, YHVH began to make him famous because Solomon was the blueprint that opened up the gate for the nation to be framed in the right way. Solomon was able to do what he was supposed to do. He was not going around saying, "Oh, look how amazing I am! Look how wonderful I am!" Solomon was busy about the work of the Lord, mediating everything the Father had given him to do. I have often found that busybodies who need to be seen and accepted by others will try to make themselves famous. These

---

[8] See Marios Ellinas, *Tables & Platforms: Forging Identity and Character for a Life of Influence*, Son of Thunder Publications, 2019. Available on Amazon.

same people seem to find the time to criticise others without accomplishing anything themselves. The key is to spend time with YHVH, to become intimate with His presence. I have always had the motto, "Head down, tail up, focus on what you are supposed to do and not on what others are doing".

Solomon was busy doing the works of YHVH within his own nation so that YHVH Himself could be made famous. His whole heart was to make the Name of the Lord famous. In everything Solomon had and did when he was being revealed within his role, he was not making his own name famous.

I find it disconcerting when I am at a conference and someone comes up to me and shakes my hand, saying, "Oh, I'm so-and-so. Here is my business card," which has got "Apostle" or "Chief prophet" on it, or something like that. A business card does not identify who you are: the works of your hands and the fruit of your labours do.

This kind of stuff totally puts me off from connecting with the people who do this. The message instantly coming across to me is, "Hey, look who I am!" We do not need to do that. We need to allow YHVH to make us famous. We do not have to make ourselves famous. When YHVH is in the full revealing process of your life as a priest, you do not have to make yourself famous. You do not have to promote yourself. You do not have to say, "This is who I am, and this is what I'm doing". Everyone else will be doing that for you. Then, others will hear what YHVH is doing by you making *Him* famous, and they will come to see YHVH move through what you are doing, not to see the sign and wonder. A standing joke within my family is that "people come to see the sign and really wonder".

It disturbs me that people have become famous out of the moves of YHVH. Then others go to see the famous person and the sign and the wonder, instead of going to see the Name of the Lord being made famous. The proof of the pudding is always in the eating. What happened to that move? Is it still going? If not, why not? What is the fruit of what went wrong there to make it stop?

> "And when the queen of Sheba heard of the fame of Solomon concerning the name of the LORD, she came to test him with hard questions. And she came to Jerusalem with a very great caravan, with camels that bore spices, and very much gold, and precious stones: and when she was come to Solomon, she spoke with him of all that was in her heart." (1 Kings 10:2 KJ2000)

The Queen of Sheba came a long distance from outside the borders of Israel, drawn by the influence of government being fully revealed. Solomon governed out of being fully revealed in the role of priestly kingship, from the place of peace. Solomon's reign was a reign of peace. The government of peace was upon his house and upon Israel because of Solomon's choices to build a house and make the Name of YHVH famous. All the borders of Israel were at peace during his reign. I often find that where there is no peace, it is because the Name of YHVH is not being made famous. I purposefully set my own heart to engage with YHVH to make His Name famous. When I am engaging with YHVH, it is easier for me not to think about what other people are thinking, doing or saying. Instead, I can think about what YHVH is thinking and focus on my task.

If I am going to be put in a position where YHVH is revealing me within a circumstance, I will not say that YHVH is revealing me but let others talk about what YHVH is doing. Do you remember when gold and gemstones were manifesting? People would go to meetings just to get gemstones. When the gold cloud was in one large church I know of, people would go just to get some gold out of the cloud. Unfortunately, we sometimes go for the wrong things. We do not go because the Name of YHVH is being made famous. We go because something different is happening, so we want to see it and become part of it, rather than wanting to be a part of the Name of YHVH being made famous.

I have seen the same thing happen within ministries where there has been a move of the hand of YHVH in a specific place. People have gone to the move to try and catch it for themselves. However, I generally find that eventually, either the move ebbs away to nothing or a system comes into operation to try and keep it going, yet the well has gone. I remember reading a book about a previous move of YHVH, which occurred when someone began to engage with YHVH. One of the old men left from that move got hold of one of his own young disciples and said to him, "If you find it, do not let it go. Do not allow it to become a system. Allow it to stay as a life flow." I have never forgotten that. It is advice I continue to engage with.

The key here is that the Queen of Sheba heard of the fame of Solomon from others.

> *"She traveled to Jerusalem with a large group of servants [caravan; retinue] and camels carrying spices, jewels [precious stones], and much [immense quantities of] gold."* (1 Kings 10:2A, EXB)

Solomon was being revealed by making YHVH famous when the Queen of Sheba came to meet him in Jerusalem. In those days, there were vagabonds and thieves on the road. The Queen of Sheba brought a huge amount of gold, goods and treasure with her and took an even larger amount back with her. Do you think the vagabonds and thieves did not know what she had? I think they did know, but they left her alone because of the extension beyond the borders of Israel of the government of YHVH. It is also fascinating that she left with far more than she brought, and nothing was taken or stolen from everything that Solomon gave the Queen of Sheba. I believe this is because YHVH overshadows and protects whatever comes from the heart of a person that is in the position of being revealed within their role as a priest and king.

YHVH will protect what He is revealing; it does not need our protection. YHVH is quite capable of doing it. He is called a *man of war* in the Word (Exodus 15:3). The moment we start to feel that we need to protect a move of YHVH is the day it will start to be concealed again, and we will lose it because we do not need to do that.

When YHVH is in the process of fully revealing you, people will come and open their hearts to you. I remember sitting at a table, talking with a multibillionaire businessman from another nation. I did not say the name of YHSVH once. I did not preach the gospel to him once. All I did was present a Kingdom and how this Kingdom operates. I was using some of these examples from Solomon and his interaction with the Queen of Sheba, presenting the dynamics of YHVH's Kingdom.

When that person left with a friend of mine and they were in the car, he said to my friend, "How do I get to know this Jesus that Ian is teaching?" I need to stress here that I did not say anything about YHSVH. I did not even mention His Name. I just presented the overshadowing of a Kingdom and what that Kingdom looks like, how it is related to the earth down here and what life looks like in the dominion of that Kingdom.

The Visit of the Queen of Sheba

When the Queen of Sheba came to meet Solomon, she did not just come to ask questions; she came to find out the truth about Solomon for herself. One of the things I and others have worked with is the issue of being true—staying true to yourself, true to YHVH, and true to what the Word really says, not to what other people want the Word to say or think the Word says. When I have Christians ask me things, I will often say to them, "I will answer you, but I will answer you from what I know". Sometimes my answer is a little bit different than they expect.

> *"And Solomon told her all her questions: there was not anything hid from the king, which he told her not."* (1 Kings 10:3 KJV)

Solomon answered all her questions. This functional role brings a full revealing of our priesthood and mediation on earth. When YHVH begins to engage with you in response to your union with Him, you become a priestly oracle of another realm. Sitting in that realm helps us unlock the mysteries of people's hearts, know their inner secrets, and be able to explain hidden things easily, even things we know nothing about.

"Solomon told her all her questions." While the queen did not ask him questions, Solomon already knew whatever questions she was pondering in her heart and their answers. When someone is communing within their heart, it does not necessarily translate to verbal communication. In Solomon's priestly role with YHVH, he was in a place that allowed him to see the deep secrets of her questions. The heart has a form of communication called *cardiognosis* (Acts 1:24). The energetic light emanations from the human heart become a form of communication with light. This is not specified in the Bible, but it is what I believe John experienced when he leaned on the chest of YHSVH (John 13:23).

When a person communicates with their heart, I call it cardiognosis, which is heart language and light language where your heart can be made fully known without you having to say a word.[9] It is a form of language of light. I believe Solomon knew about that language of light because of how he communicated with people, how he communicated with YHVH, and how he engaged with what YHVH was doing around him. I believe that Solomon was engaging in Kingdom dimensions through cardiognosis when the Queen of Sheba opened her heart and YHVH gave him deep insight into her world.

We're going to look at several important phrases from 1 Kings 10:4–5.

---

[9] During encounters in Heaven, I have seen thoughts being conveyed in light as fast as lightning.

THE PRIESTHOOD OF BELIEVERS

> *"And when the queen of Sheba had seen all Solomon's wisdom, and the house that he had built, And the food of his table, and the seating of his servants, and the attendance of his ministers, and their apparel, and his cupbearers, and his entryway by which he went up unto the house of the LORD; there was no more spirit in her."* (KJ2000)

One thing that happens when you are personally revealed in your priestly/kingly role is that everything around you begins to be affected and revealed within the measure of your own revealing. The Queen of Sheba saw all of Solomon's house. She saw several things that we need to work our way through.

Everything that belonged to Solomon, everything that was connected to him, and everything around him was in a flawless state of order due to his union with YHVH and his administration of the world of YHVH into this world. This happens when you are fully functioning as a mediator of Heaven on earth as a priest. YHVH will bring things into divine order, and everything you are doing and have oversight of will reveal the depths of your priesthood.

"And when the queen of Sheba had seen all Solomon's wisdom, and the house that he had built, And the food of his table..." (vv.4–5A): The *food of his table* is speaking about the provision of YHVH here within creation being revealed. Solomon set up cities that were to provide food for his table. It is amazing that the depth of his priesthood in personal union with YHVH overflowed into physical provision and the wisdom to understand what was needed for the season.

"And the seating of his servants" (v. 5A): When Solomon set up his table, he did not seat himself high above his servants. Instead, he sat on the same level they did, which was unheard of for a king. I believe Solomon did not feel the need to promote himself or be seen to be above others. Everyone knew who he was. Everyone knew the authority he had, and they were only too happy to be in his household. In the next segment of this passage, it is interesting to note that all the servants were dressed in the same magnificent garments as

each other. Some rabbinical teachings say that when the Queen of Sheba came to Solomon's house, she did not know which one Solomon was because all the servants were wearing the same magnificent clothing that he wore.

"And the attendance of his ministers, and their apparel" (v. 5A): Everyone had on the most glorious things they could be wearing. Every time they came to fellowship together, there was a revealing of the substance of the glory that was in Solomon's house.

"And his cupbearers" (v. 5A): A cupbearer was a servant that would taste the drink before the king in case the drink had been poisoned. If they drank the drink and did not die, then it was given to the king. A cupbearer was in such close proximity to the king that he would often become a friend. Solomon was not so important in his own eyes that he could not see the goodness in others. He positioned them in a place that would bring glory to YHVH.

"And his entryway by which he went up unto the house of the LORD; there was no more spirit in her" (v. 5B): There was *no more spirit in her* because she witnessed the full measure of the blueprint of the glory of YHVH within creation on earth and in the life of a man who lived as a true priest and mediator of Heaven. Solomon's ascent up to his throne and into the house of the Lord is frequently addressed. For me, this is a transitional gate between the natural and Kingdom realms. What started off as a physical gateway to a throne transitioned to a spiritual dimension. Solomon went up to a throne in Heaven within YHVH's realm, seen by all those in attendance. He did not just sit on a physical throne: he sat on a spiritual throne in a spiritual throne room in a spiritual city. From within the city of the Lord in Heaven, Solomon ruled on the earth, mediating as a priest of Heaven on earth. I believe this is why he was able to do what he did. Consider his ability to make gold and silver as common as stones (2 Chronicles 1:15). He made it – it does not say he mined it.

I believe that when King Solomon was seated in his position in Heaven as a fully functioning priest and king in the realm of the government of YHVH, there was a release through him of divine knowledge and ability. When someone is being revealed in their priestly function and role, tangible evidence of an increase in the level of governmental engagement will be revealed. It may be recognised without the need for the person to make a note of it to others, as the fruit becomes evident. There may also come an increase in the level of recognition from those that are around their environment, including those in authority in other cities and nations, witnessing to what YHVH is doing. This often causes those in other nations to come to them. They do not have to say anything to approve a matter; it is approved for them by others who are witnessing what YHVH is doing through them. There is a big difference between this and some of the things I see today where people are promoting their ministries or themselves. I think such self-promotion is immature. I believe that when YHVH brings us to the place of revealing us as His priests within our role and function in creation, there is a different way to handle ourselves.

"There was no more spirit in her" (v. 5B): This statement implies that the queen was overwhelmed with what she saw and heard from Solomon to the extent that she could not function physically. In some of the Celtic saints' memoirs, there are accounts of people having ecstasies where there was no more spirit in them, which they called *extasis*.[10] It is a trance-like state of ecstasy, not having the ability to speak or communicate with those around you. As she observed Solomon and his court, the Queen of Sheba, one of the most powerful women in the known world at that time, went into extasis. When YHVH is revealing the role you and I play in creation, it can have amazing effects on those who come with the purpose

---

[10] Extasis - borrowed from Ancient Greek ἔκστασις (*ékstasis*) meaning rapture, ecstasy or trance. https://en.wiktionary.org/wiki/extasis

of engaging with us. When everything we do is purposed to proclaim the name of YHVH, then He in turn will reveal us within our function and may make us famous.

> "And she said to the king, It was a true report that I heard in my own land of your acts and of your wisdom. However I believed not the words, until I came, and my eyes had seen it: and, behold, the half was not told me: your wisdom and prosperity exceeds the fame which I heard." (1 Kings 10:6–7 KJ2000)

This is YHVH doing things within creation to bring a framework so that we can become what we must become as priests, kings, legislators and oracles. I believe YHVH is about to unleash some things in creation that are completely different to anything that has been seen before. They will help frame up humanity for the future, where the full measure of the glory that YHVH has put in us will be revealed through us. When that happens, things are going to change in an amazing way.

> "Happy are your men, happy are these your servants, who stand continually before you, and that hear your wisdom." (1 Kings 10:8 KJ2000)

One fruit of being fully revealed in the role of mediating Heaven and earth as a priest is that everyone around you is happy and content. This is the evidence of an overwhelming abundance continually replenished by YHVH Himself, which reaches to those who serve you. Those who serve in your household and who are engaged with you in this process also have evidence of abundance. Everyone is able to become a beneficiary of what YHVH is doing through you.

> "Blessed be the LORD your God, who delighted in you, to set you on the throne of Israel: because the LORD loved Israel forever, therefore he made you king, to execute justice and righteousness." (1 Kings 10:9 KJ2000)

Judgment and justice are the outward expressions of the foundation of YHVH's throne. The nature of YHVH was being revealed within His relationship with Solomon. YHVH's revealing of Himself through us and to us creates an atmosphere where other people want to honour us for the Lord being in us. I do not believe that Solomon wanted any of this for himself. I believe that his whole heart at this stage was to engage with YHVH, to make YHVH's Name famous and to build Him a hallowed place. As Solomon made YHVH's Name famous, YHVH made Solomon's name famous. Yet even in being revealed and becoming famous, Solomon reflected YHVH's glory and goodness to those around him. It is interesting to note that Solomon was called the king by the Queen of Sheba, which is the tangible reality of others' testifying of the goodness of YHVH.

The reflection of Solomon on his throne follows the blueprint of YHVH's throne on earth. The function of a king is to execute justice and righteousness.

> "And she gave the king a hundred and twenty talents of gold, and of spices a very great quantity, and precious stones: there came no more such abundance of spices as these which the queen of Sheba gave to king Solomon. And the navy also of Hiram, that brought gold from Ophir, brought in from Ophir great quantities of almug wood, and precious stones. And the king made of the almug wood pillars for the house of the LORD, and for the king's house, harps also and psalteries for singers: there came no such almug wood, nor was seen such unto this day." (1 Kings 10:10–12 KJV2000)

The Queen of Sheba literally gave Solomon a king's ransom. In today's terms, it would be valued at the equivalent of about $10 billion. Solomon received all of this and made pillars and harps with it as a place of worship and a place of trading. Where riches are received, there must come the establishment of the government of YHVH. Within the king's house, there was a place of worship where YHVH could be revealed in that day.

> "And king Solomon gave unto the queen of Sheba all her desire, whatsoever she asked, beside that which Solomon gave her of his royal bounty. So she turned and went to her own country, she and her servants. Now the weight of gold

that came to Solomon in one year was six hundred threescore and six talents of gold." (1 Kings 10:13–14 KJV2000)

Solomon knew about sowing and reaping. One thing that happens when a person begins to become functional in this priestly mediation role on the earth is the capacity to sow bountifully. This is how the law of sowing and reaping begins to manifest itself through us as we collaborate with YHVH. It is fascinating that Solomon, out of his own treasury room, not the treasury of the nation, gave the Queen of Sheba more than she had given him.

Solomon went from being trained and hidden under David to being fully revealed as a priest/king when the temple was finished, to then becoming fully revealed as king and the one YHVH had engaged with to imbue with riches and glory. This story is a good way to judge what goes on around your own life, to see the substance of what happens and begin to measure whether you are functioning within your mandate. The story can help you measure the process of being revealed or whether you are being unveiled to be fully revealed. The key is the fruit that is seen, not in what you have but in what you give from the place of union with YHVH. When you walk through this process, time and time again, you will begin to see the pattern and the hand of YHVH sitting on your life. Do not run from it. Do not try to hide from it. Allow YHVH to do what He is going to do with you.

Activation

Father, today I ask for Your grace as these men and women engage and move forward in the process of becoming priestly kings.

Father, I ask that your Spirit would engage with them. I ask that You walk with them through the process, that You lead them as their lives unfold as You create environments for them. Father, I ask that they come to a point of reflective indexing of the things that are within them. Unlock the truth so that as we walk through a cycle, it does not become a stagnant place, but one that is a constantly moving, living stream of continual change, that we would truly come to the point of being fully revealed in our priestly roles. Amen.

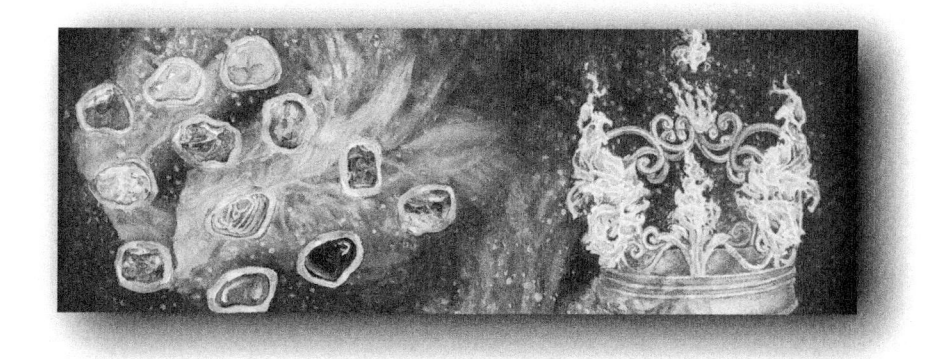

CHAPTER 6

THE PRIESTHOOD OF JONAH

In this chapter, I want to look at Jonah, a priest we do not hear much about.

Over some time, I set my heart to purposefully begin to engage with Jonah. I have become fascinated with this man's walk with YHVH, in the same way I have with Ezekiel, Moses, Abraham, Jacob and other people of the Lord.

Jonah was able to facilitate what YHVH wanted because of the way he engaged with the purpose of YHVH here within creation.

I want to talk about being a priest from Jonah's perspective, how Jonah operated and what he did regarding the priesthood. The book of Jonah shows the way YHVH initiates His will on earth, particularly with regard to humanity as a corporate group of people. YHVH went after an ungodly nation of about two million people and was able to save them through His intervention. There must have been something in YHVH's heart that drew His attention to this nation in the hope that they would respond. On the other side of this was Jonah, a man who had no time for Gentiles, who was chosen by YHVH to go to them and judge them.

The unfolding of Jonah's call to being a priest to a Gentile nation is absolutely fascinating to me.

> *"Now the word of the LORD came unto Jonah the son of Amittai, saying, Arise, go to Nineveh, that great city, and cry against it; for their wickedness has come up before me."* (Jonah 1:1–2 KJ2000)

Understand that when the Bible says the word of the Lord came to Jonah, it did not come as a voice. It came as arcing letters of light, which show the structure of YHVH's voice made real in a visible way. The living letters of YHVH moved around Jonah, forming an arc to open a window into Heaven where Jonah could observe YHVH and what He was doing. Out of that observation, he would be able to become a participant in what was going on. The words came and opened up the world of YHVH, which empowered Jonah with insight into all that YHVH would do – and he ran away from the fullness of what he observed.

When the Word comes, it does not always come as "Thus says the Lord". It may come as a swirling vortex of living letters framed in light that opens up the complete purpose of YHVH from beginning to end. I believe one reason Jonah fled was that he saw the potential for a Gentile nation to come to repentance.

In the Old Testament, the Spirit of the Lord came around and upon people; it did not come within them. This is one difference between a believer and a Hebrew. As believers today, we have no comprehension of what the Word coming upon us as a precursor to encounter is like, nor what it unlocks.

I have sat with Ezekiel in the cave and watched him stringing the living letters together. We have not engaged in the mystical part of what the people of YHVH had before Christ because as believers, understanding by Holy Spirit flows from within us. It is easier for us than it was for them and not as terrifying.

> "But Jonah rose up to flee unto Tarshish from the presence of the LORD, and went down to Joppa; and he found a ship going to Tarshish: so he paid its fare, and went down into it, to go with them unto Tarshish from the presence of the LORD." (Jonah 1:3 KJ2000)

The Word of the Lord has now become the presence of the Lord to Jonah. I believe that as a priest, prophet and oracle, Jonah was able to engage with YHVH to such an extent that he knew the heart of YHVH from what he had observed within the living letters entangling with him. I believe that the heart of YHVH was not to destroy Nineveh but to get it saved. When YHVH spoke to him and said, "Go to the city, Nineveh", I believe what Jonah was hearing in the heart of YHVH was, "My heart for humanity is such that if you go and cry out, and they repent, then I can love them". I believe Jonah knew that the heart of YHVH was not to destroy humanity but rather to love it back to life. Jonah knew that YHVH is love.

The relational connection Jonah had with YHVH was His presence being with him. Jonah was aware of the tangible, continual presence of YHVH. I believe this tangible presence was what Jonah tried to run away from when he fled to Tarshish.

When the Bible says he "went down to Joppa", that was literally what he was doing: going down. He chose to come out of his position with YHVH to go down to try to hide from YHVH above. *Going down* means he was leaving his position as a priest, coming out of his lofty place with YHVH, turning his back on what he saw YHVH doing and running away from it. In my opinion, he was terrified of YHVH's heart turning to any nation other than that of his people, especially to the people who had been so cruel to his nation. Instead of staying in the high place where he could observe all that was around him, he came down. So, when Jonah turned his face towards Joppa, it indicated he was descending from his union and connection with YHVH.

It is weird that we build walls around the places we meet with YHVH, almost in an idolatrous way. We think He is confined within the walls we have built. We seem to think that we can get away from YHVH by walking away from the places where we have confined Him. This is one of the reactions we as humans seem to have when we come into disagreement with YHVH. It shows we lack understanding that we are the temple of the presence of YHVH – the actual dwelling place of the Holy Spirit. No matter where we go or what we do, He is with us because He dwells in us. As Jonah was an Old Testament son, YHVH's presence was with him and would not leave him, no matter where he went. Wherever Jonah went, YHVH was. The question is this: Why on earth was Jonah trying to get away from YHVH? After all, Jonah knew YHVH was always with him and that he could not escape YHVH.

I think Jonah was trying to escape the reality of the living letters calling him to remember his union with YHVH, pulling him back to renew their call in his life. He was running away from the living letters of YHVH, which followed him as a moving, creating framework and window for him to observe the goodness of YHVH.

> "But the LORD sent out a great wind on the sea, and there was a mighty tempest on the sea, so that the ship was about to be broken." (Jonah 1:4 KJ2000)

Isn't it interesting that YHVH sends a wind and a tempest? The wind is described as blowing. I think that blowing is the Holy Spirit's movement over the face of the deep. In the chaos that Jonah had created by his lack of response to YHVH, YHVH was creating. I believe Jonah knew YHVH would find him.

Jonah was trying to run away, but YHVH found him and sent the Ruach, the breath of His presence, and He also sent a tempest, which was a movement up and down. This movement up and down is a remembrance of Jonah's journey up and down into the presence of YHVH due to YHVH's heart's desire to involve Jonah. The yearning in YHVH's heart for union with Jonah was visible on earth in the tempest.

> *"Then the mariners were afraid, and cried every man unto his god, and cast forth the wares that were in the ship into the sea, to lighten it of them. But Jonah had gone down into the lower part of the ship; and he had lain down, and was fast asleep."* (Jonah 1:5 KJ2000)

Do you remember someone else in the New Testament asleep in a boat when there was a tempest on the water? It was YHSVH (Matthew 8:23–24). Jonah could find the place of peace in the tempest because he found a resting place within the mystery of darkness, as recorded in Genesis 1, where YHVH separated light and darkness. This darkness is not destructive. Instead, it is a realm of unknowing and of rest in the place where there was no light but an awareness of the awe and rest of YHVH.

> *"So the captain came to him, and said unto him, What mean you, O sleeper? arise, call upon your God, if so be that God will think upon us, that we perish not."* (Jonah 1:6 KJ2000)

The shipmaster was frustrated that Jonah was asleep. How could he have a place of complete tranquillity when everything else around him was raging?

> *"And they said every one to his fellow, Come, and let us cast lots, that we may know for whose cause this evil is upon us. So they cast lots, and the lot fell upon Jonah."* (Jonah 1:7 KJ2000)

Until I looked into it, I did not understand how they found the one that was to die. Their practice was to cast lots. They would take a pile of sticks, put them in a bag and shake them around. Then, each man was to draw out a stick. The one who had the shortest stick was the one that was to blame. That way, justice would be served.

THE PRIESTHOOD OF BELIEVERS

> "Then said they unto him, Tell us, we pray you, for whose cause this evil is upon us; What is your occupation? and from where come you? what is your country? and of what people are you?" (Jonah 1:8 KJ2000)

We can see the Lion, the Ox, the Eagle, and the Man here (Revelation 4:6–7): What is your occupation? Here is a priest of YHVH and a prophet (the Man) being asked what his occupation is. What labour have you done? (The Ox). What is your country? Where did he come from? (The Eagle). Who are your people? (The Lion).

> "And he said unto them, I am a Hebrew; and I fear the LORD, the God of heaven, who has made the sea and the dry land." (Jonah 1:9 KJ2000)

Even though he was running away from YHVH, Jonah knew the heart and love of YHVH for humanity. He ran away from the love of YHVH to hide himself so that YHVH could not use him, but YHVH still found him. In the middle of Jonah's turmoil, out of the abundance of his heart, his mouth spoke. What Jonah decreed is the foundation that YHVH laid at the very beginning for all humanity to be based on. Whatever is in your heart is going to come out of your mouth:

> "O generation of vipers, how can you, being evil, speak good things? for out of the abundance of the heart the mouth speaks." (Matthew 12:34 KJ2000)

> "A good man out of the good treasure of his heart brings forth that which is good; and an evil man out of the evil treasure of his heart brings forth that which is evil: for of the abundance of the heart his mouth speaks." (Luke 6:45 KJ2000)

> "And he said unto them, I am a Hebrew; and I fear the LORD, the God of heaven, who has made the sea and the dry land. Then were the men exceedingly afraid, and said unto him, Why have you done this? For the men knew that he fled from the presence of the LORD, because he had told them. Then said they unto him, What shall we do unto you, that the sea may be calm for us? for the sea raged, and was tempestuous." (Jonah 1:9–11 KJ2000)

In the raging of the sea in Jonah's day, to Christ in a boat who calms the raging of the sea (Mark 4:35–39), the sea responds to the decree of YHVH. One of the ways that YHVH brings calm to the raging sea of our own lives is through Christ, the spoken Word. What was started in the Old Testament, Christ finished in the New Testament. Whenever you read that YHSVH does something, do not just read it as a story: go back and find out why He did what He did. Christ made a way so that no one had to run away from His presence ever again. No longer would we be unable to find YHVH if we would only turn our hearts towards Him.

> *"And he said unto them, Take me up, and cast me forth into the sea; so shall the sea be calm for you: for I know that for my sake this great tempest is upon you."* (Jonah 1:12 KJ2000)

Notice how humanity tries to work with humanity even though a word from YHVH has been spoken that is true:

> *"Nevertheless the men rowed hard to bring it to the land; but they could not: for the sea raged, and was tempestuous against them. Therefore they cried unto the LORD, and said, We beseech you, O Lord, we beseech you, let us not perish for this man's life, and lay not upon us innocent blood: for you, O Lord, have done as it pleased you."* (Jonah 1:13–14 KJ2000)

Every Knee Shall Bow

When a religious system sees the face and the glory of YHVH being revealed in a contrary circumstance, even though it does not acknowledge Him, it will still find a way to obey Him. This is because every knee shall bow, whether to confess Him as Lord or to acknowledge His Lordship.

> *"Therefore God also has highly exalted him, and given him a name which is above every name: That at the name of Jesus every knee should bow, of things in heaven, and things in earth, and things under the earth; And that every tongue should confess that Jesus Christ is Lord, to the glory of God the Father."* (Philippians 2:9–11 KJ2000)

YHVH is going to bring to Himself everything that was ever created. It is all going to be under His lordship. There is a difference between what YHVH created and what He made. Anything created as an inert object is subject to the will of the one who made it. This is why He made mankind in His image so that they would have free will to choose to come into obedience. This is about maturity and rulership. When a king comes into a conquered country, the people bow the knee. They do not acknowledge him as their own lord, but they acknowledge his governmental lordship and his seat of government, even if they do not receive him as their king.

> *"So they took up Jonah, and cast him forth into the sea: and the sea ceased from her raging. Then the men feared the LORD exceedingly, and offered a sacrifice unto the LORD, and made vows."* (Jonah 1:15–16 KJ2000)

These men worshipped pagan gods, yet because of the presence of Jonah, the living words around him and the tangible evidence of the manifestation of YHVH through creation, they could do nothing but acknowledge His government over all of creation.

> *"Now the LORD had prepared a great fish to swallow up Jonah."* (Jonah 1:17 KJ2000)

When you go into the hieroglyphic language of the Hebrews, this is not a fish as described in your English translation.

The law of first mention applies here. In the New Testament, Christ was three days in the grave and in the tomb for three days and three nights.

> *"For as Jonah was three days and three nights... so shall the Son of man be three days and three nights in the heart of the earth."* (Matthew 12:40 KJ2000)

What Jonah did in the Old Testament, YHVH responded to in the New Testament and did for humanity because a man – Jonah – had done it. If a man makes a choice to do something, YHVH then has a precedent to also do it. YHVH has given mankind free will. We are not slaves, so we have the choice to engage with YHVH's will or not. When we make a choice, YHVH can unlock what is in His heart because one person made a right choice. For example, when Abraham offered up his son Isaac, YHVH saw the evidence of the heart of a man willing to sacrifice all. Therefore, YHVH was given free right to respond by giving His all.

A man went down into the belly of the creature for three days and three nights, so YHVH had legal precedent to engage in the mystery of darkness to break corruption in humanity. I want you to see how this works. Jonah said it in the Old Testament; Christ fulfilled it in the New Testament.

Even though Jonah was in rebellion against YHVH in running away from Him, I do not believe he was in rebellion against the mandate of YHVH. Jonah knew the heart of YHVH, and this is explained a little later in the text.

> *"So they took up Jonah, and cast him forth into the sea: and the sea ceased from its raging. Then the men feared the LORD exceedingly, and offered a sacrifice unto the LORD, and made vows. Now the LORD had prepared a great fish to swallow up Jonah."* (Jonah 1:15–17 KJ2000)
>
> *"Then Jonah prayed unto the LORD his God out of the fish's belly."* (Jonah 2:1 KJ2000)

There are things I would like you to see here. Firstly, there is no fish, not even a whale, that could house something the size of a human being within its gullet and be able to breathe. A whale's gullet does not have oxygen inside it. Secondly, the acid in the creature's stomach would have been too strong for anyone to survive very long because it is designed to dissolve food such as krill shells and things like that. Finally, I do not believe this "fish" was a whale: it was an entombing of Jonah in a beast in creation in those days. No one knows what the beast was, and some things went on that we cannot explain.

As Jonah spent three days in the belly of the creature, this valley experience was a place of Jonah's deepest connection with YHVH.

> "Then Jonah prayed unto the LORD his God out of the fish's belly, And said, I cried by reason of mine affliction unto the LORD, and he heard me; out of the belly of hell cried I, and thou heardest my voice." (Jonah 2:1–2 KJV)

Jonah has gone from the belly of the beast to the belly of hell.

> "For you had cast me into the deep, in the midst of the seas; and the floods surrounded me: all your billows and your waves passed over me." (Jonah 2:3 KJ2000)

What happened here had nothing to do with Jonah engaging with the creature. Instead, this verse is talking about Jonah walking through time with YHVH.

From the beginning when YHVH set creation in place, He caused Jonah to begin to remember why he had come into creation and what his mandate in creation was. So everything that had gone on was structured around making Jonah begin to remember the mandate of YHVH for his life, to engage with him so YHVH could occupy his heart again.

> "Then I said, I am cast out of your sight; yet I will look again toward your holy temple." (Jonah 2:4 KJ2000)

"Cast out of His sight" means unable to see YHVH. Jonah had been able to see the heart of YHVH. If someone is out of YHVH's sight, they will not be able to observe what YHVH is doing. Jonah was saying he was now unable to see what YHVH was doing. This also means for Jonah, a Hebrew, that he turned his heart away from the observance of engaging with his face towards the temple. When he says, *"Yet I will look again toward your holy temple"*, the implication is that his heart was turning towards the presence of YHVH within creation, engaging again in the place of union and the sanctuary of the dwelling place of YHVH for the Hebrew people. If Jonah was in utter darkness and there was no indication of the position of the Holy Temple, it means that Jonah's heart turned again to engage with the dwelling place of YHVH. (A key to note here is that turning your face towards the position of YHVH is an act of repentance for a Hebrew person).

One of the great mysteries to Gentiles is the Hebrew fascination with and awe of the temple mount in Jerusalem. One of the great mysteries to Hebrews is the mystery presented by Paul that a believer is now the temple of the living God, the dwelling place of His presence (1 Corinthians 3:16). When these two mysteries come together in union with complete understanding from both sides, everything will change. YHVH will have what He has been looking for: one new creation (2 Corinthians 5:17).

> *"The waters surrounded me, even to the soul: the deep closed me round about, the weeds were wrapped about my head."*
> (Jonah 2:5 KJ2000)

In theory, Jonah was in the belly of a whale here. A whale's belly does not have weeds such as sea kelp and other things in its stomach. Large sea creatures like whales filter all of this stuff out before they swallow what they take in. There is symbolism here that is important for us to note. It says that these things were wrapped around Jonah's head. The question to ask is, "What does this mean?" So, let's take a moment to examine this because it is important – especially concerning the head.

If something is wrapped around your head, it shuts down your ability to hear, see, speak and smell. So, the weeds wrapped about his head indicate Jonah coming to the recognition that he was unable to see, hear or speak the mysteries of YHVH here within creation.

The waters that surrounded him point to the mysteries and secrets of YHVH that come out of the waters above and the waters below. The encompassing mystery of the Word of YHVH was beginning to engage with him again. This put Jonah in a place of not being able to run from YHVH. Yet, here he is still talking to YHVH in communion with Him. I wonder if Jonah's heart had really left YHVH or if he was simply terrified of what YHVH would do if he went to Nineveh?

> "I went down to the foundations of the mountains; the earth with her bars closed about me forever: yet have you brought up my life from the pit, O LORD my God." (Jonah 2:6 KJ2000)

Paul said,

> "Behold, I show you a mystery; We shall not all sleep, but we shall all be changed, in a moment, in the twinkling of an eye, at the last trump: for the trumpet shall sound, and the dead shall be raised incorruptible, and we shall be changed. For this corruptible must put on incorruption, and this mortal must put on immortality. So when this corruptible shall have put on incorruption, and this mortal shall have put on immortality, then shall be brought to pass the saying that is written, Death is swallowed up in victory." (1 Corinthians 15:51–54 KJ2000)

Out of what YHVH wants to do inside of him, Jonah is framing up humanity's future out of his connection to YHVH. YHVH is going to cause life to come out of corruption:

> "When my soul fainted within me I remembered the LORD: and my prayer came in unto you, into your holy temple." (Jonah 2:7 KJ2000)

> "They that regard vain idols forsake their own mercy." (Jonah 2:8 KJ2000)

What on earth is that scripture doing in the middle of this narrative with Jonah, and what is going on with him in the belly of the creature? When we do not deal with our self-life, pride instigates itself. When we mentally assent to information and do not walk it out in our life before we try to propagate it, we forsake our own mercy. We judge ourselves as being unworthy when He has already made us worthy through the blood of the Lamb.

> *"But I will sacrifice unto you with the voice of thanksgiving;
> I will pay that that I have vowed. Salvation is of the LORD."*
> (Jonah 2:9 KJ2000)

Jonah began to teach us how to find a way to YHVH's eternal world by choosing with our words to craft a doorway of access into the mystery of YHVH and to have YHSVH at the centre of our hearts.

Jonah's Dimensional Shift

It is fascinating to observe that Jonah made a clear statement about the mandate of his life by making three choices. Here we can see what I describe as the Bench of Three. These are the three witnesses that stand as testimony to Jonah's mandate and call, especially as they have to do with his personal union with the presence of YHVH around him.

1) He sacrificed to the Lord with a voice of thanksgiving.

2) He said he would pay his vows.

   Paying a vow to a prophet is leveraging. Jonah knew how to leverage what he was doing here with the presence of YHVH. He was reaching into our age, leveraging what YHVH was engaging with here within his own life.

3) Salvation. They had no idea what salvation was, except as redemption. Jonah was speaking about redemption.

It is important that we find the pattern of YHVH's fingerprints all throughout scripture.

> *"And the LORD spoke unto the fish, and it vomited out Jonah upon the dry land."* (Jonah 2:10 KJ2000)

Jonah has shifted dimensionally. In my opinion, there is no sea close enough to Nineveh to be within a day's journey of the city's borders. Scripture says nothing about the possibility of the dimensional issues of YHVH taking Jonah back to the very beginning and then shifting him back again to this dimensional reality. Jonah turned his heart: when he came back from the beginning, he unlocked the place of salvation and engaged with YHVH again. I believe that when he says "salvation", what he means is the return of the call. Jonah engaged again with his purpose and the mandate on his life when he turned his heart to the point of repentance. To a Hebrew, returning to the first estate is turning back to the perfect state of awe. Thus, one can become perfected in the process of turning back to the face of YHVH.

> "And the word of the LORD came unto Jonah the second time, saying, Arise, go unto Nineveh, that great city, and preach unto it the preaching that I bid you." (Jonah 3:1–2 KJ2000)

Jonah went through being revealed in the call, to being completely hidden in the midst of the sea and all that YHVH was taking him through, to being unveiled on dry land, and then to being fully revealed as YHVH engaged with him again through the process of brokenness to come to full life. I have always found that YHVH is a being of second chances. It is funny how we, as believers, think that if we miss something the first time, it is lost forever. For the Hebrew people, everything is circular and only increases. The latter glory is greater than the former (Haggai 2:9). Faith is so important when we turn towards YHVH.

> "So Jonah arose, and went unto Nineveh, according to the word of the LORD. Now Nineveh was an exceedingly great city of three days' journey around it." (Jonah 3:3 KJ2000)

Nineveh was a large city. In those days, it was a three days' journey to walk through it.

> "And Jonah began to enter into the city a day's journey, and he cried, and said, Yet forty days, and Nineveh shall be overthrown." (Jonah 3:4 KJ2000)

Here is another mention of three days. Three days in the belly of the creature – three days and three nights. A three days' journey. You can see the pattern. What did Christ do in the three days? He descended, took captivity captive and brought all of captivity out. What Jonah did was the reflection that Christ followed in the same pattern: entering into the bowels, unlocking them and bringing all of captivity out (1 Peter 3:18–20, Ephesians 4:8–10). So, again, here is the pattern: three, three, three, three, three.

> "So the people of Nineveh believed God, and proclaimed a fast, and put on sackcloth, from the greatest of them even to the least of them." (Jonah 3:5 KJ2000)

Jonah knew about YHVH's heart through his engagement in relationship with Him to such an extent that he knew that YHVH was Love. YHVH's desire was not to destroy but to see repentance come. The very thing that Jonah knew would happen was now going to happen. Jonah preached, and the city began to respond.

Nineveh was an ungodly city of two million people who came under the influence of the overshadowing of the hand of YHVH and the Word of YHVH that was sitting over Jonah. Here is a man who forms a trumpet for the framework of the Word and who goes through his own brokenness. Jonah had to walk through his junk so he could come to a full revealing. In that full revealing, the hand of YHVH came over a whole city of three days' journey across. Jonah's choice to obey YHVH saved two million people. Two million people came under the government of the hand of YHVH at Jonah's preaching in a single day, which is to do with going through a burial process to frame up life on the other side.

Jonah spoke, and because of the living letters around him and his engagement with the overshadowing of YHVH, the Word of YHVH began to sit over the city. YHVH's presence was there because one man made a right choice to be a priest of YHVH for a Gentile nation, to present YHVH to them in a way that they could respond to.

This is our role as priests: to be able to present YHVH to humanity in a way that creates a place of repentance and a turning of the hearts of people back towards YHVH.

> "So the people of Nineveh believed God, and proclaimed a fast, and put on sackcloth, from the greatest of them even to the least of them For word came unto the king of Nineveh, and he arose from his throne, and he laid his robe from him, and covered himself with sackcloth, and sat in ashes" (Jonah 3:5–6 KJ2000).

The way that YHVH creates an environment is for everyone from the greatest to the least to begin to acknowledge YHVH's presence and engage with Him through repentance. Repentance to a Hebrew is not saying, "I'm sorry". Again, repentance to a Hebrew is turning towards the faces of YHVH to become flawlessly perfected as He is.

> "And he caused it to be proclaimed and published through Nineveh by the decree of the king and his nobles, saying, Let neither man nor beast, herd nor flock, taste anything: let them not feed, nor drink water: But let man and beast be covered with sackcloth, and cry mightily unto God: yea, let them turn every one from his evil way, and from the violence that is in their hands. Who can tell if God will turn and relent, and turn away from his fierce anger, that we perish not?" (Jonah 3:7–9 KJ2000).

The king was picking up the very call of Jonah. Through faith in Jonah's words, he began to make a decree to negotiate with YHVH on the same level. Moses said exactly the same words to YHVH:

> "Why should the Egyptians speak, and say, For mischief did he bring them out, to slay them in the mountains, and to consume them from the face of the earth? Turn from your fierce wrath, and change from this evil against your people. Remember Abraham, Isaac, and Israel, your servants, to whom you swore by your own self, and said unto them, I will multiply your descendants as the stars of heaven, and all this land that I have spoken of will I give unto your descendants, and they shall inherit it forever. And the LORD turned from the evil which he thought to do unto his people" (Exodus 32:12–14 KJ2000).

The king of Nineveh was asking, "Will YHVH turn and repent?" *Turn and repent* means to come back to the perfect state of awe.

> "Who can tell if God will turn and relent, and turn away from his fierce anger, that we perish not? And God saw their works, that they turned from their evil way; and God relented of the disaster, that he had said that he would bring upon them; and he did it not." (Jonah 3:9–10 KJ2000)

Here was a person that was not a Hebrew, yet he heard the Word of YHVH and he took the example of Jonah's response to YHVH, going through brokenness and coming back into life. Here was the king of an ungodly nation who heard the Word, was influenced by YHVH, turned his face, came to repentance and then negotiated with YHVH, saying, "If we do this, perhaps YHVH will turn from His fierce wrath and repent" (see Jonah 3:7–9).

> "And God saw their works, that they turned from their evil way; and God relented of the disaster, that he had said that he would bring upon them; and he did it not." (Jonah 3:10 KJ2000)

YHVH repented of what He was going to do to His people, Israel, in the same way. I believe Moses knew about Jonah and was able to engage in this process to see the truth of YHVH revealed in creation. This is our process. These are the things we have to choose to go through. We must deal with our junk. This is a process we have to walk through; it does not just happen. The king did not assent to knowledge: he gave assent to YHVH, engaged with YHVH himself, and out of that engagement, he gained life for his people.

This is an ungodly king negotiating with YHVH, and YHVH responds to his repentance and negotiation. To me, that is absolutely stunning!

> "But it displeased Jonah exceedingly, and he was very angry. And he prayed unto the LORD, and said, I pray you, O LORD, was not this my saying, when I was yet in my country? Therefore I fled before unto Tarshish: for I knew that you are a gracious God, and merciful, slow to anger, and of great kindness, and you relent from the destruction. Therefore now, O LORD, take, I beseech you, my life from

me; for it is better for me to die than to live." (Jonah 4:1–3 KJ2000)

Jonah was angry because YHVH repented of what He would do in judgement. I think Jonah wanted judgement. So, YHVH had to deal with Jonah regarding his issues with judgement. Jonah chapter 4 deals specifically with the issue of how Jonah viewed a Gentile nation that he considered unworthy and had judged in his own heart. It is amazing how we lose grace for others when we judge them within their own condition, especially if they do not have the knowledge of YHVH in what they are doing.

The king positioned himself as a priest of YHVH for his people. Even though YHVH would not speak to heathen people, here is a king who created a response in the heart of YHVH to the point where YHVH said, "I will no longer do this, because what you have done is enough".

This is the process of repentance. When we repent, YHVH is able to do what He does because the little we have done is enough. To me, this speaks volumes about the love of YHVH. We next see what I would describe as Jonah having a pity party because he wanted YHVH to judge and destroy the city of Nineveh. After all, this was what was in his own heart. The scripture below clearly shows this:

> "Therefore now, O LORD, take, I beseech you, my life from me; for it is better for me to die than to live. Then said the LORD, Do you do well to be angry?" (Jonah 4:3–4 KJ2000)

YHVH is saying to Jonah, "Yes, you should be very angry, but your anger should not really be directed at Me. It should be directed at you, yourself."

> "So Jonah went out of the city, and sat on the east side of the city, and there made himself a booth, and sat under it in the shadow, till he might see what would become of the city." (Jonah 4:5 KJ2000)

THE PRIESTHOOD OF JONAH

Nineveh had already repented, and YHVH had already given them a way out. Still, Jonah was angry with YHVH, and he sat in the east. The east is the way of YHVH's coming into creation. Jonah was sitting as a gatekeeper for Nineveh to see what YHVH was going to do. He was sent to a Gentile nation, and that Gentile nation had turned to YHVH, which meant there was another group of people who were not Hebrew that were now in relationship with the presence of YHVH.

An ungodly nation that had nothing to do with YHVH turned to YHVH because one man, one priest, one person made a choice to allow YHVH to intervene with humanity. Remember, YHVH is love. All those that love are born of YHVH. He that does not love does not know YHVH.

> *"The one who does not love has not become acquainted with God [does not and never did know Him], for God is love. [He is the originator of love, and it is an enduring attribute of His nature.]"* (1 John 4:8 AMP)

The love of YHVH knows no bounds and is willing to reach over, through, around and underneath any environment to find a way to hook your heart and pull it back to Him. Yet, even when we turn back to Him, our stuff can still be raging underneath the surface, just as it was with Jonah. YHVH will reach in, hook you and pull you to Himself. He will look for any environment, any circumstance, to help you come back to yourself so that you can stand in who you are as a son.

This is the love of YHVH being revealed in creation in an amazing way. One reason I have set my heart to engage with Jonah is that there are things about his life that are so amazingly remarkable, but there is so little written about his life. In the same way as some of us are fully hidden in obscurity, here is a remarkable life that does not need the limelight and does not need to be fully revealed to find connectivity with YHVH.

Often our lives can be viewed as a fruit tree. If you begin to look at your own tree, you can examine the fruit of what is around your life. For many of us, there are measures of fruit, from fully ripe to not at all ripe. We must begin to look at the things inside our lives that are fruitful and ready to be picked as ripe. When I see circumstances changing in my life or the immediate environment changing as it did with Jonah, I ask this question: What is YHVH creating around me to provide an avenue so that He can hook into me, draw me in His love and bring me to a greater point of connectivity with Himself?

Activation

Father, I ask today for Your goodness to sit over those reading this. I ask that You would begin to put Your hook deep within their spirit being. That You would create such holy consternation inside of them that there is no way they could turn away from their yearning to engage with Your presence, Father, to be found different than they are today.

I thank You for the example of Jonah and the way You orchestrated everything around his life. Father, I want to honour the life of Jonah. I honour what You did in his life. I honour the men and women of the ungodly nation of Nineveh who repented and became a nation that walked in Your ways. Father, I want to thank You that through their precedent, You are able to create in us a way where there is no way. That You would come under, over, around us, in front of us, behind us, Father. That You would entangle us to the point where we would turn our eyes to the mountain of Your presence, that the Word of the Lord would be released, Father, in full flight, in full function; that we would be able to sit in the east gate and observe the moving of the hand of YHVH within creation. Amen.

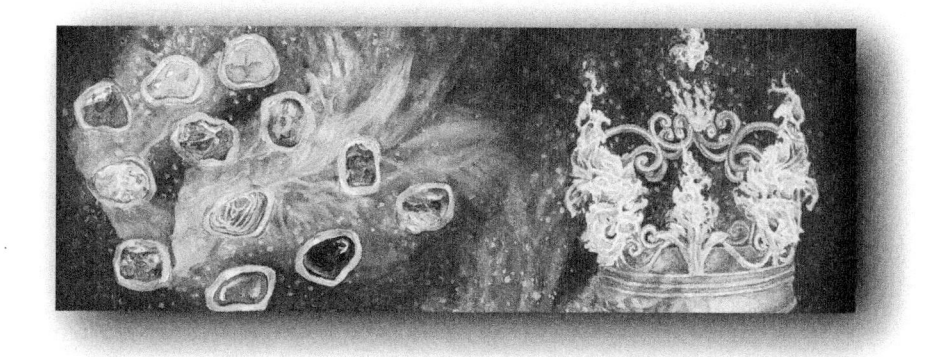

Chapter 7

THE PRIESTHOOD OF HANNAH

I have been on a journey in priesthood for a number of years. As we are shown by the example of Moses in the Bible, the nature of a priest is to present oneself before YHVH to have a face-to-face engagement, from which He may unlock or change His mind. You engage so that you can petition for others or become a way for others to have what they could never have had.

"The high priest went alone once a year, not without blood, which he offered for himself and for the people's sins committed in ignorance" (Hebrews 9:7 NKJV). I believe that when the high priest went in, the seat inside the Holy of Holies became a transportation device which would shift him all the way back to before the second day of creation. The record of Lucifer's trading started there before there was any record of sin. Then, the sin of all Israel was reconciled as the high priest engaged with the time before sin. He could then bring all of *no*

THE PRIESTHOOD OF BELIEVERS

sin back to Israel, so Israel was with no sin, all in a fraction of a second. I personally believe that the poor high priest was never seen again, which is why there was a new high priest every year.

Being a priest is important, so I started to find ways that men and women walked in a priestly capacity through the Bible. My whole bent going forward is to understand what is in the Bible about the issues of the priesthood because amazing things are going on that we may just read as stories. So, I will tell you a story in the NIV – the New Ian Version.

Elkanah had two wives. The name of one was Hannah. In Hebrew, the name is חַנָּה with the letter Nun in the middle. Nun signifies a multiplying river. Het and Hey surrounding Nun are as YHVH's breath being breathed out both at the beginning and the end, like two metaphorical hydrogen atoms. So, it is like an arc being framed over a double-seated river. The name of the other wife was Peninnah. At the beginning of the account, Peninnah had children, but Hannah did not. Elkanah went up out of his city to worship and sacrifice unto the Lord of Hosts in Shiloh. We will see why these names are important as the account unfolds:

> "And he had two wives; the name of one was Hannah, and the name of the other Peninnah: Peninnah had children, but Hannah had no children.
>
> This man went up from his city yearly to worship and sacrifice to the LORD of hosts in Shiloh. Also the two sons of Eli, Hophni and Phinehas, the priests of the LORD, were there.
>
> And whenever the time came for Elkanah to make an offering, he would give portions to Peninnah, his wife, and to all her sons and daughters.
>
> But to Hannah he would give a double portion; for he loved Hannah, although the LORD had closed her womb.
>
> And her rival also provoked her severely, to make her miserable, because the LORD had closed her womb." (1 Samuel 1:2–6 NKJV)

Remember: *"Your adversary the devil walks about like a roaring lion, seeking whom he may devour"* (1 Peter 5:8 NKJV).

As we see here with Peninnah, the devourer may come through someone sitting right next to you. It was not actually the woman. The demonic world was working through Peninnah. It knew that if Hannah had a child, there was a double river that would flow, which would completely change all of Israel. The adversary wanted that flow shut down, so he spoke words of deception.

> *"So it was, year by year, when she went up to the house of the LORD, that she provoked her; therefore she wept and did not eat. Then Elkanah her husband said to her, "Hannah, why do you weep? Why do you not eat? And why is your heart grieved? Am I not better to you than ten sons?" So Hannah arose after they had finished eating and drinking in Shiloh. Now Eli the priest was sitting on the seat by the doorpost of the tabernacle of the LORD. And she was in bitterness of soul, and prayed to the LORD and wept in anguish."* (1 Samuel 1:7–10 NKJV)

In those days, a woman could not go before the presence of YHVH in the temple. Here was a woman who was suddenly becoming a priest, taking the place of the high priest who was sitting down by the post rather than petitioning for those who came up to bring their portion to YHVH. YHVH completely bypassed the priest Himself and gave Hannah the right of access so she could present herself in front of Him, thereby operating in the priesthood before her day. Next time some idiot calls you, "Woman!", say, "Thank you", because that is what Adam named his wife in Eden, which was her first estate. The name *woman* means that you are returned to your first estate.

Hannah rose up early, so now we go back to the very beginning: light, day; darkness, night. The morning is not the beginning of the new day in Israel. Instead, the day starts in the evening, which is the mystery being unfolded. She woke up in the mystery that was being unfolded.

THE PRIESTHOOD OF BELIEVERS

> *"Then she made a vow and said, 'O Lord of hosts, if You will indeed look on the affliction of Your maidservant and remember me, and not forget Your maidservant, but will give Your maidservant a male child, then I will give him to the LORD all the days of his life, and no razor shall come upon his head.'"* (1 Samuel 1:11 NKJV)

When the Bible says something once, you read it; when it says it twice, you pay attention; and when it says it three times, it means that there is something majorly important to pay attention to here. Hannah was reminding YHVH of her status, that she was not just a woman or a wife. She was His maidservant, which means, *"The one my soul loves"* (Song of Songs 3:4 TLV).

Hannah has got some way of twisting YHVH around her little finger!

Hannah was going beyond just asking here. She was becoming an oracle. I want you to see that there is a different priesthood operating here. She had gone from petitioning to becoming an oracle and speaking a mystery. This happened before the child had even come into her womb, which I believe means that she knew the destiny of the child before he even left Heaven. Why? Because standing before YHVH takes you trans-dimensionally into the very beginning. A Melchizedek Order priesthood is happening when Hannah speaks this out into creation. Can you imagine being her son's spirit and his being standing under the Yasod, knowing his mother is on the trading floor committing him to become a Nazarite before he even arrives in creation inside her womb?[11]

> *"And it happened, as she continued praying before the LORD, that Eli watched her mouth."* (1 Samuel 1:12 NKJV)

Eli did not discern her heart – instead of her heart, he watched her mouth.

---

[11] For more on the Yasod, see Chapter 10, "Heaven's Court System".

PRIESTHOOD OF HANNAH

"Now Hannah spoke in her heart; only her lips moved, but her voice was not heard. Therefore, Eli thought she was drunk." (1 Samuel 1:13 NKJV)

We are witnessing vibrational frequencies operating within Hannah. Here is the priesthood completely revealing itself, a voice giving utterance to something that is a mystery, unlocking that mystery, and preparing a seed for birth into creation.

"So Eli said to her, How long will you be drunk? Put your wine away from you!" (1 Samuel 1:14 NKJV)

It is weird how the religious system says, "Put away the drunk. Put away the stuff we do not want to know. We are so busy doing our own thing that we do not even know you are coming before YHVH and standing as an oracle and a priest". Eli should have been doing that and operating in that realm instead of telling Hannah not to go there. Yet, Hannah went anyway because her heart was connected with YHVH, and something was going on in her affecting the world around her and empowering her to engage face-to-face with YHVH, to get hold of Him and not let go until she got her answer, because her heart said: "I am your maidservant, the lover of your soul, Lord!" This is the attitude we are to have: "I am sold out for You, YHVH". There has to be a desperation in our engaging with YHVH.

***

I had an encounter with the Holy Spirit some time ago. I had seen Him before as a pillar of fire, as a mist, and as a dove. I had seen Him in a different realm, in the dimensional realms of His world, and in the celestial arena. It is amazing to see Him, but I wanted to know Him. I did not want to know just what He is, what He does, and how He moves – I wanted the person. So I set my heart to engage with Him. "Who are You, Holy Spirit? As a Being that lives in my body, who are You?"

I remember engaging in my room. I felt a movement, a vibration. I turned, and there was a being, standing like an old, hooded monk. I knew it was the Holy Spirit because I know how it feels when He moves into the room. Holy Spirit, YHSVH and the Father each move differently and have different sounds and frequencies that they move with. I was sitting there thinking, "I am curious. I am not interested in shoulder to shoulder. I want to see Your face. I want to see what is in there. I want to see the Person." I began to engage, and I was curious – I wanted to have a look. If you are not curious, you do not get to see. I bent to a certain point where I could see into the hood, and I thought: "Now I want to see more!" I looked into the hood because now my curiosity had gone past fear... "Woooaaah!" What I saw was like moving pinpoints of light forming circles with the colours of the rainbow and fire all burning and forming an image of a face. I found myself saying, "Hello, Holy Spirit!" It changed my life because I realised that what I saw lives in me, in my body.

***

"So Eli said to her, How long will you be drunk? Put your wine away from you! But Hannah answered and said, No, my lord, I am a woman of a sorrowful spirit: I have drunk neither wine nor intoxicating drink, but have poured out my soul before the LORD." (1 Samuel 1:14–15 NKJV)

Hannah had just figuratively slapped the high priest because the high priest didn't even recognise the Presence in the chamber when Eli should have been the one petitioning for Hannah. Isn't that just like the religious system that tells you that you are deceived and teaching doctrines of devils when they do not even know what is in their midst?

***

I was hidden for 20 years in my church life. The members of my church had little or no idea that I was speaking in conferences. I would come in and out, and people would say,

"Oh, Ian was not in church." Who are we doing it for? Is it for the audience of one, or is it to get recognition from people? I used to love being in the back of the church during prayer meetings. I would get into the Presence, get up, engage and wrap myself around the presence of YHVH and do whatever was necessary. I remember being in church one day, and everybody was clapping to the three fast and two slow songs – you know, the religious system. I thought, "I cannot do this, YHVH. I am coming up because I am bored." I was bored with the methods they had to use because their DNA was so messed up. Three happy-clappies to make them engage, to open up some realms in harmony with the voice of YHVH so they could engage with their DNA.

I was sitting in the back of the church, engaging with the presence of YHVH, and I felt YHSVH walk into the back of the church. I said, "Oh, glory." I turned around, and He was looking at me, and I was looking at Him. We were having that kind of conversation where you copy what you see. I looked at him. He looked at me. He smiled, turned around and walked out. I thought, "What? You just walked out!" The church did not seem to know that He had come into the house: they carried on doing their own thing. The pillar of the religious system was governing their lives without His lordship in the middle of them. I thought, "No, YHVH. I do not ever want to be like that!"

***

So here is this poor woman: *"Do not consider your maidservant a wicked woman, for out of the abundance of my complaint and grief I have spoken until now. Then Eli answered and said, Go in peace, and the YHVH of Israel grant your petition which you have asked of Him"* (1 Samuel 1:16–17 NKJV). The Hebrew meaning of the word *peace* in this passage is *Shalom*. Shalom is a being. "Go in Shalom," not just *shalom* as peace, but "Go in the being of peace". Israel is the nation birthed from Abraham, which gives them a state in an estate. Eli is now saying, "Go in the full estate of the provision of the relationship of Abraham, Isaac and Jacob with YHVH".

YHVH introduced Himself to Abraham in Genesis 17:1 as "Ani El Shaddai", which can be translated as "I am God your supply". The English translation really does not do the Hebrew justice. To expand, the name can be further translated, "Walk yourself to My faces and become flawless".

YHVH introduced Himself to Isaac:

> "Do not go down to Egypt; live in the land of which I shall tell you. Dwell in this land, and I will be with you and bless you; for to you and your descendants I give all these lands, and I will perform the oath which I swore to Abraham your father. And I will make your descendants multiply as the stars of heaven; I will give to your descendants all these lands; and in your seed all the nations of the earth shall be blessed; because Abraham obeyed My voice and kept My charge, My commandments, My statutes, and My laws." (Genesis 26:2–5 NKJV)

When YHVH introduced Himself to Jacob before he became Israel, He said: *"I am the LORD God of Abraham your father and the God of Isaac"* (Genesis 28:13 NKJV). This created the structure of engaging with the DNA record of the relationship that another has had. The pattern was laid for us to come into the fullness of more than they had and receive the full promise they did not walk into. *"Then Eli answered and said, 'Go in peace, and the God of Israel grant your petition which you have asked of Him'"* (1 Samuel 1:17 NKJV). Eli was saying, "You will receive the full promise of all that you have never had, and you will have more than all those that have gone before you".

If you read it as a story, you will not see any of this because there is a massive interplay that you only see when you understand a little bit about the Hebrew culture, which we mostly miss with our Western mindset.

Eli just negated his position as a priest again. He gave the full responsibility for her life and her future into Hannah's own hands. It was the priest's job to have the future of all Israel on his hands once a year. Why did Eli do this for Hannah? Because he recognised a different government. There was something more in her life than was in his life, and a tree will bear fruit of its own kind.

> *"Hannah said, 'Let your maidservant find grace and favor in your sight.' So the woman went on her way and ate, and her face was no longer sad."* (1 Samuel 1:18 AMP)

We think of grace as the power to receive His will – but no, Grace is a being. Grace is one of the handmaidens of the Spirit of Wisdom. We can read into Hannah's words: "Let your maidservant, the lover of Your soul, find the realm of this being that brings me into the fullness of YHVH".

"And they rose up in the morning early, and worshipped before the LORD*"* (1 Samuel 1:19 AMP). (They rose up in the realm of the mystery of YHVH revealed in creation. This mystery can be seen wrapped up in the words *morning* and *early*.) Where was the high priest? His presence and his governmental responsibility are absent from the account at this point.

After YHVH took Abraham to count the stars of Heaven (Genesis 15:5), Abraham came back to his wife and said to her, "We are going to have a baby". She laughed because she knew that nothing worked anymore! Yet something intrinsically changed in their DNA when YHVH renamed Abram, *Abraham*. The very fact that he encountered a realm beyond what was humanly possible unlocked something in his genetic pool that his wife also caught. Sarah was already beautiful (Genesis 12:11), but the Abrahamic priesthood changed his body to such an extent that it changed her body, too. At the age of ninety, I believe she became the most beautiful woman in the known world. This is an Old Testament example of what we are going to come into.

> *"The family got up early the next morning, worshiped before the* LORD*, and returned to their home in Ramah. Elkanah knew Hannah his wife, and the* LORD *remembered her*

> *[prayer]. It came about in due time, after Hannah had conceived, that she gave birth to a son; she named him Samuel, saying, 'Because I have asked for him from the LORD.'*
>
> *Then the man Elkanah and all his household went up to offer to the LORD the yearly sacrifice and pay his vow."* (1 Samuel 1:19–21 AMP)

Before this, Elkanah had gone up to offer his sacrifice. Now, he was going up to offer his vow. What vow? The vow that Hannah had given before YHVH: "I will lend my child to You all the days of his life, and the razor shall not pass over his head." Elkanah had taken responsibility for the enactment of his wife's priesthood, engaging with the same priesthood. Elkanah was presenting that same vow before YHVH even though Hannah did not go up because the evidence of YHVH's glory was now in his wife's womb

> *"Hannah did not go up, for she said to her husband, 'I will not go up until the child is weaned; and then I will bring him, so that he may appear before the LORD and remain there as long as he lives.'"* (1 Samuel 1:22 AMP)

Unless you appear before YHVH, which requires going somewhere, you will not be able to abide there forever.

I can remember the first time I met the being who is recorded as an unbeliever in the Bible, called doubting Thomas. Do you think that Thomas was a doubter? It is a doctrine of devils that he is a doubting Thomas. The reality is that he did not believe the full measure he could have believed, but he was the only one who put his hands into the side of YHSVH. He did not touch the outside. He was the only one who was invited to put his hand into the wound. I believe that when he did, he touched another world.

> *"Elkanah her husband said to her, 'Do what seems best to you. Wait until you have weaned him; only may the LORD establish and confirm His word.'"* (1 Samuel 1:23a AMP)

Here is the dad, now becoming a prophet. He is actually ordaining his son into a full priesthood to become a prophet.

> *"So the woman remained [behind] and nursed her son until she weaned him. Now when she had weaned him, she took him up with her, along with a three-year-old bull, an ephah of flour, and a leather bottle of wine [to pour over the burnt offering for a sweet fragrance], and she brought Samuel to the LORD'S house in Shiloh, although the child was young. Then they slaughtered the bull, and brought the child to Eli. Hannah said, 'Oh, my lord! As [surely as] your soul lives, my lord, I am the woman who stood beside you here, praying to the LORD. For this child I prayed, and the LORD has granted me my request which I asked of Him. Therefore I have also dedicated him to the LORD; as long as he lives he is dedicated to the LORD." And they worshiped the LORD there.'"* (1 Samuel 1:23b–28 AMP)

She established a realm of government over the release of her son. As Western believers, we just give the responsibility for our children over to YHVH, but that is wrong. We have to lend them. Hannah is our example, you lend them to YHVH to be before YHVH forever, and then they are YHVH's responsibility. If you give them, you negate your responsibility to train them in the way of the Lord. That means that if they do not walk with YHVH, you can blame Him instead of taking responsibility as parents, but do not come under condemnation if your children do not walk with YHVH because that is also their choice.

I love my granddaughter. She is fascinating. Out of all the words she is saying now, she does not even say *mama* or *dada* yet. She says "Nan-dad" or "Grand-dad". My daughter texted me the other day: "Hey dad, my daughter is staring at a wall where there is no one and talking and pointing. I think she has got your problem!" I said, "That's my girl!"

She lent him, so: *"For this child I prayed, and the LORD has granted me my petition which I asked of Him"* (1 Samuel 1:27 NKJV). She did not say that she asked Eli to petition YHVH for her because she knew she had no right to do that, but YHVH granted it because she stepped into another age and another priesthood that gave her complete access to YHVH without Him killing her.

> "Therefore I also have lent him to the LORD; as long as he lives he shall be lent to the LORD.' So they worshiped the LORD there." (1 Samuel 1:28 NKJV)

> "Hannah prayed and said,
> 'My heart rejoices and triumphs in the LORD;
> My horn (strength) is lifted up in the LORD,
> My mouth has opened wide [to speak boldly] against my enemies,
> Because I rejoice in Your salvation.'" (1 Samuel 2:1 AMP)

She administered something here and released the four faces of YHVH around her son. She stood as an oracle and spoke a foundation over her son's life that he would be able to stand on in his future, and the things that he would operate out of. We have to do this.

> "There is no one holy like the LORD,
> There is no one besides You,
> There is no Rock like our God." (1 Samuel 2:2 AMP)

They had no idea about the rock yet, which was Christ. He had not arrived yet. She was operating out of the supply of a different priesthood.

> "Talk no more so very proudly;
> Let no arrogance come from your mouth,
> For the LORD is the God of knowledge;
> And by Him actions are weighed.

> "The bows of the mighty men are broken,
> And those who stumbled are girded with strength.
> Those who were full have hired themselves out for bread,
> And the hungry have ceased to hunger.
> Even the barren has borne seven,
> And she who has many children has become feeble.

> "The LORD kills and makes alive;
> He brings down to the grave and brings up.
> The LORD makes poor and makes rich;
> He brings low and lifts up.

*He raises the poor from the dust
And lifts the beggar from the ash heap,
To set them among princes
And make them inherit the throne of glory."* (1 Samuel 2:3–8 NKJV)

Hannah was reaching way beyond her day, talking about Ezekiel's throne of glory when she would not have had the knowledge of it. She saw something that her son was going to operate out of because she had unlocked something by lending him, engaging with him and speaking of him when he was not even in her womb yet.

Do you know why your teenagers are wandering around the streets trying to figure out who YHVH is? Is it because we did not make a decree over them to give them hope to live for the future? We were told that YHSVH was returning in the year 2000, and we would be raptured. Oh, sorry, it was 2011. Oh, it was 2016, 2017, then it was 2019 and a half… One day they may get it right, but I do not believe it will happen the way they think it will.

*"He guards the feet of His godly (faithful) ones,
But the wicked ones are silenced and perish in darkness;
For a man shall not prevail by might."* (1 Samuel 2:9 AMP)

You say, "Oh, the night has a demon". No, the wicked shall be silent in the revealing of the mystery that has never been seen.

*"The adversaries of the LORD will be broken to pieces;
He will thunder against them in the heavens,
The LORD will judge the ends of the earth;
And He will give strength to His king,
And will exalt the horn (strength) of His anointed."* (1 Samuel 2:10 AMP)

Let's talk about thunder for a bit. The Bible says that the children of Israel saw thunder and lightning. How do you see thunder?

THE PRIESTHOOD OF BELIEVERS

> *"When the people saw the thunder and lightning and heard the trumpet and saw the mountain in smoke, they trembled with fear. They stayed at a distance."* (Exodus 20:18 NKJV)

Was the thunder like the wind that blows, but you cannot see from where it comes or where it goes, but you can see the fruit of it? (John 3:8). No. According to the Hebrews, thunder is a glorified voice speaking in the middle of fire. So, when the Bible says He thunders on His adversaries (1 Samuel 2:10), what it becomes is a glorified voice speaking in fire to all that are adversaries to YHVH (Revelation 19:6).

> *"The LORD will judge the ends of the earth;*
> *And He will give strength to His king,*
> *And will exalt the horn (strength) of His anointed."*
> *Elkanah [and his wife Hannah] returned to Ramah to his house. But the child [Samuel] served the LORD under the guidance of Eli the priest."* (1 Samuel 2:10b–11 AMP)

Samuel was a boy with an unwoven purpose and destiny for his life, already engaging with the presence of YHVH, even at his immature stage. We are sons of YHVH; Samuel was a small son showing us what is coming for us in our day. The issue is getting before YHVH and standing in front of all those that are supposed to be the priests and engaging with YHVH yourself. The pastor is not your covering.

"Now Eli's sons were evil men [scoundrels; good-for-nothings]; they did not care about [know; respect; regard] the LORD" (1 Samuel 2:12 EXB). Remember that Hophni and Phinehas were the priests of YHVH? I wonder how many people today are ministering before YHVH but do not know YHVH themselves.

"This is what the priests would normally do to [… nor about their duties as priests for] the people: Every time someone brought [offered] a sacrifice, the meat would be cooked [boiled] in a pot. The priest's servant would then come carrying a fork that had three prongs. He would plunge the fork into the pot or the kettle or cauldron or pan" (1 Samuel 2:13–14a EXB). It is interesting to look at the customs of the

system we have today in church. It has sometimes become "I want more from you than I can give you". We used to have "vision catching" meetings at the beginning of every year, and it really was to get more money. Sow into the vision so we can be in the vision.

> "Whatever the fork brought out of the pot belonged to the priest. But this is how they treated all the Israelites who came to Shiloh to offer sacrifices. Even before the fat was burned, the priest's servant would come to the person offering sacrifices and say, 'Give the priest some meat to roast. He won't accept boiled meat from you, only raw meat.' If the one who offered the sacrifice said, 'Let the fat be burned up first as usual, and then take anything you want,' the priest's servant would answer, 'No, give me the meat now. If you don't, I'll take it by force.' The LORD saw that [In the LORD'S sight] the sin of the servants was very great [serious] because they ·did not show respect for [treated with contempt; despised] the offerings made to [of] the LORD. But Samuel obeyed [served; ministered before] the LORD. As a boy he wore a linen holy vest [ephod; a special garment worn only by priests]." (1 Samuel 2:14b–18 EXB)

Linen symbolises righteousness. A linen ephod is a band worn around the waist. In Revelation 1, the Son wore a linen garment with a girdle, which is an ephod, a linen ephod around His waist.[12] A linen ephod is a symbol of the power of attorney given to a king to legislate on behalf of YHVH, even though he is immature.

> "Moreover, his mother would make him a little robe and would bring it up to him each year when she came up with her husband to offer the yearly sacrifice. Then Eli would bless Elkanah and his wife and say, 'May the LORD give you children by this woman in place of the one she asked for which was dedicated to the LORD.' Then they would return to their own home. And [the time came when] the LORD visited Hannah, so that she conceived and gave birth to three sons and two daughters. And the boy Samuel grew before the LORD." (1 Samuel 2:19–21 AMP)

---

[12] "In the midst of the lampstands I saw someone like the Son of Man, dressed in a robe reaching to His feet, and with a golden sash wrapped around His chest" (Revelation 1:13 AMP).

So Samuel grew before the Lord. Samuel grew before YHVH, not before people. You must grow before YHVH before you can find the favour of YHVH and the favour of people.

> *"Now Eli was very old; and he heard about everything that his sons were doing to all [the people of] Israel, and how they were lying with the women who served at the entrance to the Tent of Meeting (tabernacle). Eli said to them, 'Why do you do such things, the evil things that I hear from all these people? No, my sons; for the report that I keep hearing from the passers-by among the LORD people is not good. If one man does wrong and sins against another, God will intercede (arbitrate) for him; but if a man does wrong to the LORD ord, who can intercede for him?'"* (1 Samuel 2:22–25a AMP)

I would say it should have been Eli who entreated YHVH for his sons.

> *"...But they would not listen to their father, for it was the LORD will to put them to death. But the boy Samuel continued to grow in stature and in favor both with the LORD and with men. Then a man of God (prophet) came to Eli and said to him, 'Thus says the LORD...Why then do you kick at (despise) My sacrifice and My offering which I commanded in My dwelling place, and honor your sons more than Me, by fattening yourselves with the choicest part of every offering of My people Israel?' Therefore the LORD God of Israel declares, 'I did indeed say that your house and that of [Aaron] your father would walk [in priestly service] before Me forever.' But now the LORD declares, 'Far be it from Me—for those who honor Me I will honor, and those who despise Me will be insignificant and contemptible. Behold, the time is coming when I will cut off your strength and the strength of your father's house, so that there will not be an old man in your house...Hophni and Phinehas: on the same day both of them shall die. But I will raise up for Myself a faithful priest who will do according to what is in My heart and in My soul; and I will build him a permanent and enduring house, and he will walk before My anointed forever.'"* (1 Samuel 2:25b–27a, 29-31, 34b–35 AMP)

The question to ask here is, who was the man of YHVH that came to the high priest, and where did that man come from? For Samuel to be growing before YHVH and growing in favour with YHVH and people, he would have already been engaging with his scroll beyond his day. Hannah already knew who Samuel was going to be in the future, which was a prophet speaking to the priest of the day.

> *"But I will raise up for Myself a faithful priest," faith-full, not faithful, "who will do according to what is in My heart and in My soul; and I will build him a permanent and enduring house, and he will walk before My anointed forever."* (1 Samuel 2:35 AMP)

What YHVH is saying is that He is going to raise up a child who is going to be faithful, who will know His mind and His heart. This is, of course, Samuel.

"And the child Samuel ministered unto the LORD before Eli. And the word of the LORD was precious in those days; there was no open vision" (1 Samuel 3:1 KJV). The reason there was no open vision was that Eli, the high priest of the day, was not in his position to receive the revelation for the people. The priest's house had become a dunghill because of the behaviour of his two sons. What they were doing was an abomination before YHVH, and as a result, the heavens closed (Deuteronomy 28:23). I find it really interesting that when the heavens begin to close, people continue to prophesy, and they start saying weird things like, "YHSVH is coming back tomorrow." When I hear that garbage coming out, I know that the heavens are closed because the priests of the house are not sitting in their posts. Whenever you find a doomsday sayer that does not tell you that there is an advancing Kingdom of which there will be no end, that is because the heavens are closed. There must always be a hope beyond tomorrow.

> *"And it came to pass at that time, while Eli was lying down in his place, and when his eyes had begun to grow so dim that he could not see."* (1 Samuel 3:2 NKJV)

Eli's eyes were closing and becoming dark, so he could no longer see. The mystery of YHVH was showing up in a place he could not understand because it had gone beyond the knowledge of his own life. YHVH was unlocking something that had been given to another generation and not to him.

> *"And ere the lamp of YHVH went out in the temple of the* L*ORD*, *where the ark of YHVH was, and Samuel was laid down to sleep."* (1 Samuel 3:3 KJV)

A young boy lay down in front of the ark, and the candle went out. One of the most important roles inside the temple is to keep the candle burning. The candle is fed by an oil ladle that has a little hole going on the candlestick that feeds the wick on top of the candlestick. If the candle goes out, it means there is no oil inside the candle holder. There is no more supply, so there is no more anointing left within the house of YHVH. The candle went out in the house of YHVH because the priest was now completely blind. Yet, there is always, always, always, in every generation, a group of people that have kept the mysteries of YHVH alive. Samuel slept before the ark. What is the function of sleep? Going into the mystery so that the mystery can be revealed in the dawn of the day. Samuel entered into the mystery of YHVH before the Ark of the Glory of YHVH, so he could bring the revelation of his day into what he was going to become.

> *"Samuel was lying down in the temple of the* L*ORD*, *where the ark of God was, that the* L*ORD* *called Samuel, and he answered, "Here I am." He ran to Eli and said, "Here I am, for you called me." But Eli said, "I did not call you; lie down again." So he went and lay down."* (1 Samuel 3:3b–5 AMP)

As a child, Samuel had no recognition of the voice of YHVH, even though he was in front of the ark. This means that Eli had not honoured his part of the covenant, which was to train him in the ways of priesthood. YHVH had to teach Samuel Himself.

> *"...Come, let us go up to the mountain of the* L*ORD*,
> *To the house (temple) of the God of Jacob;*
> *That He may teach us His ways."* (Isaiah 2:3 AMP)

Samuel stood before YHVH, who was beginning to teach him about His ways. Samuel would probably be no older than eight here. I want you to keep that age in mind.

> *"Then the LORD called yet again, 'Samuel!' So Samuel got up and went to Eli and said, 'Here I am, for you called me.' But Eli answered, 'I did not call, my son; lie down again.' Now Samuel did not yet know [or personally experience] the LORD, and the word of the LORD was not yet revealed [directly] to him."* (1 Samuel 3:6–7 AMP)

The revelation of that day had not yet been revealed for creation, but Samuel was in a position to receive that revelation because he was before the ark. The key issue is that you and I position ourselves, even though we do not know it all yet, even though we do not understand it all yet. All you have to do is take the next step. Position yourself in the next step to be where you need to be so that when YHVH is ready to do what He wants to do, He can lay it on someone who is ready and willing. I believe that is where we are today. I believe YHVH is beginning to unlock something within creation itself, and we are sitting on the cusp of what I call the event horizon. Where does it go, and what does it look like? I do not know. How long is it going to take? I do not know. What is going to be revealed? I do not know. However, I know that it is not what we have already had.

> *"So the LORD called Samuel a third time. And he stood and went to Eli and said, 'Here I am, for you did call me.' Then Eli understood that it was the LORD [who was] calling the boy."* (1 Samuel 3:8 AMP)

Eli had perceived that Samuel was being called into what Eli should have been doing. When it says that the Lord called the child, He was calling him into a mandate to operate as a priest at this early stage of his life.

> *"So Eli said to Samuel, Go, lie down, and it shall be that if He calls you, you shall say, 'Speak, LORD, for Your servant is listening.' So Samuel went and lay down in his place. Then*

> the LORD came and stood and called as at the previous times, 'Samuel! Samuel!' Then Samuel answered, 'Speak, for Your servant is listening.'" (1 Samuel 3:9-10 AMP)

I want you to see that it was no longer just YHVH's voice. The Lord Himself was now standing and saying, "*Samuel, Samuel.*"

> "The LORD said to Samuel, 'Behold, I am about to do a thing in Israel at which both ears of everyone who hears it will ring. On that day I will carry out against Eli everything that I have spoken concerning his house (family), from beginning to end. Now I have told him that I am about to judge his house forever for the sinful behavior which he knew [was happening], because his sons were bringing a curse on themselves [dishonoring and blaspheming God] and he did not rebuke them. Therefore I have sworn to the house of Eli that the sinful behavior of Eli's house (family) shall not be atoned for by sacrifice or offering forever.' So Samuel lay down until morning. Then he opened the doors of the LORD'S house. But Samuel was afraid to tell the vision to Eli." (1 Samuel 3:11–15 AMP)

Wait a minute: this is an eight-year-old boy whom YHVH has just spoken to in person – not just as a voice – and very clearly about something, and now this young boy is opening the house of YHVH? I wonder what door he opened, coming out from the night watch? Where is YHVH's house? Because we think: "Oh, he opened the temple doors." I believe the temple did not have doors on it. It had a porch with pillars on it and a massive entryway into the outer court.

> "But Eli called Samuel and said, 'Samuel, my son.' And he answered, 'Here I am.' Then Eli said, "What is it that He said to you? Please do not hide it from me. May God do the same to you, and more also, if you hide from me anything of all that He said to you."' (1 Samuel 3:17 AMP)

Eli knew that YHVH had talked to Samuel.

> "So Samuel told him everything, hiding nothing from him. And Eli said, 'It is the LORD; may He do what seems good to Him.' Now Samuel grew; and the LORD was with him." (1 Samuel 3:18–19a AMP)

PRIESTHOOD OF HANNAH

7.1: Model of the Temple at Jerusalem, 70 AD.

Shutterstock

It went from Samuel growing in favour with YHVH and people to Samuel growing and YHVH being with him. Samuel learned how to be a priest because he spent time with YHVH, knowing His mind and His thoughts, and Samuel was now being revealed as a mouthpiece within Israel.

"*He let none of his words fail [to be fulfilled]*" (1 Samuel 3:19b AMP). That sounds to me like a shift in government. Scripture says, "*Heaven and earth will pass away, but My words will never pass away*" (Matthew 24:35 TLV). So here was a man who stood like a statue in all of Israel, with authority to govern because his words were producing life. I think Samuel would have been about 18 at this point.

"And all Israel from Dan [in the north] to Beersheba [in the south] knew that Samuel was appointed as a prophet of the LORD." (1 Samuel 3:20 AMP)

Samuel began as a priest, and like Ezekiel, who also began as a priest through a different order, he was suddenly established as a prophet. Why? Because they became oracles through whom the mysteries of YHVH were made known. The priesthood that we are a part of has functioned through every single page of the Bible and has operated in mysterious ways that we have not seen but are still here. It began with Hannah and continued through Samuel. If you read the book of Samuel, understanding that he had grown into some of his calling, you can understand what he did in chapters 6, 7, and 8 when he took the stone, and all the Philistines ran in fear because of the stone that Samuel set up. This is because he goes from being a priest to a prophet or a legislator to then becoming an oracle of YHVH. *"Samuel judged Israel all the days of his life"* (1 Samuel 7:15 AMP).

The Melchizedek order priesthood that you and I are a part of was functioning in Hannah and Samuel's lives. We cannot hide from the reality that what the Bible says is possible for you and me, but we have two choices. We can reject it and say it is not there, or we can say that we do not understand it all, which is a good place to start from. "I do not understand what has been said, but YHVH, I am going to position myself anyway because when I do, then I am in a place where I can start to engage. I know that when I do begin to engage, You will sit over me and speak to me." YHVH will speak to us not just in a voice like an "outie" like the church has taught us, but as an "innie" where YHVH stands over us. That is what happened to Jacob in Genesis 28 when he went to sleep and suddenly YHVH was there talking to him. Jacob had the same measure of priesthood as the others did.

All these details are woven into what we may see as just stories, but YHVH is trying to reveal an order of priesthood that has been in creation for all of time. We just happen to be a massive group of priests now, after the order of Melchizedek, moving into a Zionic priesthood. We are going to be priests of Zion because there, in Zion, is where we came from.

Chapter 8

THIRTEEN PRIESTHOODS

In this chapter, I want to look at 13 different priesthoods in depth with you. These priesthoods are not in numerical or chronological order but have come out of my own discovery and journey into them and their function in creation. For example, the Noahic priesthood was the first priesthood of my discovery, even though it is the third one in chronological order biblically. I have referred to the Melchizedek priesthood as the 13th priesthood in other teachings, although it is chronologically earlier. I believe our priesthood is the last priesthood, and I have numbered it the 13th priesthood. When I refer to an order of priesthoods, I am not talking about a person's function as a priest. It is evident in scripture that many people operate in the function of a priest, and I have included teachings on some of these people in this book. I have been on a journey with priesthood and being a priest for a long time now, and I have found it very useful to get some background into what YHVH is trying to bring us through to.

THE PRIESTHOOD OF BELIEVERS

***

My encounters with biblical women are still new. As such, I have not yet started teaching extensively about them. In addition to the chapter on Abigail in *The Order of Melchizedek*, I have done three teachings on priesthoods led by women, which are so far unpublished. One was on Rahab: *"Only Rahab the harlot shall live, she and all who are with her in the house, because she hid the messengers that we sent"* (Joshua 6:17 NKJV). Another was on Mary, who had the priesthood of stewarding Christ up to age thirteen. Through an encounter with Deborah, I have learned about her priesthood and the realm of government she walked in. She is amazing. Barak would not go deal with the two men with lion-like faces unless Deborah went with him (Judges 4:4–16). I questioned Deborah: "Why wouldn't he go without you?" She looked at me with an expression I interpreted as, "Don't you get it yet?" Then she spoke clearly regarding our role in governing and position as priests, the operation of that government and what it looks like. Deborah particularly emphasised overshadowing, which is why I have talked about it a lot since. In the encounter, I saw Deborah and Barak stand together to engage with something that needed stewarding through the agreement of two people on earth. The protocol started in the Old Testament and Christ finished it in the New Testament. *"Again I say to you that if two of you agree on earth concerning anything that they ask, it will be done for them by My Father in heaven"* (Matthew 18:19 NKJV).

A major teaching on these priesthoods is bubbling away in the background until I have freedom to release it. I have come to understand our role in priesthood primarily through encounters with the men who have tutored me. However, for me, it is not about gender. We have been raised to think of gender. Yet I am thinking of sonship. For example, anyone can be part of the Noahic priesthood. They do not have to be male;

that was just the gender that expressed that role and function. As sons in Christ, we all can operate in the various priesthoods.

***

I was doing a Livestream conference with a group of people, and one of the speakers talked about his encounter with Eber and a book he was working on about the living letters.[13] When I heard the name *Eber*, I began a journey to discover and build a relationship with this person. Since then, I have developed an interesting relationship with Eber. Through several encounters with him, I have discovered who he is from a relational perspective. When the guest speaker mentioned the name Eber, it resonated with me because I have been looking for what I describe as the 13th priesthood for some time, knowing that it is connected to the 13th age. When preparation and circumstance meet together in something YHVH is unfolding, it unlocks a significant piece, and all the pieces start to join together to create a whole picture. The priesthoods are not in biblical chronological order in this chapter because my learning experience happened relationally.

A lot of my process has been to gain insight and understanding of what these priesthoods are, what they mean, their functions, and the outworking of their roles in YHVH's world. One of the primary objectives in anything you do is not just to build an understanding but to build a relationship with the ones you are trying to understand. It is helpful for us to engage with the people primarily involved, so we learn about the people as well as their functions. In learning about people through building relationships and observing what they do, I realised how little is recorded about the things they did. This reflects the necessity for us to engage with scripture as windows of revelation that have been recorded and need

---

[13] Aaron Smith, et al., *Friends of Eber: A Reference Guide to the Living Letters of the Hebrew Alphabet*, Mobile, AL: Scrolls of Zebulon (2018). Available on Amazon.

discovering, rather than looking at it as the conclusion of all that there is. One of the keys is not just getting knowledge about those priesthoods but trying to get to grips with what their function is.

The Adamic Priesthood

Adam is the only being YHVH has ever made from dust. YHVH created Adam as a gate specifically to engage with physical creation. One aspect of Adam's existence was his priesthood. Priesthood is only one aspect of Adam's function in creation: he was a king, a co-creator, the father of the physical manifestation of mankind, and a priest to his family. He was the connection point for his family to YHVH, as YHVH met with him in the Garden.

The Adamic priesthood was all about relationships, the development of responsibility, and the function of humanity together with YHVH. The very beginnings of YHVH's entanglement in creation come through Adam's seed line as the building blocks and foundation stone within our genealogy. This lays the foundation for our thought process and psyche as a species, and it reflects the major importance that relationships play. Through Adam's seed line, we have a record of the relational flow through us that will be a blessing for other people. The Adamic priesthood was the first recognisable priesthood, and its foundation was laid in relationship. This sets the course for the way that YHVH persistently engages with humanity, culminating in sending His Son to be our High Priest to reconcile us as a species back to Himself.

The Abrahamic Priesthood

YHVH began again engaging with humanity purposefully with the development of his relationship with Abraham, who was the head and priest of his family and nation. Abraham established a relational connection with YHVH through which YHVH began to reach out through him to humanity to establish a connection to the earth through relationship with him. There is a tradition in the Talmud that Abraham (or *Avraham*, in Hebrew) was mentored by Shem. That is why the Word says that Abraham went on a journey looking for a city whose builder and founder was YHVH (Hebrews 11:10). I believe he would have already been in the hallowed city of Salem because part of his mentorship with Shem would have involved teaching him how to access that city. The city is still accessible but not in the physical dimensional form we understand. The Talmud suggests that Salem was a city which YHVH had hallowed and shifted dimensionally on the earth into another realm because of what it represented as a physical manifestation of Heaven on earth. The unusual thing about the city of Salem was that anyone could go into it, have access into YHVH's world and be safe.

Throughout history, YHVH has been trying to engage relationally with humanity. We know that Abraham had Isaac, and Isaac had Jacob. Every time YHVH introduced Himself to one of these patriarchs, it was always out of the following context: *"...I am the God of your father Abraham; do not fear, for I am with you. I will bless you and multiply your descendants for My servant Abraham's sake"* (Genesis 26:24 NKJV). When He introduced Himself to Jacob, it was: *"I am the* LORD *God of Abraham your father and the God of Isaac; the land on which you lie I will give to you and your descendants"* (Genesis 28:13 NKJV). The framework of YHVH's relational connection with humanity began here, with an introduction going from: "You are going to know me by my works" to "I am going to be with you", all the way to Christ in us, which is a deepening of relationship.

The Mosaic Priesthood

Let's look at the Mosaic priesthood, which is called that because Moses was directly connected to it. There are other priesthoods which follow a different pattern, so I will talk about them together at the end of the chapter.

The Adamic and Abrahamic priesthoods were relational on a personal level, so the expectation would be that such a connection would continue with Moses. Yet, because Israel was in captivity, Moses was given a much larger task. It took 40 years to get Moses ready for the mandate on him. We say YHVH does not change His Word, but scripture tells us in Genesis 15 that YHVH told Abraham the children of Israel would be in captivity for 400 years. They were actually kept in captivity for 440 years. Are we seeing YHVH changing His mind here? YHVH can do anything He wants to. Moses took 40 years to get himself ready, to deal with his brokenness and manifest the call on his life so that YHVH could do what He had to do for the people of Israel.

The Mosaic priesthood was an introduction to face-to-face encounter. Every one of these priesthoods is a deepening relationship. The Adamic priesthood was the overflow from Adam's relationship with YHVH in the Garden. It then birthed into the Abrahamic priesthood, but the Mosaic priesthood was deeply personal and face to face with YHVH. The Mosaic priesthood represents face to face relationship with YHVH, which was the vital ingredient to establishing this connection point with humanity. It is interesting that Moses' face shone through his union and his encounters with YHVH, so much so that the children of Israel asked him to cover his face (Exodus 34:33–35) when really YHVH's heart was to have all the children of Israel doing what Moses did and displaying Him the same way Moses did. YHVH assigned and instigated the next priesthood, which was the Aaronic priesthood, because of the children of Israel's rejection of His desire to be face to face with them (Exodus 20:19), and their disobedience, including Moses' initial fear of presenting YHVH to the people because he had a stammering tongue (Exodus 4:1-14).

THIRTEEN PRIESTHOODS

The Aaronic Priesthood was birthed because Israel encountered the magnitude of who YHVH was, and they were terrified of moving toward Him. Instead, they said to Moses, "You go up". Due to their response to YHVH's visual manifestation and their fear, YHVH turned from face to face relationship with them to relating through a systematic process governed by many laws.

The Aaronic priesthood was initiated because of two actions. One was Moses himself not being able to speak properly, which he framed in his own language as having a stuttering tongue or a stammer (Exodus 4:10). I believe that Moses was experiencing a manifestation of the gift of tongues when he talked about the way that he spoke. Because of Moses' withdrawing from wanting to be in the front, YHVH told him that Aaron would be his mouthpiece. These two things, the children of Israel's disobedience of not moving towards YHVH when He manifested Himself and Moses' own personal fear, brought about the Aaronic priesthood.

In my opinion, it is unfortunate that a personal, relational union with YHVH was negated by the Hebrew people. One of the reasons I so appreciate what YHSVH has done is because it brings us back into relational union with YHVH, and we can have a face-to-face connection with Him. Through the mediation of YHSVH, we can be completely cleansed and made righteous in His presence and draw towards YHVH in relationship, rather than following many onerous laws. This is why Christ did away with the Aaronic priesthood, and we are now called priests of YHVH (1 Peter 2:9).

During the Aaronic priesthood, YHVH's face was hidden from humanity, and the only one who saw Him was Moses. Then those who were apprenticed by Moses saw YHVH (Exodus 24:9-10). Out of the Aaronic priesthood came the Levitical priesthood.

The Levites were a group of people that kept the law which enabled them to carry the Ark of YHVH and therefore be close

THE PRIESTHOOD OF BELIEVERS

to YHVH, but still not be face to face with Him. The Aaronic and Levitic priesthoods were established around the laws and regulations that had to do with their function and mediation around the Ark and their role for the people before YHVH. Everything was regulated by laws. YHVH's face was hidden and only seen by Moses and the High Priest once a year. This process and set of laws was the only way that people could engage with YHVH.

In observing the general way people function today through religious systems often based around task-orientated relationships, face-to-face relationship with YHVH can disappear and instead become a whole set of laws and regulations of to-do's and not-to-do's. A classic example of this is the issue of sin. People do not sin because it defiles their relationship with YHVH and becomes a regulatory law in their lives, instead of not wanting to sin because it will affect their relationship with YHVH. Our thinking needs to change from being affect-focused to becoming relationship-focused. A religious system will always move from face to face into laws of "do not". When this happens, YHVH hides His face and very slowly withdraws, and then all you have left is a shell of what used to be a habitation of YHVH's presence.

YHVH has always kept a blueprint in the earth of the secrets of each priesthood. The priesthoods have always involved a motivational heart connection with YHVH and do not necessarily function the way they are seen as typifying in scripture.[14]

Through this chapter, we will see where our own lives fit into these priesthoods. The record of the mystery and wonder of all of these priesthoods must be honoured at all times and kept functioning within creation. The full measure of YHVH

---

[14] Someone walking in the Noahic priesthood will care for creation, someone who cares for injustice could be seen in the Levitical priesthood, the Davidic priesthood loves worship, the Mosaic priesthood have to be face to face.

and the functionality of who we are as priests can be expressed and seen every day within creation. The mystery of the blueprint of the different priesthoods is kept alive at all times within creation itself.

    The Davidic priesthood came out of the Levitic priesthood. As I looked at the Davidic priesthood, David became deeply personal to me in my faith walk, face to face and also transgenerationally, crossing over the boundaries of the event horizon into the future. David's simplicity of pursuit of YHVH had him entwining with YHVH to such an extent that YHVH began to open the doors for a deep personal relationship. In my opinion, David was able to reach through all the ages and touch the Age of Zion, bringing back some of the measure of that realm of priesthood to operate within his day. David engaged with YHVH through worship, and like David, worship has remained intrinsic to our life connection with YHVH. In the Davidic priesthood, worship was deeply personal, face to face, and was able to reach into the future, which I would describe as mystical. David had an effect on the people around him because of his mystical union with YHVH and his relational place of worship, especially when he was in the cave, playing the frequencies of Heaven on his harp and singing. This is what I would describe as the mystical beginnings of a priesthood in which YHVH was trying to re-engage with creation to bring humanity face to face with Him again. David touched the future, and I believe he was able to bring it into his day because he said things like: *"Do not take Your Holy Spirit from me"* (Psalm 51:11 NKJV) when the Holy Spirit had not even been given yet. He brought the Ark through the wilderness to the House of YHVH, and thousands of people were worshipping 24/7 when the glory of the Lord came upon the Ark and upon David there (2 Samuel 6). David saw that worship would be the container to house the manifestation of YHVH in creation in this way and surrounded the Ark with thousands of worshipers who became the veil that overshadowed the Ark.

THE PRIESTHOOD OF BELIEVERS

As we move into the different priesthoods, the contexts of the way these people operated with YHVH will become more evident. The Zadok priesthood, which I am calling the Tzadoic priesthood, was a group of people who separated themselves unto YHVH and followed very strict rules and guidelines. *"Zadok (the priest) and his fellow priests lived before the congregation tent of the Eternal in the high place at Gibeon* (1 Chronicles 16:39 VOICE). From my perception and understanding at this point, the Tzadoic priesthood was known for its singularity in the pursuit of holiness before YHVH. The Tzadoic priesthood is amazing. If we look at the meanings of the living letters used for Zadok's name in the ancient text, the Zayin was a weapon, the Dalet was the door, and the Qof was the view from behind time. When we read Zadok, we are seeing a weapon that is the doorway behind time, which points to unlocking mysteries and the keeper of mysteries, like who Eber was.

The next priesthood I want to look at is the Melchizedek priesthood, which has been woven into all the other priesthoods in some measure because of the necessity for maturity and knowing the heart of YHVH. I have recorded lots of teachings on the Melchizedek Priesthood, what it means, the process, how it operates, what is done and the way it moves. I have also published a book called *The Order of Melchizedek*, so I am not going to repeat that teaching here.

The last priesthood that is connected to this flow is what I call the Zionic Priesthood, which I see as the priesthood to whom the mysteries of the future were unveiled. Much of the function of the Zionic priesthood is seen in the flow of revelation and the administration of the mysteries of YHVH and in the secrets of YHVH being released in creation. Part of the Zionic priesthood is reflected here in creation and found in the upper waters and the lower waters (Genesis 1:6). The lower waters are the reservoir of the mysteries of YHVH that are not yet revealed, and the upper waters are to do with the secrets of

THIRTEEN PRIESTHOODS

YHVH not yet revealed. All of this is based on maturity and responsibility. The Zionic Priesthood are the priests of the city of Zion and are already part of the Cloud of Witnesses. This priesthood is all about being in the place of full union with YHVH. It is part of the reflection manifesting through us of this priesthood that gives us entry into that city.

The Zionic priesthood is really about the priesthood of the future, which reaches into the realm of infinity. There is always a moving forward from the realm of the eternal world of YHVH to the realm of infinity; infinity enfolds itself into the eternal world, creating an overshadowing circle of priesthoods.

As priests of YHVH, we replace the covering cherub as reflected in the Davidic priesthood. This enables us to stand before YHVH, becoming the priests of YHVH and looking into the unfolding measure of YHVH at all times. The Zionic priesthood gives us the ability to mediate the revelation of the way YHVH wants to entwine Himself with creation through humanity, to bring the record of light through humanity and to creation itself.

> *"For the creation eagerly awaits the revelation of the sons of God. For the creation was subjected to futility—not willingly but because of the One who subjected it—in hope that the creation itself also will be set free from bondage to decay into the glorious freedom of the children of God. For we know that the whole creation groans together and suffers birth pains until now—and not only creation, but even ourselves. We ourselves, who have the first fruits of the Ruach, groan inwardly as we eagerly wait for adoption—the redemption of our body."* (Romans 8:19–23 TLV)

The Word says that all creation is groaning for our revealing. This includes our physical body, which is also part of creation. We are groaning within ourselves for the revealing within the structure of our physical body of the manifestation of our future. This is to do with the metamorphosis out of human genealogy into YHVH's genealogy which brings us back into position as illuminations, giving our light to the earth, going beyond this "now" and giving our light to creation. The Zionic priesthood is the priesthood of the future. All these priesthoods are a reflection of the nine stones that were stripped from Lucifer's body. The whole process of the revealing of these priesthoods within the role of humanity before YHVH, how we are represented in their function and what our function is as a species empowers us to unlock who we are.

YHVH engages with us to bring us to the point where who we are in Christ is fully manifested and revealed. This positions us to be able to turn outwards and administrate YHVH to creation through the faces of our Father. There were twelve stones on Aaron's breastplate as high priest (Exodus 28:15-20). I realised that as well as the twelve stones, there was also another element, which was the gold that the stones were mounted into. As I was working through this process, I asked YHVH how this works, as it is woven throughout all the stones, keeps them together and is very functional. The answer is that the thirteenth priesthood is the fabric that holds all of this together, just as the priesthood of YHSVH is what holds the fabric of all the other priesthoods together and empowers them to be functional. For me personally, it does not matter where you position Him without the mediation of His priesthood, whether He is the first or the last or anywhere in between. It is like having a golden thread woven through every strand of a tapestry: without that strand, there is no picture. Because YHSVH laid down His life in the very beginning as the foundation stone and laid the foundation for the revealing of our priesthood through His passage through death, YHSVH is the priest of humanity. As our high priest, He mediates us into our role to reveal YHVH Himself. First in us and then through us as we are woven into the fabric of the desire of YHVH for the fulfilment of our purpose in creation.

Through what YHSVH has initiated as our high priest, we are able to come through Him as our veil. As we do so, He begins to order everything in us with the purpose of bringing us to the place of being priests of YHVH through the process of maturity.

This gives birth to the last priesthood that is going to be revealed in creation. As a funny way to express it, we could use the "You'it" or the "Youic" priesthood!

You are it – there is no other priesthood that is going to come after us. We are the final priesthood. This was one of the key reasons that YHSHV initiated our Priesthood. Through union and relationship, the Father positioned us to be able to gaze upon Him, replacing the covering cherubim and being able to mediate what we are observing through Him into all of creation.

You are it. I believe our priesthood is all about us growing in maturity and becoming the priests of YHVH. None of the others, even YHSVH Himself, were ever called the priest of YHVH. You and I have been called, through the blood of YHSVH and what He did to birth us into our role, to fulfil the mandate YHVH originally gave to humanity. Our responsibility as the only ones and the last priesthood to be revealed in creation as priests of YHVH is to bring the completion of the knowledge of YHVH into full bloom here. I want to stress again that we are "it"; there is no other priesthood after us. We are the final priesthood that will ever be until a new Heaven and a new earth are formed. It is all about you and me.

These two priesthoods are the last priesthoods to be fully revealed and known about, and they become the bridge between the old and the new. Through His Son being our priest, YHVH was restoring humanity back to Himself in relational union. This created the bridge between us and YHSVS's priesthood, mobilising our priesthood into existence to be able to unfold the full purpose of YHVH's heart and His design for humanity as His representatives. This leads into the thirteenth age, which is creating a new Heaven and a new earth.

These three become the bench of three of the last days. These are not necessarily in numerical order but are interwoven with one another:

- Our (Youic) Priesthood
- Melchizedek Priesthood
- Zionic Priesthood

In my opinion, at this stage, the operation of these three create the three-fold bond to present the sovereignty of the human race, seated as the centre chain between all three.

Our priesthood as the Priests of YHVH represents YHVH Himself in creation.

The Melchizidek priesthood operates the process of rulership and the government of all of creation, including the administration of wealth.

The Zionic priesthood has to do with the function of the city of Zion's government and its overshadowing of the earth.

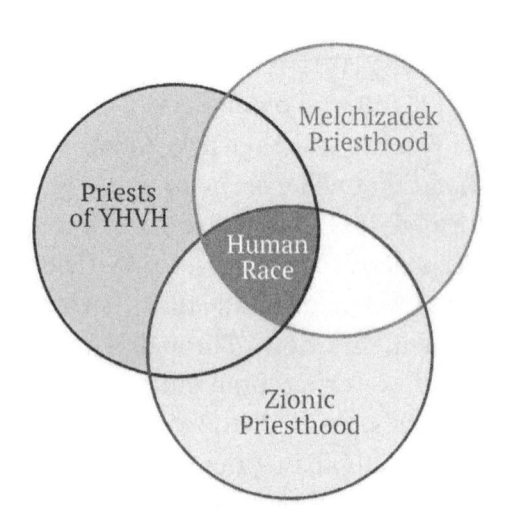

8.1: The Interwoven Bench of Three Priesthoods

THIRTEEN PRIESTHOODS

These three are positioned purposely as a Beit Din.[15] Through this union and government, the rule of YHVH will be extended out into all of creation.

This makes eleven priesthoods so far mentioned. Over time my discovery of the Eberic priesthood came through a pursuit to engage with the mysteries of YHVH found in the Living Letters. In my journey through this and through divine appointment, YHVH brought me into relationship with Eber. As a keeper of the structure of the Living Letters, Eber's life was centred around the unfolding and wonder of all that pertains to their mystery. I believe Eber was alive on the earth in a physical way before the flood occurred in Noah's day. It is interesting to note that Eber was not on the Ark. I believe YHVH transformed him and moved him trans-dimensionally in the same way as He did with Elijah in the ascending whirlwind (2 Kings 2:11). Eber is now positioned in the mountain of the mysteries of YHVH as the keeper of the cave of the wonders and secrets of YHVH. The Eberic Priesthood now makes twelve priesthoods:

- Adamic
- Noahic
- Abrahamic
- Aaronic
- Mosaic
- Levitic
- Zionic
- Davidic
- Melchizedek
- Tzadoic
- YHSVH
- Eberic

---

[15] Rabbinical Court: "A Jewish Court serving the needs of both Jewish and non-Jewish people in issues of disputes. The Beit Din is a Jewish court of law composed of three rabbinic judges, responsible for matters of religious law and the settlement of civil disputes (Google Dictionary). Beit Din is a Rabbinical Court that has been the foundation for Jewish law and living throughout history and around the globe. Procedures and decisions based on the Torah, Halacha and Talmud assure correct and fair decisions that involve any issue of dispute" www.thebeitdin.com.

THE PRIESTHOOD OF BELIEVERS

Another priesthood was in the midst of all this, thirteenth priesthood. For me, this is the most important priesthood because it is the last one that is ever going to be manifested in creation. It comes through the union of man and YHVH, which sets mankind in a preeminent place and position within the structure of what YHVH has planned. This thirteenth priesthood is discoverable in the scripture that says, *"...the one about whom these things are said belongs to another tribe, from which no one has officiated at the altar"* (Hebrews 7:13 TLV). I have named this the *Youic* priesthood, which is actually *Your* priesthood – the name is my humorous attempt to create a name to match the "ic" format of the others. Our priesthood is manifested as the last one in chronological order and now makes thirteen priesthoods. I am aware that there are many other expressions of priesthood all the way through the Bible that reveal a function of priesthood, but this is different to an order of priesthood.

I am going to try to create some understanding of the Noahic Priesthood. To me, Noah is the bridge between two estates of the physical earth, pre-flood and post-flood. Due to his position, he was able to mediate as a bridge between the destruction of the old to the unfolding of the new. As a priest of the earth, Noah was able to take what was pre-flood and store it so that when the flood subsided, he was able to bring that life back out onto a new physical platform. Some extra-biblical accounts describe Noah as a really freaky looking being when he was born, but you will not find that in the Bible we read today.[16] You can find some of this in manuscripts that were studied by the rabbis connected with Israel's history.

Noah was the mediator between the union of the upper waters (the spirit life) and the lower waters (the natural life). Through his obedience to the blueprint YHVH gave him, Noah proved his willingness to serve YHVH, and being able to

---

[16] It is postulated that Noah may have been born albino in colouring. See the *Book of Enoch* and other extra-biblical works.

mediate as an earth-bound son, he established himself as the only one to be priest of the earth.

The four key priesthoods that flow through my discovery process are the priest of the earth, the priest of humanity, the priest of YHVH, and then Eber. In my opinion, the first three set up the Beit Din, or the bench of government for creation. As the steward of the mysteries of the Living Letters, Eber becomes the fourth face of the side of a cube. This unlocks the possibility for the complete revealing of the four faces of YHVH.

I was completely fascinated with Eber, and over a period of time, I set my heart to engage with him. I wanted to know who this man was that the Bible talks about in very vague terms. There is so little knowledge available about him until you start digging into ancient rabbinical teachings and ancient books of the Hebrew people. From those sources, you start finding that Eber was quite an unusual person. I wanted to go all the way back to just before the Tower of Babel was built when all the seed lines came out of the east and people settled to dwell in the plains of Mamre. This was all of Cain's seed line coming out from the east of Eden back into creation, through the East Gate, coming back into the earth to become part of the blended gene pool of humanity. Reptilian seed lines, Men of Renown and human seed lines were all woven together in this conglomerate mixture.

It is surprising that Noah had a flawless genetic code when the rest of mankind's genetics were mixed. As I have stated before, Noah was a very unusual being, so let's get back to Noah's father and Eber. I believe these two formed an arc by agreement to keep the knowledge and record of the oral mysteries of the living letters on the earth. Because the letters were living, their objective was to keep their reality and mystery functional within creation and to keep the knowledge of their application within creation. This is why the Hebrew language is so important (particularly the pictorial expressions – the ancient hieroglyphic Hebrew).

The human beings on the earth at that time gathered together on the plain of Mamre. In an attempt to bypass the necessity for holiness, they wanted to build an entry for themselves back into the realms of YHVH. They were trying to bypass the key component of the union of YHVH and mankind. Through a corrupt process negating this necessity, they began to arc together and what started off as a physical manifestation of mortar and tar grew into an attempt to engage the spirit realm, to build a gate. At this point, the temple in Heaven was still defiled because of what Lucifer had done. It was not cleansed until YHSVH took His blood and cleansed the heavenly temple to make a way for you and me, in a fallen estate but made holy by Christ's blood, to have unlimited access to YHVH Himself (Hebrews 9:11–14).

Through the blended seed lineage and the sons of God still on the earth in a physical way, the knowledge of Heaven's accessibility and that world's realm was available due to the sons of Gods' personal experience of that realm. The sons of God's first estate was a light covering of glory that gave them unrestricted access to the realms of YHVH. The tower was built through the mirror of corruption in an attempt to build access to regain their first estate. It was built by the common union of their fantasies and desires, using the fabric of their own mystery and their understanding of light technology, woven together with corruption by polluting the very fabric of the function of the Living Letters. All of this was being used by the sons of God, in corporate union with those that were gathered together in Mamre in an unrighteous way, to weave together a fabric of their own creation as a gateway to create what they wanted in Heaven. It was an attempt to build a spiritual gateway through knowledge, by the realm of fantasy, from their own desires. By this time, the DNA of mankind was corrupted by the intrusions and overshadowings that occurred over this period (Genesis 6:1-2). From what I can see, it took around the same length of time to attempt to build the tower as it took Noah to build the Ark (over a hundred years). The tower was never completed. At the same time that Noah received the blueprint of the Ark, the corrupt blueprint for the building of the tower was being manifested from the knowledge and corporate union of the sons of God coming together with the rest of humanity to create their own desire.

It is fascinating to watch the attempted implementation of what the sons of God tried to do. They would never have been able to even attempt this if mankind's seed-line was not involved in what they were doing. The point I am making here is that the inheritance mankind had been given was being used to help manifest what the sons of God wanted. Without mankind's involvement, this would not have been possible, which shows the importance of the stranded DNA cord of mankind with regard to its ability to be able to host mystery.

It is interesting also to note that there was no way back or return for the sons of God that had put off their first estate. Through what was to come in Christ, mankind would be given complete access to the fulness of YHVH's Kingdom again, having the ability to bypass everything to do with the law to come into union with Him. The sons of God wanted access to the power of the provision of that Kingdom without establishing relationship, responsibility or accountability.

The foreknowledge of what would be given to mankind became the driving force for the sons of God to put off their first estate, thinking that they would be able to have the same inheritance as mankind, wanting what humanity had been given: the right to rule in all of creation. This is what our priesthood is all about and why it is so important that we fulfil the mandate and come into full maturity to be able to be YHVH's representative in all of creation.

Eber and Noah's father are believed to have been the only two outside of Noah and his family who did not participate in the building of the Tower of Babel. During an encounter I had with Eber himself, as we were discussing what happened to him (he was not on the Ark when scripture says (Genesis 6:21–23) that YHVH destroyed everything that drew breath), he told me that YHVH moved him dimensionally out of the physical creation so that YHVH could judge creation. Due to YHVH moving Eber as the keeper and steward/priest of the secrets, function and mystery of the Living Letters, they were kept holy and sacred, becoming the woven fabric of his priesthood.

I set my heart to engage with Eber because I wanted to know who this man is. The way that I do this is to first set my heart to engage with the person and honour the mystery of the life they led here in creation. I have learned over the years that this does not happen instantly, in the same way that relationships do not happen instantly. They are built personally rather than functionally. I would then turn my heart to go into the mountain of YHVH, to drink from the wine of the record of their life that is stored in the Wine Room in the mountain of YHVH. The Word says,

> "Taste and see how good Adonai is.
> Blessed is the one who takes refuge in Him."
> (Psalm 34:9 TLV)

Once I have done this, I allow my heart to ponder over their life and begin to engage with them. My purpose is to honour their life, to sit in and honour the mystery of who they are as a being, desiring to build a relationship with them. I do not want to get what they had; I want to build a relationship so I can understand who they were and what they had. Out of this understanding, I learn how to engage with them and become an observer of their life as they walk with me through it, with the questions I would ask. As I walked through this engagement over a long period of time, I had an encounter with Eber that completely revolutionised my life. It was through this encounter that I discovered who Eber was.

THIRTEEN PRIESTHOODS

In my first encounter with Eber, I had no grid for what I was seeing. Eber first appeared as a moving white cloud with strands of white silken thread woven around him that continually moved, which made him look like a white whirlwind. I could see the vague shape of a human form sitting in the middle of this. Very slowly, these strands dissipated inward until I could no longer see them on the outside of him. Looking at his physical form, what now appeared to be his skin was these same silken threads. Through asking many questions, I learned that his physical entity was being held together by YHVH's words. These mysterious functional Living Letters were completely part of his life. It was from him that I initially learned how to weave the fabric of the Living Letters back into my human recorded DNA strand. My encounters with Ezekiel helped this to become functional in my life.

Eber has been positioned as a priest and a steward, on the mountain of the mysteries of YHVH, as the keeper of the cave of the wonders and secrets of YHVH. Eber's priesthood is to keep the knowledge of the mystery and function of the Living Letters and the wonder about them alive in creation. As a steward and a gatekeeper, he is actively involved in presenting this to the sons of YHVH, who turn their hearts to engage with these mysteries. Through Eber's tutoring, I was able to see the way the Living Letters functioned and how they were connected through scripture. The Bible says that creation is framed by His Word, and scripture has a role within the metamorphosis that we will go through to become like Him.

> *"God, who at various times and in various ways spoke in time past to the fathers by the prophets, has in these last days spoken to us by His Son, whom He has appointed heir of all things, through whom also He made the worlds; who being the brightness of His glory and the express image of His person, and upholding all things by the word of His power, when He had by Himself purged our sins, sat down at the right hand of the Majesty on high."* (Hebrews 1:1–3 NKJV)

I want to note here that my only access point to all of this is through Christ. He is the only righteous gate that gives us access to all of these realms. I go through Christ, through His blood, body and the torn veil that He provided for us. Establishing a relationship with Christ is central to all that I do. This is the beginning point of what John described in Revelations when he said he was in the spirit on the Lord's day (Revelation 1:10). I am not interested in just connecting with the spirit realm but connecting with the realm of YHVH in the spirit. Remember, both corruption and incorruption are around you at all times in the spirit realm. Whichever one you lean into is going to become the source of your supply. I know personally which one I want, and I choose it through Christ. I have done a teaching about the standard to be able to judge every encounter by, to be sure it carries the evidence of all that YHVH is, called "The Twelve Strands of Judgement", which is available from www.sonofthunder.org.

Adamic, Abrahamic, Mosaic

These three priesthoods are a reflection of the relational connection built by these individuals with YHVH as He reached in to engage with humanity. All these priesthoods reflect a depth of union with YHVH Himself in friendship. It is interesting when you hear people today talk very specifically and persistently about everything we do being all about relationship; this is their singularity and focus. It is the function of these three priesthoods, either in combination or as individual priesthoods, being reflected and carried and present within the community of the Father. These three sit as a bench as examples of the way relationship is reflected within them.

Aaronic, Levitic

These two priesthoods are to do with the necessity of the Word and its establishment within the way YHVH is presented and the way an individual presents themselves to YHVH. When you meet people who are functioning out of the blueprint of these two priesthoods, the common thread running through their language is the statement, "You must have the Word". They generally end up being teachers presenting biblical truths. Outside of Christendom, this is often reflected on the earth in people who become teachers in different areas of society.

Davidic, Tzadoic

The Davidic and Tzadoic priesthoods have to do with worship, connectivity with YHVH and the set aside life. In conversation with these people, they will often talk about the importance and necessity of having a life set apart for the service of YHVH. This is reflected in the solitude of monasteries that involve worship as an intrinsic part of the lifestyle. Many people connected with the administration of this order of priesthood today will be worship leaders, on worship teams and people who listen to worship music on a continual basis. In communicating with these people, their whole focus is on worship as the singular most important aspect of a believer's life. There is nothing wrong with this, and they are engaged with this order of priesthood. This type of person thinks that anybody who is not worshipping is missing the mark in ministering to YHVH. The Levitic and Aaronic priesthoods think that anyone who does not have the Word is falling short of truth in their lives. The Adamic, Abrahamic and Mosaic priesthoods believe that anyone who does not have face to face relationship with YHVH is missing out on the mountain-top experience of divine revelation. Each of these priesthoods will tell us that we need to be like them. It is important to recognise the importance of every one of the functional pieces of the priesthood and make room for their administration within the corporate body of Christ, each playing their part.

Noahic

The Noahic priesthood was a prime example of a priesthood whose administration and care were directly related to the earth itself. When you look at the function of this priesthood today, you will find that people carrying the blueprint and heart of this priesthood are directly related to the care of the earth. A classic example of this in the earth today is the young man who is seeking to wipe out the plastic waste in the oceans. Many of these people are involved in local communities, caring for wildlife and in the preservation of key areas of nature. When you talk to them, it is almost like they cannot see anything else because this is the most important part of what is needed for them. Sometimes we have named them tree huggers and nature lovers. It is just the natural outworking of the Noahic blueprint to love creation the way YHVH loves it.

Melchizedek

Much of the order of this priesthood has been discussed in my book, *The Order of Melchizedek*. The blueprint of the Melchizedek priesthood is often expressed in financial stewardship, governmental protocols, a fantastic capacity for the presentation of verbal ideas, and entrepreneurial endeavours. One aspect of the Melchizedek priesthood is complete submission to the Holy Spirit in such a way that He is able to speak through you in the spirit, in tongues, and in your natural language to unlock the secrets of YHVH in a way that others can understand. This is what Paul was referring to when he wrote,

> "I will pray with the spirit [by the Holy Spirit that is within me] and I will pray with the mind [using words I understand]; I will sing with the spirit [by the Holy Spirit that is within me] and I will sing with the mind [using words I understand]. Otherwise, if you bless [and give thanks to God] in the spirit only, how will any outsider or someone who is not gifted [in spiritual matters] say the "Amen" [of agreement] to your thanksgiving, since he does

not know what you are saying?" (1 Corinthians 14:15-16 AMP)

The main function of the Melchizedek priesthood is to do with relational union with YHVH, where you know His mind and His thoughts and are able to communicate these without the need to be recognised by others, from a place of hiddenness.

Eberic

As mentioned earlier, engaging with Eber was one of the most amazing experiences I have had. It is fascinating that the blueprints of all the priesthoods have always been on the earth in some way, often completely hidden from the face of others. YHVH has always kept these records on the earth, purposefully woven into the fabric of the lives of people. I have found that if people who carry the blueprint of the Eberic priesthood are not inspired by the current face of Christendom, they will often get involved in the occult world and the deception that is around it. This is just the cry of the heart of a person unable to find YHVH, who slides down the pathway of destruction. In Christian circles, many of these people would be seen as prophetic, but they may have no concept of this because of the lack of language and expression within the contemporary church system for what they carry as part of this blueprint. Much of it is being uncovered today with the insatiable desire to be relationally connected with the mystery of the Living Letters and have personal encounters with them. This is not just learning how to read a language, but a deeply felt draw towards the relational aspect, in the way that these Letters weave themselves within the record of who we are.

Many of these people are also those that seem to have been able to see spiritually all their lives. It is easy to get frustrated at times by those who can just "see". Part of the expression of people that are connected to the Eberic priesthood is the innate ability to see dimensionally. They are often unable to express it in a logical way that people can understand and are sometimes called weird or too spiritual.

One of the key aspects of engaging with all these priesthoods is learning to not allow the function of your personal priesthood to negate what is operating in another's life through their priesthood, but to learn how to engage with them all. It is important that we recognise each other's priesthoods and learn how to embrace them with the same measure of love that you would show if you saw someone operating out of what you operate from. The key to all of this is to have the centricity of the Word as our foundation and keep relational connections with each other while also engaging through worship. All of this is based around relational connections with one another, not task oriented but relationally focused. These people become a reflection of the Eberic priesthood's blueprint and mystery remaining in creation. It flows together and moves in and out like a river.

The next three priesthoods, the Zionic, YHSVH's and Youic (our priesthood), begin to reflect the future.

Zionic

The Zionic priesthood is generally recognised in people who are future-focused. They are often excellent businesspeople. I find that people who carry the blueprint of the Zionic priesthood will generally have a five-year plan for their lives. Many of these people have become stuck, trying to discover the future, particularly regarding world events, but not recognising that they are the future themselves. It is strange how within each priesthood, there seems to be a bent towards becoming fixated in a particular way, without the ability to properly express what is speaking from within them. These people will often become involved in government or within big structural organisations and make fantastic CEOs of companies. They also make great town planners, structural engineers and businesspeople. An expression of the Zionic priesthood is seen in the corporate world by the draw to be connected and part of a franchised system. Many people recognise that belonging is important. The unfortunate part is that just belonging does not make you exactly what they are in their expression of the Zionic priesthood. Much of their focus is on the union of all believers and the desire to bring everyone into unity. Some of these people are found in the music industry, where fame seems to attach to them very quickly, and people begin to idolise them. The same thing seems to happen in Christendom, where someone becomes idolised by other believers for what they carry. Up to this point, I have not pushed too much into this priesthood, but it will definitely become a focus in the future for me. Some of my funniest encounters have been with those that are in the Zionist priesthood, particularly my first encounter when the matrix opened to be able to see into that arena. I had assumed that these priests of Zion were all austere and very focused because of my past encounters with them outside of their natural setting. Since this encounter, my whole belief system about them has changed, and I now recognise that they are different when they are in their function than when they are outside of that role. Because these people are very future-focused, they often find the book of Revelation centrally significant.

YHSVH

One of the key priesthoods connected to who we are as sons is the priesthood of YHSVH Himself. It is fascinating how many people try to be Him, not realising that we do not have to. We only have to become like Him in nature and in character. I think it has been to our great detriment that how we function within the current church belief systems, particularly around the area of intercession, is not talked about. It is not our function or our role to present others to the Father. This is YHSVH's role, given to Him specifically by the Father because of His passage through death to redeem mankind to the Father Himself. This is why He is called our mediator (1 Timothy 2:5), who presents us and prays for us to the Father.

One of the things that YHSVH accomplished, which we would be unable to do, was to tear the veil to give others unrestricted access to the Father. Our role now is to walk in and out through that veil, to show others how to accomplish this and come into union with YHVH, to share life with Him in His world.

YHSVH's priesthood is a reflection of submission and complete yieldedness to the Father's purpose for His life, walking through obedience in complete honour of the Father's position and His own blueprint being fulfilled on the earth. The process of redeeming mankind to the Father paved the way for the birthing of this priesthood into creation. The reflection of YHSVH's priesthood is often seen through the experiences of people who position themselves in complete service to others. One of these people in our day is Jackie Pullinger, who has laid down her whole life to serve the drug addicts of Hong Kong.[17] Our role is not to mediate others to YHVH but to mediate YHVH to others, and she is a classic example of mediating YHVH to others through the reflection of YHSVH's priesthood on earth.

We seem to have got things backwards in what we present to those around us regarding our role. I sometimes think that avoidance or lack of knowledge has been a key component to us not becoming the priests of YHVH that we are supposed to be. As our knowledge of our priesthood and what we are mandated to increases, I am hoping that it will release many from the burden of trying to be something they are not called to be. I know that in the past, many people have spent much time trying to engage through traditional processes of presenting others to YHVH. This process needs to be changed to us

---

[17] *Chasing the Dragon: One Woman's Struggle Against the Darkness of Hong Kong's Drug Dens* by Jackie Pullinger withAndrew Quicke. Minneapolis, MN: Chosen Books, 2007.

presenting YHVH to others, which puts the burden on us to deal with our lives in connection with YHVH's world and realm. I have often found it easier to avoid dealing with myself by looking at others and having my focus on them. Sometimes this is great, but it is not always the right way to do things. As priests of YHVH, our role is to present the Father to others and to mediate from our position in Him what we are experiencing there in His world, here on the face of the earth. Mediating means bringing that which is in Heaven over that which is on the earth and becoming a reflection of that which is in Heaven.

Youic (Our Priesthood)

The final priesthood that I have engaged with and will continue to move forward in is our priesthood. When I was thinking about giving a name to the priesthood we operate in, with all the other priesthoods having an "ic" at the end of them, I thought it would be hilarious to call ours 'youic'. Really what it means is that you are in charge. It is our responsibility, and it is given to us to become the priests of YHVH. This is a journey that we go through, and it is not something that happens immediately. It begins as we immerse ourselves into relationship with the Father and learn how to mediate for our own lives, face to face. We walk through and deal with our issues and brokenness before Him through the process of deepening relationship and coming to maturity, and then we begin to become a reflection of what we are beholding. From this position, we can then turn and bring what we have been beholding to bear on the face of the earth.

Walking face to face with YHVH and learning through the mediating of our own issues teaches us His response to our brokenness and corruption. This then teaches us the necessary skills when it is our turn to respond to the corruption that is around us. Our role is to mediate YHVH to creation, which is completely different from the current stance of trying to mediate creation to YHVH. For example, in the church age, we have presented others to YHVH through much intercession. Our role is being completely reversed as we mature into our priesthood to now present YHVH to others. The key objective is to become a reflection of our Father's face, His desire and His will, which is mediated through taking dominion over corruption. Firstly with the earth, then reaching into creation.

It is important that we start in Jerusalem (Acts 1:8), which means starting with ourselves. We cannot take another through something we have not gone through ourselves. It is our experience that is the teacher, and it allows us to understand the mind and heart of YHVH's response to us. I have found too many people trying to mediate for others who have not yet walked through their own issues without even understanding the heart of YHVH for themselves. The development of our relationship with YHVH through this process teaches us how to engage with the heart of YHVH, which is the key objective because it builds a depth of relationship. Companionship with our Father is the objective so that we can remain with Him and share life with Him in His world.

One of the greatest positions we can take is to govern creation and all that it occupies. This is the final component of maturing into what we have been destined to become. Many issues arise when we want the great without doing the small first. If we do not do the small, we miss the patterning of the great, and the great will fall down around our ears. It is easy to turn the focus outwards instead of turning the focus inwards to build union with YHVH. As the process of restoration of our own lives proceeds and deepens into union with YHVH, our hearts will very slowly begin to turn outwards from inside the relationship. At this point, we begin to see what YHVH is unfolding. Too many of us try to solve what is around us by seeing it as a task instead of seeing the relational aspect as the key. YHSVH said that He only did what He saw the Father doing (John 5:19). It is from this point of relationship that we will be able to do what we see the Father doing, which is not the same as waiting on earth to hear a voice tell us to do something. That was a church age teaching that negated the need for the face-to-face engagement and relational union that is necessary with YHVH.

Out of this intermingling and joining with YHVH, the union of our spirit and His Spirit beginning to entwine together, the distinction between the two becomes very hard to distinguish. This is seen in the scripture that says, *"He that is joined to the Lord is one spirit with Him"* (1 Corinthians 6:17 NKJV).

The deepest part of our future is going to be the unfolding of a new Heaven and a new earth, which cannot be done unless we walk in this place of union with YHVH. As we mature through this process, we will be able to reach right into the heart of YHVH to see the future and mediate what is necessary to bring change to the earth. This cannot be done through a mental assent to information alone, and it can only be done from a place of maturity. I have found so many people who think they're qualified to function without experience simply because they have heard a teaching and have some understanding of it. This is not so in YHVH's Kingdom. Mentorship and apprenticing are key components to the way YHVH functions with us and teaches us, not just with instruction but with life experience within His Kingdom. Again, I want to make a statement here that it is *"on earth as it is in Heaven"*, not in Heaven as it is on earth.

The images of all of these priesthoods are reflected out through us into creation, often being expressed by our individuality to create the diversity of the expressions of YHVH. As a corporate body, when we function together, we understand which priesthoods function through us. People often have one predominant operational priesthood that they function in, usually with two others which support that predominant function. I am not limiting YHVH in saying we will only have three because, in the end, I do believe that all of these priesthoods will be reflected through us as we come to the full maturity of sonship, but it is important that we anchor somewhere and work outwards from there. It is important that individual expression is given room to function, even within the understanding of the other twelve priesthoods operating within our life. The blueprint of YHVH can be expressed through us as a corporate body. Because of the differences in expression, it is important not to try to make others be like you but find where we each fit and function from there. All of these priesthoods have always been in creation, functioning in some way because the blueprint has had to remain in creation so that YHVH had a record on earth to work with.

There is no set formula for how the expression of the priesthoods function within our lives, except that it is often seen through the drive in our heart. This drive helps us to identify the expression of a particular priesthood within us, which reflects the blueprint of YHVH's heart. This reflection is the burden of responsibility that is given to us to express within creation. We need to stop worrying about what other people say and get hold of what YHVH wants for us in our lives so that we can each walk out what we have to do within creation itself.

All of these priesthoods are important, but our priesthood as priests of YHVH is the most important. None of us is excused from the process of maturing in our function as priests of YHVH and coming to the point of being able to mediate on earth what we are an observer of in Heaven. The Bible repeatedly calls us the priests of YHVH:

> "You shall be named the priests of the LORD." (Isaiah 61:6 NKJV)

> "To Him who loved us and washed us from our sins in His own blood, and has made us kings and priests to His God and Father." (Revelation 1:5–6 NKJV)

It is time to learn what it means to be a priest in Heaven, learning how to mediate even to the point of arguing your perspective with the Father from a place of maturity. This is seen clearly through Moses' involvement when YHVH wanted to destroy the people (Exodus 32:9–14). It is important to realise that having an open and honest discussion, even a heated one, is not just an argument, but it can be a way that helps develop respect, honour and relationship. When we develop this skill, we are able to live in the reality of a relationship where nothing is hidden. It is often said that the Hebrew people argue a lot. It is interesting that when they do, it does not often break relationships because it is coming from a mature standpoint. The way of discussion has to be learned through experience and cannot just be learnt from a book as knowledge. I personally have found that the Father loves nothing more than a good, lively discussion! I have pursued this pathway on several occasions and have thoroughly enjoyed it.

Throughout this book, we are looking in-depth at how to become a priest, what it means to function and operate as a priest, and how to represent YHVH in creation. Maybe you have never thought about this, but you are YHVH's representative. He has chosen you and called you to be His priest, not the priest of man, not the priest of the earth, not the priest of anything else, but His priest alone. Of course, out of this, there are many expressions that give us individuality, added to the matrix of the whole. All of us will be woven into the fabric of the union of His heart with us, and from this place we will begin to understand the mind of YHVH.

Our function is not just to settle in one style of priesthood but to find out what is in our hearts, the deepest yearnings of our inner being towards YHVH and to engage with His presence. To be able to move into what YHVH is wanting, function as a son and be displayed as a priest. YHVH can then position us to become mediators of the blueprint of His dreams for us here in creation.

The Zionic and Melchizedek priesthoods, together with our priesthood, form a bench of three. The Zionic priesthood is about the future, the Melchizedek priesthood is about government, and our priesthood is focused on YHVH. This bench of three will govern all the other priesthoods and bring them into order and correct functionality. This is why I said that all of us are called to our priesthood. Not all of us are called to become priests of Zion. These other two priesthoods are functions that we can learn. The Melchizedek priesthood includes the functions of kingship, priesthood, sonship, legislator and oracle.

There is no specific order that we need to operate in, for example, Adamic, Abrahamic, Eberic, and Noahic, because you can operate in the Davidic priesthood as your first function. It is not that these are a decreasing order of priesthoods or an increasing order of priesthoods: they are all independent priesthoods. Very often, our priesthood can be discerned by the way we function practically in the world around us today. We may function mainly within the Davidic priesthood, with a little bit of the Adamic priesthood and some of the Eberic priesthood, meaning we are operating in part of one face and part of another. Eventually, I believe that we will all be operating from all of these, which I believe is full maturity, coming into full measure. Christ in me, the hope of glory (Colossians 1:27) is going to bring us into the full measure, and all the priesthoods will be applicable to us.

I believe that what YHVH defines as a priest is all of these priesthoods put together. For example, the twelve priesthoods would be a circular pattern on the outside, with our priesthood as the thirteenth in the centre, being the hub that is able to facilitate everything that is necessary through the other twelve. The outer layer of the twelve priesthoods would be the outworking of the complete expression of YHVH being visibly seen within creation. This is why the function of our priesthood is so important in correlation to all the others. You and I will be the definition of all of these priesthoods in the end. All of this, every one of these priesthoods, is going to become our function. In the same way that the twelve stones on the priest's breastplate were held within gold, our priesthood will be the seams of gold holding all the others in place. We will present YHVH to all of creation through these priesthoods. Our role as Gentiles is to provoke Israel to jealousy by our priesthood and union with Him until we all join as one new people within YHVH, the "all within all", to see what He is doing here in creation (1 Corinthians 15:28).

Activation

Open up your heart. We often try to take new information in and assimilate it with the information we already have to bring order to it so we can figure out how it all works. I can guarantee you will not be able to figure it all out, so in the end, what we have to do is to honour the mystery. I invite you to join with me to engage with this.

Father, as Your people, we come together in corporate union, we come up into Your presence, and we engage You through the veil, through the blood of YHSVH and present ourselves in Your presence. Father, we want to honour the mystery of the priesthoods that You have released within creation to fashion and help bring the record of Your glory back into creation. YHVH, however these fit together, we want to honour the mystery and not try to figure it out, just honour the blessing of being part of a priesthood and part of the future where this is going to be unlocked for us.

Father, I ask as these men and women each engage with this mystery that You would give them an idea, make known to them the blueprint of their own lives and where they are structured, not as a limitation, but as the beginning of the all in all. All that is in You is going to be all that is in us, and we will be able to function out of all of this. Reveal to them the priesthoods they are currently functioning in to help them understand their own life flow.

When we get confused about how another behaves, Father, I ask that You would create a capacity for us as believers to honour what we do not understand, to recognise what we do understand, and to give You the glory because all glory belongs to You. Holy Spirit, today as a global family, we thank You for the call to be the priests of YHVH and the last priesthood that will ever be revealed within this creation. Lord, in the days and the age to come, in the new Heaven and the new earth, I ask that You would help us to engage with our blueprints to find the measure of joy within our priesthood and creation itself. Father, bless these men and women today. I thank You for them, and I ask that You help unlock the truth of this mystery for each one of us. In the name of YHSVH HaMashiach.

Chapter 9

THE CANOPY OF ANGELS

Because of the aid that can be secured through the angelic realm within our Father's house and in all creation, understanding the angelic is an important aspect of engagement as a priest. Unfortunately, many of us do not engage the angelic, and therefore we are often left with our assignment incomplete because we have not purposefully engaged with angels.

Angels are sentient beings in the service of YHVH. They engage with humanity and aid us in our purpose on earth as sons and priests of our Father. Angels are spirit beings who have a soul but do not have a physical body expressed in the way that we have a physical form. It is fascinating – when we actually look at our physical bodies, the question to ask is, "Are they real?!" As human beings, this is our reality, but as YHVH-spirited beings, our bodies are the functional tools that enable us, as spirit beings, to touch the physical world. Everything about the angelic is spiritually dynamic. Within the confines of the physical world, our own bodies are an intensely patterned formation, an energetic system created by the accumulation of photons of light being observed.

Our awareness of the Kingdom spirit world around us begins to unfold as we mature and become more spiritually aware. As we step into the priestly authority we have, our interaction with the angelic begins to take on a new form to facilitate what is needed. Please note that I never pray to angels or engage them like slaves. They are servants of our Father's house who willingly cooperate with YHVH's design and desires.

Everything in the physical world has come out of the eternal realm of YHVH, whether it has a physical or spiritual structure. Angels are real. To better see their role within the function of Heaven, it is helpful to understanding them as a community. When biblical records first began, very little was told about where angels were, what their function was, or where they came from.

I do not believe angels were created when creation was made. I believe they were there from the eternal realm before the beginning ever was, before the days of old, before His works of old, before all these patterns of the unfolding of YHVH, before creation was even framed in the beginning. We know very little about them in the beginning realm, let alone the creative realm or the spirit realm. Angels are beings that have been with YHVH for eternity.

Michael and Lucifer (one of the two cherubim over the Ark or over His presence) (Exodus 25:22), were in the eternal realm before creation was framed. That means that the angels were all there even before Lucifer fell. So, before creation was there, they were there.

We have treated the angelic realm as something to keep at arms' length instead of allowing it to be right here where we are. Some time ago, I was body surfing at the beach with my son-in-law, who had a Go-Pro camera. In a picture he took, an angel is in full view. The angel's head is sideways, and he is surfing with me in the water on the top of a wave! It is not a made-up apparition. You can see the angel's face and wing structure in the water with me. If there is a community of angels, how close do they live to us? Do we realise how many there are around us? They are here, and we should not ignore them.

9.1: Ian and the Angel in the Wave

Years ago, when I first started talking about the angelic, a renowned speaker stood up and said: "Anyone who talks about angels and says they are in a relationship with them is deceived". Yet that same person talked about demons all the time. I thought to myself, "How can that be? What is wrong with the culture we have grown up in? What are we missing?" A third of the Bible is about angelic encounters in one way or another. If there is that much volume devoted to the angelic in the Word, maybe a third of our spirit life should be connected to angels.

Where do angels come from? They were created by YHVH. They have a will, they have emotions, they feel, they worship, and they have all aspects associated with a complete expression of the soul.

Many believers think of angels as structured as humans but with two wings. Some look like that, but many angels are beings and creatures. The Seraphim and Cherubim are examples of creatures we call angels. The Ophanim are wheels full of eyes with no human-structured form, yet we call them angels. I am saying this to help you become aware of the reality of the word *angel* meaning "messenger". As you and I are spirit beings, they too are spirit beings, but they have different roles than we do within creation and the function of the Father's house.

I have always treated the angelic realm as part of a family assigned to me that I can build friendships and relationships with, particularly those specifically assigned to me from the very beginning. There are two big differences between them and me: I have a physical body I can operate through, and I am a son of YHVH. Angels are perpetually *in the presence* of YHVH, whereas we as sons are actually *in* YHVH Himself.

What astonishes the angels about us is that YHVH has positioned you and me so that He can live in us. He does not live in angels. YHVH created them out of the life flow of who He is, as a reflection of part of Himself. The angelic realm's fascination with humanity can be summed up in this question, "How can the God of this universe and all of creation choose to live inside a two-stranded human being?"

If we go back to the very beginning, we see the role Lucifer and the other covering cherub had over the Ark of the presence of YHVH. Through the nine stones on their bodies, the revelation of YHVH was displayed and reflected to the rest of creation. It happened like this so that creation would not crumble at the impact of a direct visual revelation of YHVH when He displayed Himself in His glory. They were created to reflect His glory, like a mirror.

The reflection of the glory of YHVH would come off the stones on the bodies of these two beings. Please do not get caught in the belief system that says these two beings are currently over the Ark of YHVH: they are not. That is our role now. As priests, we are to reflect the full measure of what we are seeing into creation and reveal the mystery that YHVH has revealed in us as His sons. Then the angelic realm is able to understand who we are. When we, as sons, start operating in some of these arenas, as we speak and display Him as priests, they sit back and watch the reflection of the glory of YHVH coming out from us into creation. They wait for this to be spoken because it is the mystery that is being revealed.

Do angelic beings have families and reproduce of their own kind? I do not know. This is one of the hairy questions I have been asked, and it has been fascinating watching the response to these kinds of questions. Everything about our Father is always about family.

I have seen angelic beings that carry a feminine form and angelic beings that carry a masculine form. If we look at the Seven Spirits of YHVH, they include both feminine and masculine gendered beings – as with humans, there are males and females. If we are made in the image of YHVH, male and female, then that gendered process must be in every being YHVH has created. He does not create them just because He wants to. He creates them with a purpose.

I have often looked at the descriptions of angels in the scriptures. Some can eat food, and some cannot. Sometimes there is a physical manifestation of one form of an angelic being and not of another. There are astonishing descriptions of encounters with angels that Ezekiel had, yet many people only think of angels as little beings sitting on clouds, playing harps. We have no concept of what they really are.

> *"In My Father's house are many mansions; if it were not so, I would have told you. I go to prepare a place for you."*
> (John 14:2 NKJV)

Do angels have families? Of course they have families – but are they the same as ours? Do they have young angels? I am not saying whether they do or do not. I am posing the question.

If everything about our Father is about family, we need to recognise that they are a part of our family. They are servants of our Father, but they are also part of their own family. When a servant serves in a household for over 50 years, they become part of that household and can receive part of the inheritance of that household (Genesis 15:2–3). Our confinement to the physical world has limited our understanding of the dimensional world. In my Father's house, there are many mansions, many dimensions. The word *mansion* should really be translated as *dimension*.

We mustn't take the physical reality we live in and try to apply its operation and function to the Kingdom spirit world. What goes on in the Kingdom spirit world is very different to our physical reality, but it follows the same blueprint as YHVH Himself.

YHSVH was not talking about a mansion in Heaven where we are going to go and play our little harp forever, worshipping Him. That is one aspect, but that was not all He was talking about. When I look at this, I say, "Father, I do not understand". I need to get to the point of knowing nothing. In knowing nothing, I can begin to learn everything.

Angels listen, and angels love us. We have no idea how much they love humanity! They are fiercely loyal, like doting grandparents. I have seen them arguing about people within the body of Christ. "Oh, he is better than that one." "Why is that one better?" "Well, they are doing this really well." "No, this one is better because of this." They do not fight physically as we picture fighting, but they have animated discussions. YHVH wants animated discussion because that is what a family is about.

I had to deal with how the church age and generic historical images had shaped my belief system of what angels were. The Law of First Mention can set a precedent in our neural pathways for something to be seen as truth that is not true. It took me months to deal with the images of angels I had in my mind from the church age.

Why have we not been taught about the realm of the angelic and all the aspects associated with angels? If we look in the Old Testament, it is all there.

Do not have a corporate ascension to try and engage with an angel. Purposefully engage in developing relationship first, privately, in your own time. Do not do it publicly. Remember, our focus is within YHVH's Kingdom when we do all of this, with the Word as a centring plumbline in everything we do. We cannot do this outside of the knowledge of the Word, as it is the basis for our understanding of this realm.

When I think back to my first encounters with the angelic realm over 40 years ago, some were hilarious. As our relationships develop with the angelic realms that surround us and the angels which have been assigned to us and are also entwined with the Cloud of Witnesses become more clear to us, each angel's character begins to come to the fore. Some of them are absolutely hilarious! Most seem to have a very dry sense of humour. I remember talking with a friend of mine in a car, and his two angels were sitting in the back. He looked at them. They turned to one another and asked, "Is he looking at us?!" They spoke in a casual, humorous, mocking way because most believers do not see them, let alone acknowledge them. When my friend told them he could see them, they were surprised and shocked. "This is not the way it is supposed to be!" But we are supposed to be aware of the angelic realm and function with an understanding of it.

One of the first times I had an angelic encounter, and I still knew very little about the angelic realm, I was preaching in a religious church in New Zealand. It was one of my first experiences speaking somewhere by myself outside of the church I belonged to, so I was not expecting angelic interventions. The church building had a big A-frame roof which must have been 15 metres high, and there was an angel there, which was about five metres tall. I was busy speaking when the spirit Kingdom realm opened up, and I saw an angel spinning around the beam in the roof like a gymnast on horizontal bars. Every time he stopped at the top, upside down, looking at me, he would say, "Go, Ian, go!" and do another spin, cheering me on while spinning. I was in the middle of the meeting, looking at this angel and trying to speak. I stopped talking, looked, and thought, "What on earth is that?" People in the meeting could feel the presence of the angel. I have since seen that angel on many occasions and now recognise that he is one of the courtiers of the angelic realm around me.

Angels have a definite sense of humour. I have had them set me up like YHVH does. He is "sneaky-sneaky," and they have learned how to be sneaky because they watch YHVH being sneaky with us. They will set you up to have a laugh just to see how you respond, especially when you are in a relationship with them. Some of the funniest times that have had me laughing out loud in meetings have been when they have set me up to see how I would respond.

I think they are so used to family life that they treat us as family because we are family to them. Of course, we are far more than just that to our Father, and because of that, we are far more than just that to them. They are friendly and welcoming, and they want us to know that.

In many discussions, a question has been alluded to that has never really been satisfied with an answer. I am going to do a similar thing here because we all need to discover some things for ourselves. Some of YHVH's secrets are for our ears only. The question is, where did angels come from? We believe they were created by YHVH as part of the completion of all creation. The angelic realm and the world of the angelic occupy much more than creation itself. This includes the realms going back to the beginning, to the everlasting, to His works of old and into the eternal realm (Proverbs 8:22–24).

THE CANOPY OF ANGELS

I believe angels are spirit beings that have a complete functional soul-being in them without being connected to the physical realm. I believe YHVH breathed His Spirit into us, which is YHVH's life force, and then man became a living soul. That means the union of the physical and the spiritual created the expression of the soul. I think our understanding of an angel's soul is limited by our understanding of how a human's soul operates and functions.

People take their belief systems regarding how physical harm can happen to us as physical beings and try to apply that to what happens in the angelic realm. This is wrong. I have never found an angel that lost a battle or was damaged by anything that was corrupt. Sometimes angels need help from another angel with greater authority. We see this when the angel bringing Daniel his answer from YHVH needed help from Michael (Daniel 10:10–14). Angels keep contending until they win; they do not lose battles. They do not fight in the way we think about fighting. Their position of government and the presence of YHVH that they live in continually becomes the preeminent force they use to contend for positional authority.

> *"Yet Michael, one of the mightiest of the angels, when he was arguing with Satan about Moses' body, did not dare to accuse even Satan, or jeer at him, but simply said, 'The Lord rebuke you.'"* (Jude 1:9 TLB)

Michael's statement is a reflection of angels' authority as servants of YHVH. It is important to note here that their service is at will, not constrained in any way, whatsoever. An example of this in the physical world is seen in the way that when the sun comes out, it will melt a snowman, just because it is and has the power to do that. The angelic realm operates in a similar way.

Part of being a priest of YHVH and mediating our Father's image to creation includes learning how to direct the angelic. Do not think that you can command them in anything. They are servants of YHVH's household and therefore servants of ours, and their inheritance is being in His presence. Even as servants within the household of YHVH, angels are referred to as princes (Daniel 10:13 NKJV). This must be the position in our hearts when we are engaging with the angelic. Everything must be done with honour.

The angelic realm has absolutely no grid for our corruption. They wait for the incorruptible seed in us to begin to engage with them. They are not caught in time as we are, so if we do not engage with them for what are long periods of time for us, they just sit and wait. I have often heard them wonder, referring to us, "Why don't they see us?"

I have seen angels use swords for judgement, but not in battle. Nothing that is corrupted can touch angels because they are light, and darkness cannot penetrate light. The demonic cannot decapitate an angel or put their swords into them. The angelic realm comes in and takes over. We currently have false belief systems about the angelic being vulnerable to the demonic because that is how we see ourselves. We think that angels are like us, but they are nothing like us. Angels do not suffer the same things we do with the physical form of death: angels do not know any death. When angels turn up, victory comes. *"The angel of the LORD encamps all around those who fear Him, and delivers them"* (Psalm 34:7 NKJV). As they surround us, angels bring the Light that wins. Trying to apply our human understanding to angels does a massive disservice to the Kingdom of YHVH.

Redemption and Salvation

The only angels that were corrupted were those that fell with Lucifer (Revelation 12:4). There is no redemption for those.

Restoration was given to inert things (things that have no will of their own, such as the earth), while salvation was given to humanity. When YHVH creates things, they are inert. When YHVH makes things, such as the angelic, they have a will of their own. Animals have a will in their own ecosystem, but they are subject to human will when they encounter us (Genesis 1:26).

The earth is going to be able to be restored because it is inert and subject to the will of that which YHVH made to have dominion over it. YHVH made the angelic realm to be a functional part of all that He created. YHVH Himself is the one that has divine authority over that arena. Once the angels fell with Lucifer, there was no pathway and no journey back to redemption for them. They chose their estate. The consequences will be meted out to them. Please do not have ascension groups trying to get them redeemed because we cannot. I want to reiterate again: free will, salvation and redemption have been given to humanity alone. These are not available for any other sentient being that YHVH has ever made. It is so important that we understand the significance of humanity within the structure of our Father's house. He provides an avenue of redemption for us because of the corruption we have been subject to.

An angel's soul is not covered with a physical form. Their soul expresses itself through their spirit being's ability to communicate with all of creation and their functionality with us as a being. When we see an angel, what we see is a manifestation of the soul of the spirit being that is the angel. When we see a human being, we see a physical manifestation of our physical body that is an expression of our soul's union with our spirit. However, because angels do not have a physical body as we do in this physical world, we see their full expression as there is no covering.

What you see is what you get. I love that about angels – what you see is what you get, nothing is hidden, and what they are is what they are! They do not appear to get any older in this realm, as they are not caught in time. YHVH is ageless. He looks old, but He is not. He is mature. The same thing seems to happen with the angelic. They, too, are ageless because they have been with Him forever. Angels are not subject to the physical restrictions that we are in our corrupted physical form. We are also subject to the passage of the physical sun over our bodies if we live under its government, as according to scripture, it numbers our days. *"Then God said, 'Let lights appear in the sky to separate the day from the night. Let them be signs to mark the seasons, days, and years'"* (Genesis 1:14 NLT). *"Then I hated all my labor in which I had toiled under the sun..."* (Ecclesiastes 2:18 NKJV).

Due to the limitations of our framework of time, we think that Michael must be older now than he was in Ezekiel or Daniel's day. There is no time in that world, so angels do not get old. They just are. Part of our problem is that because time is functional here, we do not realise there is creative light there.

This stuff does not affect my salvation. It does not affect my belief system about the gospel. It does not affect my belief system about the blood of YHSVH. What it does do, though, is make me appreciate the full measure of the household that we are part of.

A few years ago, Grant Mahoney and I were looking for a building to buy to become our centre, and we walked into what is now our building for the first time. It was weird because I could see an angel in the building, and it looked at me. Because of that angel, I knew that the building was ours. I remember saying, "How much is it? We want to buy it". It was because of the angel. That angel has not left.

There are positions and positional angelic beings that are with us for a period of time, acting as counsellors from the instructions they have been given and tutoring us until their assignment is complete. Then when we shift, it is not a dishonour for them to let us go because we are still family. They do not lose anything. The relationship changes, but it is not broken. I guarantee if you went and engaged with those angels, they would still be there and be as happy to see you as before, but their level of responsibility towards you would have changed.

THE CANOPY OF ANGELS

Seraphim are not dragons. They are like a burning, fiery phoenix. They do not have a physically structured form like we do. They burn, but they are not dragons. I want to make sure we understand we are not to go out to try to redeem dragons. A dragon is a being in a corrupted estate that has fallen from its angelic estate. We cannot redeem them. If you try to redeem them, you will get burnt in the wrong way and caught in deception. There is no process of redemption for them. Redemption was not offered to any other sentient being. It was only given to humanity.

Angels are sometimes 150 meters tall. I describe one as looking like a 40-story skyscraper, with six wings encased in a capsule of burning fire of the glory of YHVH. They are terrifying! They are not cute, tiny little angels that you go play with. They are all business. They are throne-carriers of YHVH's glory: be aware of this. Relationship is built over years of knowing that they are with us. The angel that was with me surfing in that wave has been with me from the day I got saved and has intervened and helped me in a lot of ways within my Christian life. That angel has specifically helped me see where deception is, showing me a way and opening a window for me to see.

The encounters I have had with one particular being are always terrifying, but I love them. When I encounter it, I know things are going to change in my life. The first time I encountered it, I thought, "This thing looks like an Ophanim and is just like a wheel of eyes". That was when YHVH gave me my new name. That is why I am called *Thunder* or *Son of Thunder*, a glorified voice speaking in fire. It would be better to call this being a sentient creature of YHVH. Notice I am calling it a *being*, not an angel. I heard a sound like a rushing wind, like a jet taking off. I was in my lounge at home in New Zealand, and I was terrified out of my wits, not knowing what was going on. I was so terrified that I was hunched over on the floor. This thing picked me straight up off the ground. It had the appearance of an eagle's head, but the outside of the head looked like a burning fire. The eagle's head appeared to be inside the head of the being that was burning on the outside. There were wheels on the side of it. The wheels moved and also burned with fire.

YHVH will often use the angelic to reveal part of our scroll to us. This being took me out of my room and into YHVH's world, over the Crystal Sea, which is before His throne (Revelation 4:6). As we came in over the Crystal Sea, I could see the mountain of His glory and the Crystal Sea that is before the mountain, but it did not take me to the mountain. As the being brought me closer to the Crystal Sea, it started looking like a carpet at a distance, with little shapes in it. The shapes looked like translucent white crystals. As the creature brought me closer and closer, the mottled surface of the Crystal Sea grew bigger and bigger until every single one of those threads came into focus, and I could see they were beings worshipping YHVH. As we came closer and closer, the creature slowed down and went over the top. What I saw were transfigured people that looked like pieces of crystal, looking up at me, saying, "Please, Ian, teach us how. We do not know how".

At this point, I received my assignment to do what I needed to do within creation. I was taken straight into what I would describe as the laver of fire that was in the middle of where YHVH's throne is. I got caught in that flame of fire, and YHVH came and gave me my new name.

I can remember asking YHVH to show me what it would be like to be in a place where there was no corruption. It was not just asking, it was a very strong desire, and this opened up an encounter with what appeared to be a fiery chariot. I remember the same sound of rushing wind started to happen. This being took me straight out of my lounge, out of the earth and accelerated away into the solar system. The earth filled my vision and then got small. I saw the moon go by, and then our solar system started going by. I was drawn out from beyond our solar system, out through the place of the ice, and then very slowly, our galaxy started forming in front of me. At this point, I was terrified and thinking to myself, "How am I going to get back?"

I was outside our solar system in "Nowhere-ville", where there is no corruption and nothing, just the void of darkness, which is not corrupt. It is the mystery of YHVH being fully manifested without a grid of knowledge for what you are beholding. The feeling that the peace of YHVH gives is the guiding factor for everything I do regarding how YHVH leads me now. It is in that peace that goes beyond understanding that I know YHVH is engaging with me. I felt it. There was no chaos. There was no nothing. Then the angelic being started laughing. I discovered it was laughing because its next step was to take me back at the same speed it took me out of my house. I did not know why it was laughing, but I soon realised it was laughing at the sheer joy of being able to engage with me, especially for the return journey that was coming. If I could have had a conversation with it, it would have said something like, "I am so glad I get to take you back, tiny human – let's see how you can handle speed (ha ha!)".

**

When I was in Singapore, I had an encounter while I was first starting to learn about the angelic realm. I saw an angel that looked like fire and structurally looked human, but with wings. The angel had a sword in its hand, which had the appearance of a small bolt of lightning. At that stage, I was trying to get to grips with what I saw, as I knew nothing except the little bit that I had learned through my journey as a believer so far.

The encounter lasted about three hours. I now know the angelic being was the Holy Prince Warring Angel of Singapore. This angelic being showed me how the angelic structure is arranged over an individual's life, a family's life, a business, a building, a territory, a church, a city, a region and all the different angelic structures that are associated with these. They are all connected to this process. This happened in a three-hour period in Singapore when I should have been sleeping.

The most amazing thing was that this angelic being left a red feather that was about ten inches long and three inches wide on my pillow. It was huge! It had a firm structure, but when you blew on it, it would go translucent, and you could hardly see the feather when it would start to move.

I was so excited in the meeting. I opened my Bible and took the feather out to show it to the people in the meeting. After I put it back in my Bible and went and did ministry sessions, I forgot my Bible in the church. I came back to pick my Bible up, and the feather was gone! Either the angel removed it because I showed it off, or somebody stole it. I have never had another one like it.

Whenever I would go through these encounters, I would say to YHVH, "I need to know this is real". I cannot go to scripture and show you how an angel is assigned to a person, assigned to a family, the marriage covenant, the opening of a building, or assigned to us under the Shepherd's rod. There are no scriptures that specifically speak to those things. However, this functionality is very real.

Their assignment to us and their role with us helps to precipitate the opening of the spirit world and the Kingdom world's physical appearance. Oftentimes an angel will precipitate the physical appearance of the Kingdom world opening, which is recorded in scripture (Luke 1:5–13 and 26–33, Judges 6:11–7:24, Matthew 28:2–8). About 25 years ago, we were in an African church in Seattle. During that point in time, orbs were being seen in photographs until photographers changed the frequency of the light flash so you could not see the orbs anymore. The senior pastor was at the back of the church because we had hired his church, and he had always wanted to see the physical manifestation of YHVH. This was a

79-year-old man who had served YHVH since he was 16 and had longed for supernatural manifestation. He took a photo and freaked out because the whole front of his church was filled with a massive, big, round, white ball. I turned around and looked at the pastor and said, "Today, you are going to see something".

First, a long, spindly feather floated down out of the air. Then it started to literally rain small feathers. They did not look like bird feathers; they were long, spindly feathers. When they moved in a breeze, they would become still, disappear and then materialise again. The heat of peoples' hands would make the feathers rise into the air and disappear. The feathers would then reappear above their hands again.

This was the first time the minister had seen anything like that in his entire life. He was at the back of the church, crying his eyes out in great sobs, seeing the manifestation of YHVH like that for the first time. This is how sensitive angels are to your needs if you give them a chance.

When Kay and I flew into Israel and landed but had not yet engaged, we were travelling in the car to the hotel with one of the guys who was supposed to be the tour guide. He could not be the tour guide but still wanted to meet us anyway. As we were in the car, I saw a flash. I turned around, and looking up, I saw the Holy Prince Warring Angel of Israel had just come through a door. I could see the door, and I could see this angel coming through. I picked my phone up and took a photo. In the photo, there is a massive arched door and a silvery being you can see flowing into the atmosphere, coming to the door. The Israeli man in the car had not seen many angels. He asked, "What are you doing?" I said, "I am taking a photo of an angel that came to the door because I started engaging". I showed him the picture on my phone, and it blew him away. Angels are very involved in everything we do when we go into other nations.

Do you realise that we are also classified as a messenger, which means an angel? Jacob (Yakov in Hebrew) saw angels ascending and descending. *"Then he dreamed, and behold, a ladder was set up on the earth, and its top reached to heaven; and there the angels of YHVH were ascending and descending on it"* (Genesis 28:12 NKJV).

YHSVH said, *"And I also say to you that you are Peter, and on this rock I will build My church, and the gates of Hades shall not prevail against it"* (Matthew 16:18 NKJV). You will also see angels ascending and descending like that: *"And He said to him, 'Most assuredly, I say to you, hereafter you shall see heaven open, and the angels of YHVH ascending and descending upon the Son of Man'"* (John 1:51 NKJV). It is not angels with wings that we are talking about here. This is about messengers ascending and descending. Ascending is where you go up into something that is higher in authority and glory than where you currently are. If we look at the angelic realm currently, it is already in an ascended state because they live continuously in His presence. YHSVH was talking about the ascension and descension of those who are within who He is, as messengers within His Kingdom. It is upon this rock of ascending and descending that His church was supposed to be built.

Angels cannot descend into a physical environment. They must materialise into a physical environment. It is the descending, the going up and coming down that is sovereignly given only to us as YHVH-spirited human beings. *"For I have come down from heaven, not to do My own will, but the will of Him who sent Me"* (John 6:38 NKJV). We are the only ones that can ascend and descend and bring life to the earth as messengers of YHVH. The word *angel* means *messenger*. We are the messengers of our Father, able to go up and down. Another aspect that fascinates angels is that we have the capacity to go into their realm and into the realm of the Father and come down out of that realm into this one, bringing out from YHVH's realm into creation as a priest, administering what we have observed. The blood of YHSVH and what He has done there for us gives us the ability as a priest to do what we do and gives us the sovereign right and free access instantly into His realm from this world.

Do not try and limit the angelic realm to the earth. There is far more out there in the universe than we realise. It spans billions of light-years, with many galaxies, some that can be seen and some that cannot. We do not fully know what is there because that is still a mystery for us to unlock.

Everything that exists, even if we do not observe it or have a reference for it, is still real. Please do not get mixed up between the angelic realm and the beings that live in the nanoworld. The nanoworld is an energetic particulate system that has a government of its own kept in divine order by the voice of YHVH. There are beings moving in the fabric of the voice of YHVH. Do not get mixed up between the colouring, synaesthesia and the energetic appearance of that realm and the angelic realm.

Engaging with the angelic realm does not negate the necessity for union with YHVH, relationship with Christ and the union with the Holy Spirit within you. In talking about the angelic realm, I do not neglect those relationships, but it is like building a relationship with people that I am close to. I do not disassociate my union with my Father to build a relationship with a person on the earth when I shake their hand, greet them and say, "Hey, let's get to know one another".

My union with YHVH carries on behind the scenes, even though I have relationships here with physical people. I am not idolising the people I am in relationship with by being in a relationship with them. It is the same when you come into a relationship with the angelic realm: it does not mean you are idolising angels. Do not allow people to say you are treating angels like an idol when you are just in relationship with them. I do not treat people as an idol when I am in relationship with them. They are part of the family we associate with. It is the same with the angelic family. YHVH designed us to be in the angelic realm, as well as in the realm of the angels.

The realm of the angels is their home. That is where they live. The realm of creation is where the functional part of their service to YHVH happens. They desire to see His will completely unfold within creation, and there is a beauty in the connection and synthesis of this together. The angels have always desired to be with us and around us because of the way the Father has treasured us as a sacred possession. One of the greatest motivations for angels to be assigned to us is that they get to do life with us, watch over us and see our journey with the Father. Their desire is to be with us in what we do. In the journey to maturity, it will become appropriate for us as sons to learn how to give instructions to the angels we share life with. Never command them to do anything. They are there by their free will, not as a slave to your wants. They always respond to maturity, not to immaturity. I have at times instructed angels to do things through working together in relationship, but I have been put in a position to have to do that. The relationship is like a co-labouring together for something important.

I do not pursue the angelic realm by saying that I want to see the angelic. The pursuit comes from the normal pattern of a lifestyle that helps it to unlock. I have found that the key is having a subconscious tether that the angelic realm is real and an expectation to observe it and be a functional part of what is going on.

I find it helpful to engage with the angelic realm by going through the process of encounter. Go through the blood, through the veil and then engage by praying in the spirit. When I am engaging like that, I am like John, who said, *"I was in the Spirit on the Lord's Day"* (Revelation 1:10 NKJV). I am engaging, praying in the spirit, and I will hold it there. I am not trying to look at something, just sitting and being in wonder at YHVH's presence. My heart is tethered to engage, to see what I might see. When you look at what happened with John, he goes into a massive encounter with the being that we read about in Revelation 1. John says,

> "After these things I looked, and behold, a door standing open in heaven. And the first voice which I heard was like a trumpet speaking with me, saying, 'Come up here, and I will show you things which must take place after this.'"
> (Revelation 4:1 NKJV)

This happened after the Revelation 1 encounter, which means he did not stop looking.

When we go through an encounter with YHVH, there is a union between us and YHVH, and we interface together with Him. We begin to investigate His world, going through a gate of invitation. This has been an easy way for me to engage with this realm. I do not go striving to try. As our relationship with YHVH grows, our invitation opens into the angelic household, which is connected to everything that is YHVH's and His function.

When you meet an angel, do not try to figure it out and give an interpretation to everything you are seeing. When you see it for the first time, just see it. That is the invitation to build a relationship. Then go back into it over and over. Sit and watch. Sometimes I am observing, being somewhere else, doing something, or seeing an angelic realm move.

Angels seem to me to have a very dry sense of humour, and when you rub shoulders with them as a son, and they participate with you in activities, eventually they become more like brothers than angels. Let me assure you, they love to play jokes. I think that is one of the reasons YHVH sits in Heaven and laughs (Psalm 2:4) because He would find some hilarity in different species of beings (angels and humans) enjoying life together in His Kingdom.

When Grant saw me sitting over a cloud in Japan, the cloud was the same angelic host that I know is with me. The Word talks about how Christ could have sent more than twelve legions of angels (Matthew 26:53). I do not pursue angels, but I am conscious of them, and I am tethered into that realm with a desire for relationship.

We must recognise that angels are not slaves to YHVH. They are servants in His house. A relationship with a slave is completely different from a relationship with a servant. A servant is there willingly; a slave is there by compulsion. Angels want to build relationships with us. They are there willingly and willingly get involved with us. When you see an angel, do not try and get its name, just build a relationship. Say "Hi" like you would to a stranger and see what the response is. The angelic realm functions similarly to the human realm. Sometimes you take a gift (like a burning coal of fire to a Seraphim); sometimes, you introduce yourself and bring your new name as a conversation starter.

The Angelic Canopy

> *"Then I looked, and I heard the voice of many angels around the throne, the living creatures, and the elders; and the number of them was ten thousand times ten thousand, and thousands of thousands."* (Revelation 5:11 NKJV)

The angelic canopy, as I have seen it, has ten layers, and it is important for us to understand their function. Each layer of those ten has a sentient administrating angel that oversees it. This is set up in the same way described elsewhere in this book: there is the Bench of Three, which is the government of the realm of the angelic, and seven administrators who release that government into the atmosphere. You and I stand in the middle of all of this. We are supposed to be facing each other as priests, administering the revelation that we observe together, as sons, into the world.

These layers are very important for us. By the way, this is only ten layers of angels, but there are something like 38 different kinds of angels. These are just the ones that are around the throne. There are many more.

THE CANOPY OF ANGELS

Angelic Canopy		Heaven of Heavens	
METATRON	CHAYOTH		Creatures
RAZIEL	OFANIM		Spheres
TZAPHKIEL	ER'ELIM		Mighty ones
TZADKIEL	CHASHMALIM		Shining ones
GABRIEL	SERAPHIM		Burning ones
URIEL	MALACHIM		Messengers
HANIEL	ELOHIM		Judges
MICHAEL	B'NAI-ELOHIM		Sons of God
RAPHAEL	CHERUBIM		Covering ones
SANDELPHON	ISHIM		Warring ones

Heaven

9.1: The Angelic Canopy

1. The first layer at the top level is called the *Chayoth*. These are known as the holy living creatures. There are 21 different kinds of creatures I have personally had encounters with. They are not all in the Bible, but they are all in the realm of the Kingdom. YHVH has opened up little doorways in His Word for us to uncover the bigness of His provision already out there. YHVH is not contained in His Word. He is bigger than the Word, but every encounter must have its basis in the testimony of the provision of the Word of YHVH and the covenants He walks in, in righteousness, holiness and truth. I question any experience I have outside of those parameters. When I am in the middle of the glory, in the Father, looking out into the throne, and I see creatures coming in, I believe those creatures to be of Him, or they would not be able to be in His presence, speaking to Him while I am watching what is happening from inside Him. That is the only way to be around the throne. If you come from the outside in, you will get shocked and never go back in again.

"At that day you will know that I am in My Father, and you in Me, and I in you" (John 14:20 NKJV). Are you a spirit being on the outside looking in, or are you on the inside looking out? The only way to be around the Father and understand what He is doing is to be inside the realm of eternity. When you are in the realm of eternity, all of eternity begins to open up and unlock for you, and therefore you are in the Father. If you are in the Father, what devil in its right mind is going to come at you? Your heavenly Father will make short work of it.

The sentient administrator in this level is *Metatron* (who is not Melchizedek), who keeps the timing of everything. He lives in the mountain of gold that is in Eden, where the Father comes out of the glory realm, shedding His glory, full of gold. Metatron lives inside there with three eagles and other sentient beings from that arena. All these things go on in the realm of Eden. He is also the key keeper and key maker for every doorway in Heaven. David got some keys from worship, one of which is the timeline, opening up the ability to go backwards and forwards in time. In my opinion, David knew that and lived out of our day. The key of David is living out of the future today, bringing the future into today and living out the expectation of the future in today. David said things like "Take not your holy spirit from me" when the Holy Spirit had not yet been given. *"Cast me not away from thy presence; and take not thy holy spirit from me"* (Psalm 51:11 KJV). David is an awesome member of the Cloud of Witnesses to engage with.

If you want to engage the men of old, the wine room of the cellar of the mountain of YHVH is a place where the wine of every person's life is stored. The record of the glory of YHVH poured out into them is stored in wine bottles in the wine room, with a record of their DNA and the sound of who they were in that day. You can go and get access to that. Anyone of any generation who has ever walked with YHVH has wine stored in that wine room. If you want to know what their walk with YHVH was like, you go and taste their wine and then you can see that the Lord is good.

2. The next layer is the *Ofanim*. They are known as the wheels, and their sentient administrator is named *Raziel*. If you didn't already know, could you tell by looking at the moon that it is a three-dimensional ball rather than a flat wheel? So, when Ezekiel described seeing wheels (Ezekiel 1:15–21), he was not seeing the rim of a wheel. He was seeing a ball within a ball within a ball. Ofanim are very important in the function of the realm of YHVH.

3. The next level down is the *Er'elim*. Their sentient administrator's name is *Tzaphkiel*. When you start talking about these things, they start showing up. Once, I was at the dinner table with my daughters, talking about the wheel within the wheels and the eyes around the angels. One of my daughters said, "Daddy, I wonder which eye I can poke, hahaha!" She lifted her hand with her forefinger extended and poked into the air with it, and a feather fell out of the middle of the air from just above her finger. She cried, "I poked his eye! Daddy, what do I do?" and I said: "Nothing, it is just laughing at you". This stuff has to be normal; it should be a part of normal life for our children to experience this side of the Kingdom. One of our most important roles as a priest is to teach our children not to be afraid of the mystical side of YHVH's Kingdom. Your children will always do what you do, not what you say. We must set the example.

The Er'elim are known as the mighty ones. They are the powerhouses that get stuff done. In the Hebrew culture, there is an angel described as being 500 walking years tall. That is about 13.5 million miles, which is further than from here to the moon. That height is many times taller than the width of our sun, which is about 860,000 miles wide. That is one angel, and we have 10 million. The layer of angels which surrounds YHVH's throne and your life (because He dwells in you) is terrifying to behold from the outside. The Er'elim administer the justice of Heaven when court proceedings reveal something that needs to be mandated on the earth. They go and get it done. So, when you need something to be done, you say, "Father, I release the angelic covering of the Er'elim to come and stand with me."

When I was in Namibia, we were going after this thing out in the sea that has a gate into Africa, which brings stuff into Africa and trades on the blood of Africa. This thing sits out there, stopping men and women from coming into the knowledge of salvation, which is what the spirit of Apollyon does. I have never seen a scripture that talks about the hunter angels, which go into the highways and byways and cause men and women to come into salvation. I knew they existed, but I had not yet learned how to function with them. Their goal is to destroy the yoke on the earth of the demonic entrenchment that sits around cities, nations, tectonic plates, and our galaxy. We went after the gate of this thing, and I went into the Kingdom realm. As I was beginning to move toward this gate, I took a step and heard a movement on either side of me, like people stepping forward together in unison. I looked to my right and to my left, and all these angels were looking at me with their swords drawn. These are not little fluffy angels. They are huge, monstrously strong! If you've seen the movie *The Incredible Hulk*, you'll have an idea of what these things look like. They were looking at me, and I was looking at them, going, "Yes!" I took a step forward, and they all moved forward. When I did that as a son, I saw that they did the same thing. Then I did my normal Ian thing. I stepped back, stepped forward, then stepped back and forward again. I was enjoying watching them and having a bit of a joke with myself. Then they realised what I was doing – it was a good family joke, but we were still about serious business. I did not go looking for that, though. The encounter happened out of my union with YHVH and unfolded from that place. When you engage Kingdom stuff and begin to move with the angelic realm, the angelic realm moves in engagement and cooperation with you.

The Book of Jasher[18] talks about a lot of this stuff. When they fought, the first arrow fired in every battle had an angel's name on it. The first spear that was thrown had an angel's name on it. Every shofar that they blew had angels' names on them, and the shields that stood in the front all had angels' names on them. They knew the angel's name or nature, mandated by the written character of the name, would give it authority to function. This is the old covenant (before Christ). Under the new covenant, so much more is available to us regarding the role of the angelic around our lives.

4. The next layer down is called the *Chashmalim*. Their sentient administrator's name is *Tzadkiel*. They are known as the brilliant ones or the shining ones. That is where you get the word *chameleon* (the animal that changes colour). When people first close their eyes and begin to engage the Kingdom realm, they often see shifting colours, and they say, "Ian, all I see is colour. I am sick of seeing colours". Well, you are actually seeing an angel. The Chashmalim have swirling colours in the Kingdom spirit world, and they come as a cloud of colour. They are very interested when you begin to move in the Kingdom realm because they want to be around the glory that is on your life. So, the moment you start to engage, they engage with you to observe the realm of YHVH around you. We think we are so cool as human beings. We see in the seven colours of the rainbow with four base colours. In Heaven, there are 27 different base colours. We see four base colours, and we think we are amazing because we can see the seven colours of the rainbow. There are other colour spectrums currently in the

---

[18] "The Book of Jasher, which means the Book of the Upright or the Book of the Just Man, is a book mentioned in the Hebrew Bible, often interpreted as a lost non-canonical book" (available on Wikipedia.org).

physical creation, such as ultraviolet, infrared, microwave, and radio. When you are in the Kingdom, the dimensions of every one of these spectrums open up in colour to you and can be observed as a spirit being.

If you were to take the true colours of the rainbow, put them on a disc and spin it at 3800 RPM, the disc would go grey and eventually turn white. If you take tints or shades of those colours and do the same thing, it would go grey and then turn black.[19] Whatever you are engaging is seen in the spirit world by the refraction of the colour index of your life. You bring glory light out of Heaven, which has the appearance of being white.

5. The next layer is the *Seraphim*, whose leader's name is *Gabriel*. The Seraphim's role is to administer the burning coals of fire.

> "...I saw the Lord sitting on a throne, high and lifted up, and the train of His robe filled the temple. Above it stood seraphim; each one had six wings: with two he covered his face, with two he covered his feet, and with two he flew... Then one of the seraphim flew to me, having in his hand a live coal which he had taken with the tongs from the altar. And he touched my mouth with it, and said: "Behold, this has touched your lips; your iniquity is taken away, and your sin purged." (Isaiah 6:1–2, 6–7 NKJV)

It is important to note that the blood of Christ has now accomplished all of this for us. Having the Seraphim engage with you with a coal of fire is a very interesting process to walk through. Our sin is purged from us, and our transgression is removed from us. It is not about what YHSVH did for us when He went into the realm of Heaven. He has already worked within us, empowering us to go into the realm of the Kingdom. When we are in the Kingdom, there is a preparation work that goes on in the arena of holiness within our genetic code that is important as part of our preparation for service as a priest of YHVH. The Seraphim's function is to prepare us for service. That is why it

---

[19] See Newton's colour wheel.

was only after Isaiah had the coal of fire touch his lips that he began to remember his mandate from the very beginning when he was released into the earth. This was when he heard YHVH saying: *"Who will go for us?"*, then Isaiah was able to say, *"I will go"*, and YHVH said: *"Go to this nation of hard hearted people"* (Isaiah 6:8–10).

6. The next layer down is known as the *Malachim*, and their sentient administrator is *Uriel*. They are known as the kings. These are the ones who bring the judgments of YHVH to pass on the face of the earth. I have had a bit to do with some of these beings. When you are involved in the Celestial Council with the judgments of YHVH, you need to authorise the Malachim to outwork their function. They are the ones who deliver the justice of YHVH onto the face of the earth.

7. The next layer down is known as the *Elohim*, and their sentient administrator's name is *Haniel*. Many people have seen the Elohim, which have a human structure with wings. I call them "look-like-man angels". It is amazing how when we see something that is similar to our appearance, we accept it much easier than we would otherwise. For some reason, we seem to feel safe. The early church knew a lot more about the function and role of the angelic realm in daily life than we do today. That is why when Peter came knocking on the door, and the lady ran to the others saying that Peter was at the door, they told her that she must have seen his angel (Acts 12:5–17). They often had interactions with angels, and this realm was a reality in their culture. We have to be educated about the angelic realm because we do not have it in our culture.

We have covered the seven, which are not the governmental seven. YHSVH said, *"If anyone desires to be first, he shall be last of all and servant of all"* (Mark 9:35 NKJV). The lower layer of the Bench of Three governs the realm, which are the ones that are closer to the person of YHVH. I am not talking about the function of the angels that are around the throne. I am talking about the layers that are at the bottom of the

THE PRIESTHOOD OF BELIEVERS

diagram. We have the realm of the angelic occupying space around us all the time.

8. The next layer down is known as *B'nai Elohim*. Their sentient administrator's name is *Michael*. These are known as the sons of YHVH, which YHVH created in the first creation. Some of these left their first estate, gave away the name of their covering and got into the atmosphere of the earth. When they entered the atmosphere of the earth, they engaged with women, and giants were birthed in the land (Genesis 6:4). The B'nai Elohim hold the thrones that are not occupied, hold the governmental seats of dominion of the thrones on the mountains and hold a portfolio of that function. They hold them until we come to maturity, and they can give us a portfolio of the function of that mountain.

9. The next one down is the *Cherubim*. Their sentient administrator is *Raphael*. I have done teachings on the Cherubim, who are known as "the covering ones". They have a function in Heaven around the throne, and it is good to interact with the Cherubim when you worship. The reason you worship is to say, "He is holy, they are holy, you are holy". That is why they say "Holy, holy, holy": three *Holies*.

10. The last one is known as the *Ishim*. The Ishim are the closest things to the prince warring angels of nations. They engage the supernatural Kingdom for and on behalf of nations. Their ruler and sentient administrator is *Sandelphon*.

Wherever the glory of YHVH is, there are 100 million angels sitting around that glory, and when they begin to administrate around that glory, and they begin to manifest inside that room, you have got a 100 million strong battalion of angels at your fingertips. They will guard and protect the glory of the presence of YHVH. There are another 70,000 that go before you to scatter the enemy and another 100,000 that form a rear-guard around your life. You can add 170,000 to the others now, so you can see that you have a personal angelic escort or household of your own.

THE CANOPY OF ANGELS

YHSVH said, *"...do you think that I cannot now pray to My Father, and He will provide Me with more than twelve legions of angels?"* (Matthew 26:53 NKJV). We carry YHSVH's image, and we carry His likeness. Therefore the same thing applies to us, too, today. It is time we started relating with the angelic realm. Tomorrow morning when you get out of bed, say hello to your angels rather than focusing on binding the principality of this or that place, or taking dominion over whatever demon. We need to begin to actively engage with the angelic realm here.

There are another 37 different kinds of angels I have encountered that are not necessarily part of the ten layers that surround His throne. A list is provided below.

Kinds of Angels

1. Judgement Angels bring the judgement of YHVH on the face of the earth
2. Watcher Angels watch over the presence of YHVH and the mandate of the authority of YHVH
3. Salvation Angels bring in the release of golden nets of harvests
4. Angels of Glory radiate the manifestation of the glory of YHVH
5. Angels that guard the Gates
6. Angels that carry scrolls and bring the scrolls. The scroll angels are like lions
7. Angels that seal the testimony of YHVH, that bring the seals of YHVH on the face of the earth
8. Territorial Angels carry the mandate of YHVH's territory and the realm of His dominion into the earth's atmosphere
9. Dispensation Angels carry the times of transition in the realm of the spirit for the assignment of the earth
10. Angels of Assignment are assigned to engage the realm of the Kingdom on the face of the earth
11. Angels of Art release artistic ability into the lives of people
12. Angels that administer grace into people's lives

13. Angels of holiness that release the glory and manifestation of holiness around your life
14. Angels of healing
15. Angels that gather
16. Angels that bring the anointing
17. Angels that bring provision
18. Angels that carry the mantles of those that have walked in the past, to deliver the mantles on the face of the earth, around the lives of those they are sent to
19. Angels of worship
20. Angels that blow the shofar or are the sound of the voice of YHVH
21. Angels of the treasury that carry and release treasure and finances out of the Kingdom realm to us.
22. Angels of incense that carry the fragrance of YHVH around
23. Angels of revival
24. Angels of portal that carry the doorways of Heaven
25. Angels that bring delivery or bring deliverance
26. Warring angels that YHVH sends
27. Angels of covenant that bring the inheritance of the sons of YHVH onto the face of the earth
28. Angels of wisdom
29. Angels that look like pillars that stand
30. Angels of celebration
31. Angels that bring the radiation of the glory of YHVH
32. Angels that commemorate certain events in the realm of history
33. Angels that bring revelation on the face of the earth
34. Angels that carry the mandate of the power of YHVH on the face of the earth for you and me
35. Angels that are sent on missions in the earth
36. Angels that look like men that are sent on missionary endeavours to preach the gospel
37. Angels that are known as the angels of the Lord that radiate the glory of YHVH, that make a way for the Father to turn up

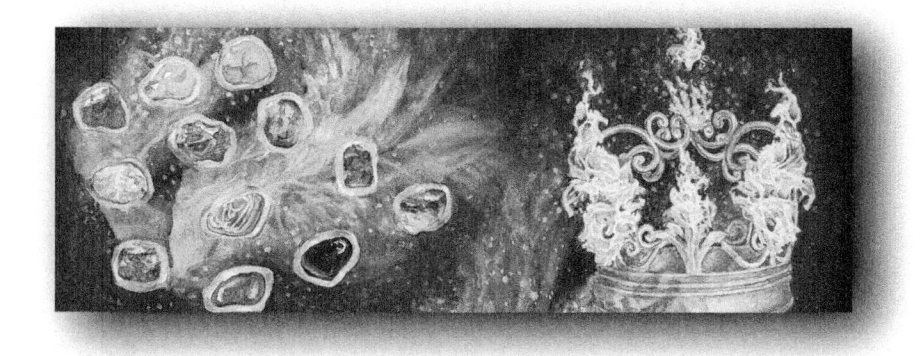

Chapter 10

HEAVEN'S COURT SYSTEM

In this chapter, I want to talk about Heaven's court system. I heard someone say that while YHVH will not violate His Word, He often violates our understanding of His Word. YHVH is bigger than the book. The Bible does not contain YHVH; it only reveals Him. Rules never establish relationship: they only help maintain it, and guidelines help increase the depth of a relationship.

One of the key aspects I have learned about the ten courts of Heaven is their system of government. The heavenly government is set up with the Father, Son and Holy Spirit on the throne, forming a Bench of Three, or *Beit Din*, and the Seven Spirits of YHVH before the throne, forming a Bench of Seven. These two come together to form the Bench of Ten.

This pattern was reflected directly in the Hebrew culture of rulership within the local synagogues, which created a

THE PRIESTHOOD OF BELIEVERS

reflection of "as it is in Heaven". In the synagogue, the roles of the seven are designed specifically to interact with, connect and impact the local Hebrew community. The Bible says we have the Father, Son and Holy Spirit sitting on the throne, which is the Three in One, and we have the Seven Spirits of YHVH that dwell before the throne. If you hold this in your head and heart, everything else about the way YHVH works will flow from the same pattern and thought process and will follow the same image that has already been established in Heaven. At the bottom of The Court System of Heaven diagram is creation itself.

10.1: Explaining the Bench of Ten

To me, creation and the earth are synonymous with one another. The earth is not all of creation, but it is part of creation, and YHVH called it all Heaven in Genesis.

> *"Then God said, 'Let there be a firmament in the midst of the waters, and let it divide the waters from the waters.' Thus God made the firmament, and divided the waters which were under the firmament from the waters which were above the firmament; and it was so. And God called the firmament Heaven."* (Genesis 1:6–8 NKJV)

HEAVEN'S COURT SYSTEM

When He created the firmament, YHVH called it all *Heaven*. I frame it all together as Heaven, even though we as believers have often separated the earth out of Heaven. The Mobile Court sits within the earth's atmosphere and can sit in the earth or just above the earth and engage with creation. It is not *Heaven* as in "the abode of YHVH and the dwelling place of everything else to do with YHVH", but about the 35 per cent of the known universe, which scientists call knowable matter. The other 65 per cent is dark matter, unknowable matter, which we are beginning to get more understanding about.[20] The Mobile Court forms the basis for a type of menorah directly connected to the Bench of Ten.

The base of the menorah lays the foundation for the way Heaven's court system functions. The Mobile Court forms the base of the menorah, which is connected into creation and can move down into creation for us. The Mobile Court is where you learn process. It is the starting point, not the end point, and you need a functional understanding and ability to participate within the Mobile Court system before you can move in any of the other court systems. Once you understand the Mobile Court, you get the right to be invited up. Do not assume that you can move into all the courts because you know about them. This is where spiritual knowledge and information become dangerous because knowing about something does not mean you have the ability to function with it or be a part of it. The only court that is accessible to you and me instantaneously as believers, through activation, is the Mobile Court. We all have access to this court to be judged, and this is the only reason we go there (review Chapter 3, "The Mobile Court," for more).

Many people hear about the other courts and say, "Oh, I'm going to go to all the other courts now", when they have not been invited. We assume we can go because we have the knowledge of them. Do not try to go just because you have

---

[20] "Universe Weighed and 'Found Wanting'," SpaceRef, March 8, 2001, http://www.spaceref.com/news/viewpr.html?pid=4055.

knowledge; go when you are invited. We are invited when we are mature enough to handle the responsibility of what goes on there. Everything that goes on above the Mobile Court has to do with the realm of Heaven and its function within creation.

The Court System of Heaven

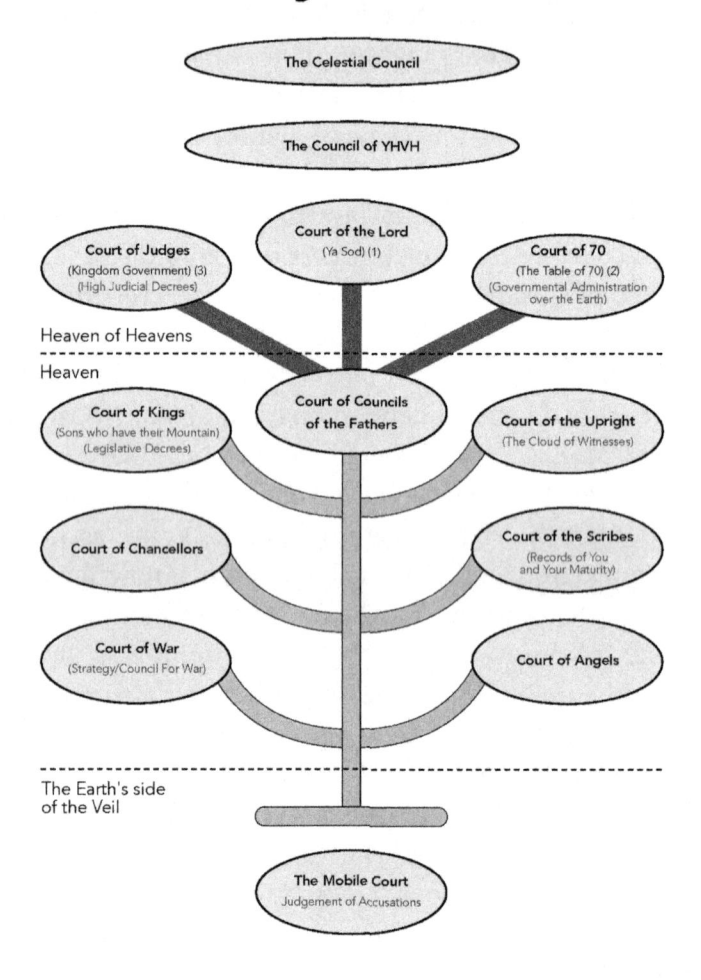

- The Celestial Council
- The Council of YHVH
- Court of Judges (Kingdom Government) (3) (High Judicial Decrees)
- Court of the Lord (Ya Sod) (1)
- Court of 70 (The Table of 70) (2) (Governmental Administration over the Earth)

Heaven of Heavens
— — — — — — — — — — — — — — — —
Heaven

- Court of Kings (Sons who have their Mountain) (Legislative Decrees)
- Court of Councils of the Fathers
- Court of the Upright (The Cloud of Witnesses)
- Court of Chancellors
- Court of the Scribes (Records of You and Your Maturity)
- Court of War (Strategy/Council For War)
- Court of Angels

The Earth's side of the Veil
— — — — — — — — — — — — — — — —

- The Mobile Court (Judgement of Accusations)

10.2: The Court System of Heaven

No devil or demonic spirit has access to these higher courts. There are ten different court systems, and as mature sons, we are the only ones who can access them. The only court anything of a corrupt nature has access to is the Mobile Court. We have the right to move in and out of these court systems, going by invitation up the ladder to those that sit above this menorah. The Bench of Ten is structured the same as the menorah. There is a main prime court with two courts on each side, and each has its own court system and governmental processes.

The three courts at the top establish the Bench of Three that govern over the other governmental systems connected to creation and how it functions within YHVH's house. The first court on the right-hand side is the Court of the Angels.

The Court of the Angels

This court administrates every angelic assignment released from Heaven to flow through into creation or the earth. Whenever a person is born, all the courts operate until the angels are assigned and come through into this physical realm.

The angelic court is the last point of authorisation and contact before an angelic assignment is released. This includes everything that has gone on in every court above it that has authorised an action to be facilitated through the angelic court, which impacts creation and the earth. The angelic realm receives its assignments from here, which give a mandate to do whatever is necessary.

Do not assume that because you can go to the Mobile Court, you can also go to the Court of the Angels. You and I must be invited by the chancellors connected to each court. Do not go just because you have knowledge. You go because you have been invited to come in and participate in some way with what is going on or to learn how to function within a court.

The Court of the Council of War

The next court on the left-hand side is the Court of the

Council of War. This was the third court I went into after ascending into the court system. Many of these courts are structurally set up like a menorah. When I moved from one to another, it was like going through a passageway. The best way for me to describe this is that it's like how oil is drawn up through a menorah's centre hole to keep the fire burning at the top. It was in these passageways that I had some of the encounters I have talked about with Abraham and with Noah. It is important to realise that this is a place of observation, not participation until we understand the function of our role and the way the courts function. I spent six months just watching and observing how everything functioned. This is where mandates are received and given to facilitate what is necessary within creation, always filtering out through the other courts. Mandates do not go through the Mobile Court. Remember, the Mobile Court is activated by you to facilitate your being judged. What comes from the other courts flows out into creation and has nothing to do with the Mobile Court. The Mobile Court has a separate function to the courts above it, but it stands as the support for the base of the menorah, or court system. The Court of the Council of War taught me much about the functionality of our words, actions, deeds, intents and desires. Our thoughts, intents and desires are all part of this process.

This court taught me how to establish myself as a son, to get my desires, thoughts and intentions in the right place, and it tested my faith and hope, which were important pieces to the puzzle. If you have wrong thoughts in the Court of the Council of War and you want to increase your understanding of one of the other courts, you are not given an opportunity or invited until you deal with your internal issues and become more mature in your thoughts and actions. We need to understand the protocols of each court. Practical learning is vital for any form of participation.

Invitations to move into these various courts have always come through the mentorship of those assigned to me, who watch over my observance and share breath with me in conversation about what has gone on. We discuss anything I have observed that I do not understand. This is all about discipleship, mentoring and training. Once you are qualified, the invitation will come to explore these further realms of our Father's government. Let me assure you that YHVH is not in any hurry regarding our maturing in these areas. It has taken me years and years to process through this, to even understand what the courts were, let alone to participate and have a function in them.

One thing that helped facilitate my participation was spending time meditating over the overall court structure and engaging in conversation with those assigned to me. It has always seemed to me that conversation develops relationships with those who operate within the structures of these different courts. I met many members of the Cloud of Witnesses here who testified to my role outside of creation. They have since become mentors, staying in their positions. Every one of my mentors has been connected to the Cloud of Witnesses and has been involved with me in different ways through the years.

I mention this to show how flippant people can be when they engage with this process. It is important to note at the beginning that this is not a place where you go to get what your own desires, thoughts and intents want. I sometimes hear people say, "I've gone to the Court of Angels to get this". We cannot go to the Court of Angels to get anything. We go there to receive. Observing how assignments filter down to this court and are released into creation is one of the greatest places to learn the function of the angelic realm. It is where we receive a lot of information and input. We do not go there to get something.

The Court of Scribes

The next court is connected to the right side of the menorah. It is known as the Court of the Scribes, and it sits on the right-hand side in the house.

THE PRIESTHOOD OF BELIEVERS

> *"...One man among them was clothed with linen, and had a writer's inkhorn at his side...."* (Ezekiel 9:2 NKJV)

This being, known as a scribe or record keeper, records every action that YHVH does, everything to do with what YHVH is doing, what you and I do, what angels do, and our function within that. I learned some time ago that a bench of three scribes follows me, recording every single thing I say. This includes what goes on in the unknown parts of my heart, which comes out as a vibration in my physical form. Our thoughts, intentions and words are seen in the spirit world and are written down. That knowledge really began to put positive peer pressure on my life to deal with my stuff.

This court is directly connected to the library in Heaven. The library in the Father's Mountain has massive vaults with books of records kept about every single person, their behaviour, and everything they have ever done. Every deed, thought, and intent they have ever had in their heart is recorded.

> *"But I say to you that for every idle word men may speak, they will give account of it in the day of judgment."* (Matthew 12:36 NKJV)

Everything that has ever come out of you or you have said is recorded. That is why it is so important to have the blood of Christ available for cleansing and restoration as preparation for our position, so we can maintain a positive, forward motion in our journey. We must actively engage with the blood, activating its ability to cleanse the record of our life and remove the enmity of the record held against us. The blood of Christ expunges the record of corruption that is kept about us (Revelation 1:5). I spent a year and a half walking through the years, months and days of my entire life, systematically applying the blood to all of it. I spent another year and a half walking through the internal records of images that went on inside my imagination of things that had occurred in the past (see Chapter 12, "Human Genetics", available only in the NFT version and Limited Edition). Keeping short records is most important regarding these books in the library.

The library is in YHVH's mountain, but you cannot go through the Court of the Scribes to get your own information. You have to go to YHVH in the library and see the records there. Then you come back to the Court of the Scribes and ask if you can bring the records down into the Mobile Court to deal with your stuff. Do not go there just because you have spiritual information and knowledge about what the library is. We access the court system through invitation and experience, not just through knowledge of it. I am teaching you the knowledge of it because it is important to understand the court protocols that are needed in these areas. When I first released this teaching many years ago, YHVH shut it down because many people did their own thing and did not follow protocol. People acted like children who threw their toys around and did not clean up after themselves. We must deal with the need for affirmation and the need to be seen to be spiritual, which are very detrimental to the body of Christ. These things have caused massive disruption to the maturing process because people have not wanted to grow up and deal with their stuff.

The Chancellors' Court

The next court is known as the Chancellors' Court, which is above the Court of the Councils of War on the menorah. This court sits within the Bench of Ten, in the centre of the three courts we have discussed so far.

The Chancellors' Court administers the protocols of every higher court into some of the lower arenas. I spent two years in the Mountain of the Lord learning about the function and role of a chancellor. I have spent much time sitting in this court observing, learning how protocols are written, understanding decrees and how they operate, how creative light operates in conjunction with this and how the imagery of the court system operates. In this court, I learned about the outworking process governing all judgments through the Mobile Court. I learned how to be an advisor about some of this, my functionality in the Chancellors' Court, and the other three courts. The Chancellors' Court is directly connected to the other three courts and is part of the judicial government directly associated with them. The other three courts are responsible to the Chancellors' Court for everything else that goes on.

The Court of the Upright

The next court is the Court of the Upright, which is about the Men in White Linen. It is on the right side of the menorah above the Court of the Scribes.

> *"Therefore we also, since we are surrounded by so great a cloud of witnesses, let us lay aside every weight, and the sin which so easily ensnares us, and let us run with endurance the race that is set before us."* (Hebrews 12:1 NKJV)

It is fascinating how much we do not know about the Cloud of Witnesses. Within the congregation of the Cloud of Witnesses, there are the Men in White Linen, the Spirits of Just Men made Righteous, the Ever-Living Ones, the Men of Old, the Ancient Ones, the B'nai Elohim and the Shin Elohim. They are all direct witnesses to us doing the seemingly impossible, which is to host the presence of YHVH within us. The Court of the Upright is their functional role, which is directly related to creation. The Cloud of Witnesses also plays a big part in the mentorship process and as witnesses who testify to our journey within both the physical and spiritual realms. The Cloud of Witnesses' role within this court is primarily to oversee and observe the authorisation of what has passed within the heavenly court systems as it is worked out in and around us. Those that operate within this court can also be involved in other courts within the judicial system of Heaven. This court sits above some others (refer to Heaven's Court System diagram below). Heaven's governmental system is based around the Court of Ten, which is reflected in creation in the governmental processes of synagogues. Everything on earth must be a reflection of that which is in Heaven. I have always found it important to follow the same patterning that is present in a reflection from Heaven. It is very helpful to recognise these patterns, as they are all through the Word.

All of this is my personal experience over more than twenty years of walking through the governmental court system of Heaven. It is referenced and alluded to in scripture but not specifically taught, so I do not have many scriptures to rely upon.

A friend that I honour as a father in the faith is an ex-High Court judge with a background in law. He and his wife are amazing people. He reviewed what I teach about the Heavenly court systems through the lens of his knowledge of the way earthly courts function and operate. He found many similarities between the heavenly court systems and the general court, High Court and Supreme Court in New Zealand in the way they all operate with the different layers of courts.

Before we entered creation, when we voluntarily cried out, "Father, send me, I will go!", we received our scroll and passed under the Shepherd's Rod or the House of the Father's government. This is very similar to what Isaiah experienced when he received his mandate for the Israelite nation (Isaiah 6). Isaiah remembered what he had gone through and why he had been released to come into creation with his assignment. This occurs at the very beginning of our journey into creation, as the Cloud of Witnesses testifies to our union with creation. At this point, many in the Cloud of Witnesses choose to become involved with the life of the person they are testifying about. It is interesting to observe how the Court of the Scribes records all of the beginning part of our journey and how the Court of the Angels then receives their assignment to our scrolls. In the Court of the Angels, we are assigned two specific angels to walk with us as spirit beings until our completion within creation. The Chancellors' Court engages with us, and the Court of the

Councils of War supplies what is necessary for our lives as we outwork it in creation.

When we come out of the eternal realm, we come through this process and are born into creation. In some way, all of these courts have a part to play in our life before we reach the earth and start our involvement as spirit beings in the physical world. I have often found that the Cloud of Witnesses are more involved in our meetings and gatherings than we realise. As my personal awareness of them and their function around me has grown over the last ten years, my relationship with them has developed and increased, and we have found that they have been more involved in meetings. Their choice to be assigned to us and engage with us was made before we even came into this physical realm.

If we go into the Kingdom realm and make demands, we are considered immature. When I did this, I was taken through a period where my thought processes, motives and belief systems were retrained and restructured until I became more responsible in my approach. There is a lot of grace given to children to grow in understanding and maturity in YHVH's world, and much nurturing, training and teaching given to us about the ways of our Father's house. However, I found that if I continued to behave like an immature son, I was disciplined in a different manner and kept at bay until my behaviour changed.

> "And you have forgotten the exhortation which speaks to you as to sons: 'My son, do not despise the chastening of the LORD, nor be discouraged when you are rebuked by Him; For whom the LORD loves He chastens and scourges every son whom He receives." (Hebrews 12:5–6 NKJV)

I feel quite frustrated at times with the lack of maturity within the body of Christ. I see many using information and spiritual knowledge to present an image of maturity to creation, especially in our priesthood responsibility to the Father, in presenting His face to creation. We think we can go and do as we like, just because we have knowledge. It would be like giving the keys to a powerful car to a 15-year-old who does not understand the responsibility but wants to drive their parent's car because they can drive a go-kart around the track. It does not work like that. Please do not try to be super-spiritual or try to be someone you are not. Be who you are and learn how to grow. YHVH will teach you this. You do not have to get freaked out that you might be far behind or that you might not be recognised. It is important that our journey with YHVH moves forward into what He has designed for us. I have found that many of us have to deal with the need for recognition from people to be something more than we are.

The Court of the Kings

The Court of the Kings sits on the left on the menorah and on the next point up on the Bench of Ten.

You and I cannot function in the Court of the Kings unless we have sat on our dais and throne and occupy our mountain in the realm of Heaven. When we sit on that seat, we learn how to govern from there as kings and priests.[21]

> *"...To Him who loved us and washed us from our sins in His own blood, and has made us kings and priests to His God and Father, to Him be glory and dominion forever and ever. Amen."* (Revelation 1:5–6 NKJV)

As I teach in the chapter on Ezekiel, he starts his journey in an immature state.[22] We have to go beyond the immature state, journeying through our own lives, to come to Ezekiel chapter 10, where we are positioned as mature sons. As mature sons, we are able to be a part of handling responsibilities to do with the earth and our calling to it, including the responsibility for life and death. *"To everything there is a season, a time for*

---

[21] See the chapter "Government of the Seat of Rest" in *Down to Business*.

[22] See Chapter 13, "Ezekiel's Process of Maturity Through His Priesthood," available in the Limited Edition.

every purpose under heaven: A time to be born, and a time to die; a time to plant, and a time to pluck what is planted; a time to kill, and a time to heal, a time to break down, and a time to build up" (Ecclesiastes 3:1–3 NKJV). YHVH's desire has always been for us to present His face to humanity in a mature and responsible way. This court deals with major responsibilities. We do not go in here to make demands. We get a position here when we assume the seat of responsibility for what YHVH has revealed through us and to us, for the realm that sits around us. The Court of the Kings is for those who have their mountain, sit in their mountain, understand their dais and their seat of rest, and understand what the rod of the sceptre of YHVH in our hand is for. *"We all know that everyone fathered by God will not make sin a way of life because God protects His children from the evil one, and the evil one can't touch them"* (1 John 5:18 VOICE).

By the time you and I get involved in this court, the devil is immaterial to who we are in creation, our eyes are no longer on what he is doing, and he is irrelevant to our life. Why do we go after every devil under every stone and worry that we are in such a mess? When we do that, we frame the world around us with a focus on corruption and the corruption engaging with us. That becomes our source of supply. Whatever you look at, you are going to become like. As I have understood more about who I am as a son and the power of life and death in the tongue, I have realised that the very patterning of my words can create a house for corruption to exist in. If I am focused on the demonic, it can use the power of my breath and my words to create a frame for its existence. We will be held to account for every word that comes out of our mouth, whether corrupt or righteous. *"But I say to you that for every idle word men may speak, they will give account of it in the day of judgement. For by your words you will be justified, and by your words you will be condemned"* (Matthew 12:36–37 NKJV).

The Court of the Kings is about great responsibility. At the point we gain access here, we will have learned about our responsibilities in and how to engage with all these other courts.

The lowest court is the Mobile Court. It is not the highest point. The Mobile Court's operation and function are the beginning point of learning how to operate in the judicial system of Heaven. This does not happen overnight through information you hear or read in a teaching. I have found that so many people gain information and immediately try to become the master of that situation instead of journeying to maturity within that environment. It has taken nearly 38 years of my life to understand this process. The Mobile Court is the starting point of the invitation to the rest of the courts. We need to spend years engaging with this process. People say to me that there seems to be so much work to do. At least you will not have to try to figure out what these courts are, but you can start with this chapter as a background to help you process your journey. It is not surprising that it could take ten or more years to understand this process and for it to become established in and around your life.

For me, the tipping point of revelation happened when the Age of Melchizedek opened on the 20th of December, 2012. When this age became accessible, it opened up the mystery of our priesthood and our function within this age. Our understanding of being a king, a priest, an oracle and a legislator came to the fore after this point.

Court of the Council of the Fathers

The Court of the Council of the Fathers is the final one concerning the expression of our priesthood within creation. It sits on the top of the menorah and also sits at the top of the Bench of Ten.

This court is based on mature sons who have discipled others through to maturity and who understand and have participated in the functions of all the other courts. You and I cannot just go there. We do not go into this court to demand anything. Grace will initially be extended to us in toleration of our ignorance and bad behaviour, but if this carries on, opportunity will be given for correction by having us removed from the court so we can grow in our understanding and function by being an observer for a period of time. In this position, it is expected that we will act responsibly and maturely, having honour as the focal point in everything we do. These courts are directly connected to the function of the Seven Spirits of YHVH within our life.

Everything moves in the same pattern: Father, Son, Holy Spirit and the throne; and The Seven Spirits of YHVH who dwell before the Father's throne. This pattern was reflected in synagogues, with the Bench of Three and the seven below them that governed the communities that the synagogue operated in. This followed the pattern of "as it is in Heaven". We must learn how to operate and function in these other courts because of the importance of the three courts that overshadow the other seven courts at the top. These three courts are very important in our journey as a priest going forward into maturity.

The Court of the Judges

The court in the middle is the highest court of all, and with the other two courts, it leads on from the Court of the Council of the Fathers. We cannot participate in these three courts above until we have sat in the Court of the Council of Fathers. The first one on the left is the Court of the Judges.

The Court of the Judges can be seen in the Old Testament, where people judged Israel. The Bible is clear that we will judge His courts and His house.

> "Thus says the LORD of hosts: If you will walk in My ways, and if you will keep My command, then you shall also judge My house, and likewise have charge of My courts; I will give you places to walk among these who stand here." (Zechariah 3:7 NKJV)

A level of maturity is needed here for judgement. The Court of the Judges is about responsibility and being able to handle any consequences that may come from irresponsible action in these courts. Where we have walked through our mistakes and learned from them, we can be involved in this court. To operate in any of these three courts requires maturity and responsibility, as well as a lifestyle of honour, which must be reflected in our practical life here on earth. This is not just a spiritual exercise or activity we do.

As with the Bench of Three, we need to be mature to be involved in any of these arenas and have life experience in governance and whatever else is related to our function within this governmental system. YHVH's Kingdom world is like a multiverse, and this is just one piece.

We learn how to judge by being judged in the Mobile Court, which lays the foundation for us to later stand in the Court of the Judges. This is a great responsibility and is connected to the next court, as they are connected three in one, like the Godhead. Everything is woven into the fabric of all of this.

The Court of Seventy

The court above the menorah on the right is known as the Court of Seventy. When I first went through this several years ago, I called this the Celestial Council, but I have learned since then that it is not and is actually nowhere near the Celestial Council. The Court of Seventy is also known as the Table of Seventy, which comes from Exodus, where Moses took Aaron, Nadab, Abihu, and 70 of the elders up the mountain where they sat at a table before the Lord and ate. In this court, there is a round table surrounded by 70 seats. There is also a Bench of Three that supervises the whole thing.

> *"Then Moses went up, also Aaron, Nadab, and Abihu, and seventy of the elders of Israel, and they saw the God of Israel... But on the nobles of the children of Israel He did not*

lay His hand. So they saw God, and they ate and drank." (Exodus 24:9-11 NKJV)

The bench at the Court of Seventy is connected to the function of the Bench of Three but also to the Father, Son and Holy Spirit. It is the same pattern. The Court of Seventy is directly connected to the earth and to all adjudication regarding anything to do with maturing sons on the earth. The maturity process is training others to replace you and doing away with your role and function there. One of the biggest frustrations for me is the knowledge that so few of those in the Court of Seventy have trained anybody to replace them and to function within the same realm that they function in with their sonship and government.

It took me about three years of watching and seven years of experience in this court to get to this stage of the process. In total, this was about ten years. Not one day, not one week, not two weeks in each place. This is a maturing process. Here you will learn about who YHVH is and how He governs creation. The whole objective is to grow, to mature as a son so we can govern in our Father's stead. This is a lifestyle and a life process. It does not happen overnight. It can take up to 20 years of your life to walk through this process. It does not happen just because you have spiritual knowledge.

The Court of the Lord

The last court in this area of the heavenly court system is the Court of the Lord or Yasod of YHVH. When you and I, as spirit beings, receive our commission from YHVH to come into creation, we must pass through the Yasod of YHVH. This is where we receive our commission to work out (toil) and outwork (unfolding) our involvement in the physical realm of creation. This is for the inheritance YHVH has for us if we still have our physical bodies at the end. If we do not have our physical bodies, then we do not have an inheritance in the physical world, just in the spirit Kingdom of the Father.

HEAVEN'S COURT SYSTEM

The Court of the Lord or the Yasod of YHVH is where the Bench of Three is, which is the Father, Son and Holy Spirit. As we mature in the understanding of our function and role as a king, priest and son, our position within the Godhead unfolds, and we are able to view what YHVH is doing through the Yasod of YHVH, for *"in Him we live and move and have our being"* (Acts 17:28 NKJV). From this position, we will operate as sons, moving as stewards of what we are observing. Our role is to be priests of YHVH, presenting Him to creation as a result of our observation in the court system. Our role then becomes more action-orientated to all of creation.

The Court of the Lord sits at the top above the menorah with the Court of the Judges and the Court of Seventy as the Bench of Three over the rest of the house.

10.3: Complex Overview of the Courts

This whole system of government sits over the earth and creation. The Mobile Court is the key place for its function and final outworking within the earth. When you and I come into the Mobile Court and engage with it, everything else agreed upon in the other courts above filters down through the Mobile Court to come into creation. That is why when you and I come into the Mobile Court and acknowledge any accusations against us from the accuser, the accusations are dealt with succinctly and in the fastest way possible.

YHSVH is not just our advocate who paid the price to make the Father's "Not Guilty" verdict possible; He is also our mediator. He knows the function of all the courts, and He operates through all of them.

> "And the Lord said, 'Simon, Simon! Indeed, Satan has asked for you, that he may sift you as wheat. But I have prayed for you, that your faith should not fail.'" (Luke 22:31–32 NKJV)

All these courts are one mountain, where YHVH sits at the top.

Synagogues are set up in the same way, in the shadow of the Mountain of YHVH, which is also the House of YHVH. Everything to do with the functionality of all these courts goes on within the Mountain of YHVH. This understanding is referenced when the Bible says, *"And when he had sent the multitudes away, he went up into a mountain apart to pray"* (Matthew 14:23 KJV). He went in the mountain made up of these courts to engage, to get the secrets of what YHVH was doing in the Kingdom realm. Then in His daily life, He could walk Kingdom secrets out, functioning and operating within creation as He outworked from all that is above the Mobile Court.

The Council of YHVH

If we put all of this together, there is another realm that operates above these court systems, which I call the Council of YHVH or the Sanhedrin. It operates at a circular table (see diagram 10.2, The Court System of Heaven). This council also has 70 members. Assignments are given from here in creation to humanity. This is a direct reflection of the Court of Seventy, which it is connected to and interfaces with. I gained a lot of insight into the workings of this council by researching how the Sanhedrin of Israel functions regarding judicial governmental decisions as a corporate body. Another realm of government is above this, recognised as a mountain connected to this one, called the Celestial Council.

The Celestial Council

The Mobile Court occupies space and is engaged in the Kingdom of the Earth. The next seven courts occupy the realm of the Kingdom of Heaven, and the three at the top occupy the realm of Heaven. Our Father's House occupies the Heaven of Heavens with the Celestial Council and is reflected in the Table of Seventy. The Kingdom of YHVH operates from within a believer and is the matrix that YHVH moves through us into the physical world. I am aware of no courts in this arena, but the results of all the other courts flow through us as priests when the Kingdom of YHVH manifests itself.

Some people say they go to the Celestial Council. The first time I went into the Celestial Council, I was scared witless. When I first began to speak about this arena, I called it the Galactic Council because I had no other way to frame what I was seeing or my participation. I have since been corrected and told that it is the Celestial Council, so I now use that term.

The Celestial Council is like the United Nations. It has governmental authority over creation. It is also a place where the movement of the unfolding liberty of the sons of YHVH and their jurisdiction within creation is seen before it happens. This is to do with the mysteries and secrets of YHVH being manifested within creation through the maturing of the born-again sons of YHVH.[23]

The Celestial Council is also directly connected to the earth regarding the movement of tectonic plates. This arena is all about responsibility, and any consequences incurred from decisions made in this arena are borne by those within this

---

[23] The beings referred to as sons of God, who put off their first estate, have no access and no relevance to these arenas of Heaven because they are corrupted and Heaven is all in light. The day Christ cleansed the heavenly temple with His blood was the day all corruption lost access to this estate.

THE PRIESTHOOD OF BELIEVERS

Council. The Celestial Council has 365 seats that all need to be occupied. Eighty-five seats are assigned to humanity to reflect the importance of our role as sons within our Father's House.

It has taken me years of training to learn how to engage with all of this. Please do not try and be spiritual. Just *be* yourself. Learn how to *be* instead of trying to be something. Learn how to be who you are. Do not worry if someone else seems to be in front of you. Enjoy your journey and the responsibility you currently have. Do not try to become something you are not.

Moses went up with the 70 elders and sat at the table with them (Exodus 24:9–11). Moses and Joshua were then called up a higher mountain into the House of YHVH (v. 13). Then Moses was invited up the mountain by himself to come face-to-face with YHVH (v. 18). There were three distinct levels of Moses' journey. Each had to do with a level of relational connection and union with the Father Himself, which enabled Moses to represent the nation of Israel when YHVH was going to wipe them all out, other than Moses and his line (Exodus 32:7–14).

From the Beit Din at the top, decisions are accumulated, come down through each court level and are passed down to impact creation. I hope you can see the onward flow and pattern of how the mountain of YHVH operates.

***

Do not be scared if what you have been doing or saying has not been quite right. Just stop and start again in the right place. Your entry point is the Mobile Court. Hopefully, this chapter has given you a framework for understanding the maturing process that we all go through. As priests of YHVH, we must understand the mediation processes of all of these courts and the dispensation of the Messiah, which is easily entreated, full of loving-kindness, merciful and gracious. The most impactful period of our existence as a species lies in front of us. As priests, we have been given the enviable task of mediating a complete change in creation. Enjoy the journey!

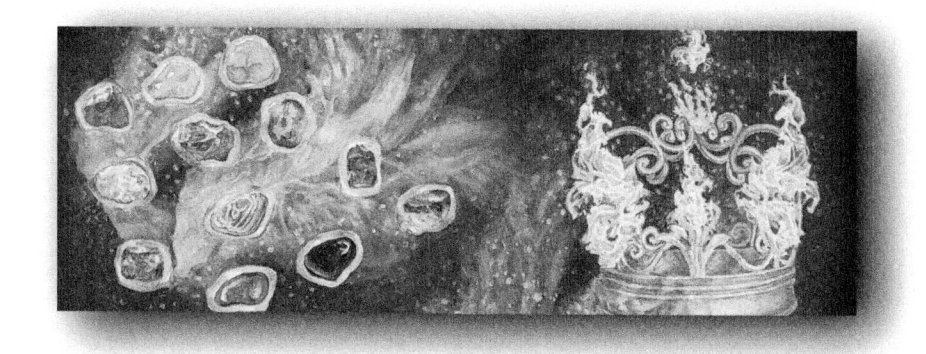

Chapter 11

HE MADE THE HEAVENS

The menorah is a very important aspect of our life with YHVH. Not only because of what it symbolises, but it bears the image of a cross-section of true life and our triune being. Each of the layers is a bowl that is a reflection of something in the realms of Heaven.

The menorah has three circles, each one being a bowl or container for something that has a specific function in the realms of Heaven. There are connections between the four corners and the four spirits, the four points of the compass and the four winds and between the four elements and the four portals of Heaven (refer to diagram). It is the same on both sides. In the Hebrew understanding, everything is circular. As the beginning is, so shall the end be. Everything goes around in circles. YHSVH is the Alpha and Omega, so He is the same yesterday, today and forever, which means that as it was yesterday, so it is going to be forever. YHVH does not change. All He does is increase the responsibility. YHSVH did not do away with the Old Covenant. He fulfilled it and gave us a greater responsibility. We are called to become gatekeepers and engage with the Lord in all of these arenas, not just the Kingdom of the earth. *"Lift up your heads, O you gates! And be lifted up, you everlasting doors! And the King of glory shall come in"* (Psalm 24:9 NKJV). When our government is lifted up, everlasting doors will open up because everlasting doors respond to correct government.[24]

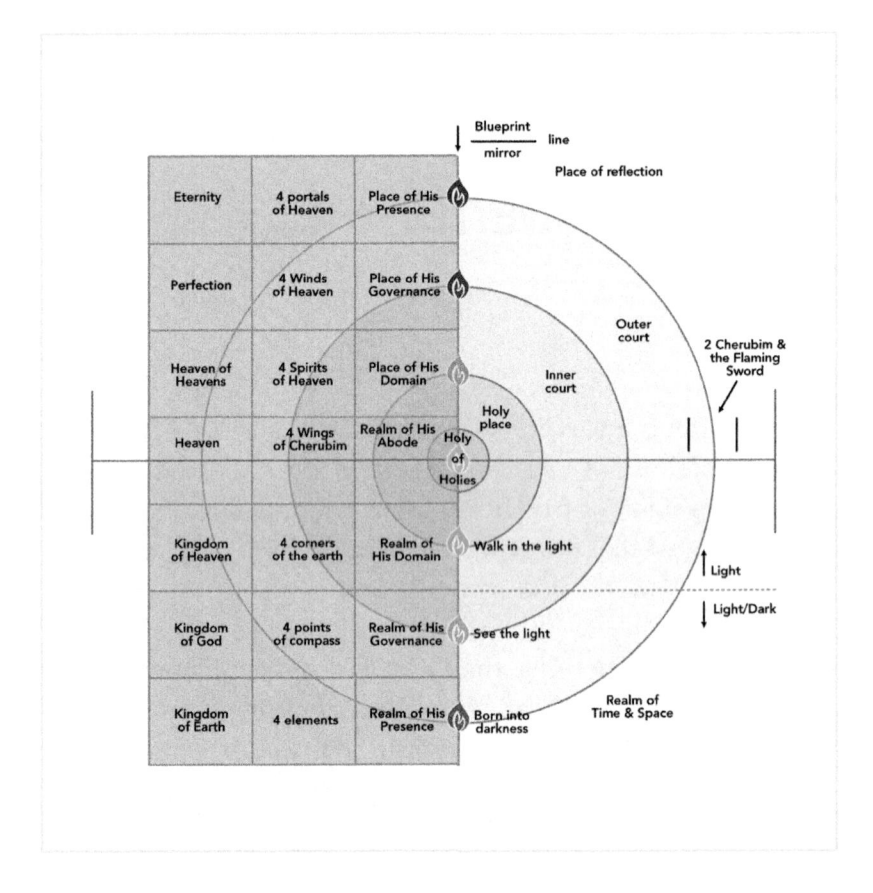

11.1: The Menorah and the Realms of Heaven

---

[24] For further teaching on this, see my book *The Order of Melchizedek*, available on Amazon.

In the diagram, on the right-hand side of Heaven, we have the four wings of the two cherubim covering the Ark of YHVH.

One of the most important aspects of our life as a son is to be able to come into union with the Father and engage with Him, heart to heart. If we do not do this, we will not find our fulfilment as a son and will always be earthbound Christians.

In the next layer up are the four Spirits of Heaven we find in the Bible (Zechariah 6:5). These four Spirits of Heaven are not part of the seven Spirits of YHVH.

The four Spirits of Heaven guard the passageway of the breath of YHVH. They engage it and bring it through the realm of the Heaven of Heavens into the realm of Heaven.

The breath of YHVH can then go from Heaven into the other realms of Heaven. It is the function which carries His voice with all that is needed to keep creation within its framework. Without the breath of YHVH, nothing would be alive because it carries the completion of who He is from the very beginning.

In the next layer up are the four Winds of Heaven found in Ezekiel: *"...He said to me, 'Prophesy to the breath, prophesy, son of man, and say to the breath, "Thus says the Lord GOD: 'Come from the four winds, O breath, and breathe on these slain, that they may live.'"'"* (Ezekiel 37:9 NKJV).

The four Winds of Heaven are not just inert things. They are sentient beings that have a specific protocol or function in the realms of Heaven.

The next layer has the four portals in Heaven, which are the gates of entry for the creative light of the dimension that we physically live in. Everything flows out of the realm of eternity through these different arenas of the Kingdom, flowing down to reach the earth and manifest in the earth. This manifestation is first seen within the heart of a believer when the flame of YHVH is ignited within them and will be seen in its fullness when the sons are glorified and bear His image. The nine-branched menorah has the added dimensions of time and

THE PRIESTHOOD OF BELIEVERS

space, which frame those branches represented by this menorah.

I am just introducing this teaching in this book. For more on this subject, see my teachings at my Son of Thunder website (www.sonofthunder.org).

Activation

I want to thank you, Lord, that You tore the veil to make a way open for me to be able to come into the realm of Your presence. I step forward through the veil and thank You that You died to make a way for us into the world of our Father, where we can engage the supply of all that You have in that world. Father, today by faith, we ask that this world we live in would be affected by the supply of what is in the realm of Your presence.

Father, we move forward through the veil into the realm of your presence. According to the book of Zechariah, when Joshua the high priest showed up and the first thing You saw was a filthy garment, You didn't condemn. You didn't criticise. All You said was to change the garment (see Zechariah 3:3–4). And today, Father by faith, I ask that You would change my garment, from what I am, into who I am. Father, I receive righteousness as a gift while I stand here in Your presence today. I receive it as a cloak around my life. Thank you, Father, for the covenant of Your Names that are woven into the cloak of righteousness that I receive from You around my life. They are hanging in the realm of the provision of Your Kingdom in the atmosphere of the presence of Your tallit.[25]

Lord, I reach up, and I engage with the tzitzit of the tallit. I put my hand into the tzitzit today, and I draw on the supply of the names of YHVH for my life in this world. I draw on it while I stand here in Your presence Lord, and by faith, I step back

---

[25] A *tallit* is a fringed garment worn as a prayer shawl by religious Jews and Samaritans. The tallit has special twined and knotted fringes known as *tzitzit* attached to its four corners.

into the realm of the earth, bringing the provision of YHVH with me. I release the provision of the Lord into every circumstance and situation of my life. Into my business, into my finances, into my relationships with people, into relationships with my family, into my relationship with my wife, I release the provision of YHVH to come into its fullness. I administrate this from the realm You've given me, Father. By faith, I thank You that You tore open the veil through what Your Son did to give me unrestricted access into the realm of Your presence. Through faith, I engage the fullness of my future. I choose to walk within Your presence, in the light where You dwell. Father, today, I lift my eyes up into the realm of Your glory and government. Amen.

About Ian

Ian Clayton is the founder of Son of Thunder Ministries. He passionately pursues a life of understanding and getting to know who the person of YHVH really is. Ian travels itinerantly by invitation throughout New Zealand, Africa, America, Europe and Asia ministering, teaching, equipping and mandating people to become sons of God.

Ian's heart in founding Son of Thunder is to have an avenue to put strategies and keys into believers' hands to enable them to actively participate in the reality of the realms of YHVH's Kingdom and to experience the empowerment of life as the spirit beings we were created to be.

Ian trains and equips believers to give their lives in a persistent, passionate pursuit of the person of YHVH, enabling them to discover that their lives are about the preparation for oneness and unity with YHVH for the purpose of becoming mandated and authorised ambassadors of His Kingdom. His passion is to reveal to the sons of YHVH the purpose of the power of the attorney of YHVH within them, removing the sense of powerlessness and hopelessness that is often attached to many in the body of Christ when they are confronted with the reality of the spirit world that surrounds them.

Find out more at Ian's website, sonofthunder.org.

The Priesthood of Believers is published by

Son of Thunder Publications

sonofthunderpublications.org

Printed in Great Britain
by Amazon